What enhances and constricts mental space – space for reflection, for feeling, for relating to others, for being open to experience? The author addresses this question in the light of two sets of issues: first, how we locate psychoanalysis in the history of thought about nature and human nature, with particular reference to Cartesian mind-body dualism; second, which psychoanalytic approaches are most useful and resonant with our experience, as contrasted with scientistic versions of psychology. He then turns to key concepts which bear on these issues: culture and cultural studies, transference and countertransference in the analytic space, psychotic anxieties and other primitive processes, projective identification and transitional phenomena. In each case he gives a careful exposition of the history of the concept and the debates about its scope and validity, in individual and social terms, including group relations, racism and virulent nationalism. Particular attention is paid to the *kinds of accounts* of human experience which are most enabling, as opposed to those which diminish the richness and depth of experience. This is, then, a book about the problematic idea of mental space and about the concepts which the author has found most helpful in understanding what enhances and threatens it.

ROBERT M. YOUNG, Ph.D., is Visiting Professor at the Centre for Psychoanalytic Studies, University of Kent. He is a psychotherapist in private practice, teaches on various trainings in England and abroad and is a Member of the Lincoln Centre and Institute for Psychotherapy and the Institute for Psychotherapy and Social Studies. He studied philosophy at Yale and was for many years a don in the history of the biological and human sciences at Cambridge University and a Fellow and Graduate Tutor of King's College. He subsequently worked in cultural politics and made a series of television documentaries – 'Crucible: Science in Society'. He founded Free Association Books and was its Managing Director for ten years. He is the Editor of the quarterly journals *Free Associations: Psychoanalysis, Groups, Politics, Culture* and *Science as Culture* and the author of *Mind, Brain and Adaptation* (Oxford, 1970, 1990) and *Darwin's Metaphor: Nature's Place in Victorian Culture* (Cambridge, 1985).

MENTAL SPACE

ROBERT M. YOUNG

Process Press 'only purity of means can justify the ends'

London, 1994

for Lucy and Linda

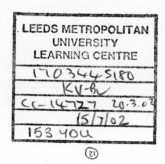
Published in Great Britain in 1994 by
Process Press Ltd.
26 Freegrove Road
London N7 9RQ

© 1994 Robert M. Young

A CIP catalogue record for this book is available from the British Library.

This book was composed on an AppleMac iiSi, and typeset by Archetype.

Printed in the EC by the Cromwell Press

The motto of Process Press is a quotation from *Darkness at Noon* by Arthur Koestler
(Cape, 1940; reprinted Penguin, 1947, etc.), Penguin ed., p. 207.

CONTENTS

PREFACE

My title is meant to be startling and intriguing. 'Mental space' is a contradiction in terms. The mental and the spatial were *defined* in modern thought so as to be mutually exclusive. The essence of the mental is thought; the essence of the spatial is shape or extension. How they relate is a profound and unresolved mystery at the heart of modern philosophy.

Yet 'mental space' has a pleasing ring to the psychoanalytic ear. It conjures up a congenial place for thinking, for reflecting, for rumination, for nourishment. It connects readily to comforting boundaries – containment, being held in mind. It also connotes capaciousness, relative freedom from feeling crowded, from mental claustrophobia.

Between the contradictory sense of 'mental space' and the appealing one lies a surprising set of interesting problems. One of the most interesting is the place of our most basic feelings in human nature, and the best way of representing them, in a world of minds and bodies. Where do stories about people find a place in the light of the conceptual scheme of philosophy and science? Put more broadly, how does culture relate to those frameworks? I wrote this book to explore these problems and in an attempt to make a contribution to a richer, more enabling sense of the proper, undefensive and non-omnipotent place of psychoanalysis in culture.

My philosophic and humanistic purposes intersect with the fact that I have found the ideas of Melanie Klein and others working in the tradition she founded to be the most resonant with my own experience of the psycho analytic approaches I have encountered in my reading, my own analyses and in supervision and teaching. You could say, then, that this is a book about the problematic idea of mental space and about the concepts which I have found most helpful in understanding what enhances and threatens it.

I say again that I am exploring, while trying to achieve some clarity about certain key concepts, for example, countertransference, psychotic anxieties, projective identification, transitional phenomena, in order to work some things out for myself and to offer food for thought. My training in philosophy and the history of ideas has led me to approach these concepts historically and conceptually. I hope this perspective will complement the clinical one which is more usual.

Please don't be put off by my lists. I am writing at the intersection of many disciplines and literatures and am seeking to make the sources more accessible. Allusions which will be commonplace to one group of readers will be new to others. Although it may irritate some readers, it has been my experience that many appreciate some guidance to unfamiliar debates.

I am told that the chapters have very different tonalities or moods. This is intentional.

Islington, September 1991 – March 1994

ACKNOWLEDGEMENTS

Dr. Sydney Klein helped me to find the space in the internal world to think about these matters and inspired me to do so with as little jargon as can be managed. Dr. Colin James helped, too, and drew my attention to the significance of Winnicott's ideas on mental space. Martin Stanton created the academic space to explore my ideas and supported and encouraged the early stages of my research and writing. Bob Hinshelwood has been my pupil, teacher, supervisor, mentor and colleague throughout my clinical training and in a number of joint projects where his enabling ways have been indispensable. He has also provided comments on drafts of a number of chapters and was then characteristically generous enough to give me the benefit of a meticulous critique of the whole revised manuscript, including comments on practically every page. Joe Berke has provided ongoing collegial and personal succour and – in his writings and by virtue of his sardonic humour – has reminded me again and again that I must give due weight to people's malicious, destructive side.

A reading group for many years encouraged all of its members to work out their own ideas, no matter how inchoate they seemed at first. Thanks to Barry Richards (who set its course during that period), Karl Figlio (an inspiration to scholars), Margot Waddell (who introduced me to Kleinian ideas and, in particular, the idea that all knowledge is mediated through the mother's body), Les Levidow (whose singleness of purpose is exemplary) and Paul Hoggett (whose writing moves me). Victor Wolfenstein has provided sharp criticisms of certain chapters and passages and has commented critically on the extent to which my Kleinian perspective contradicts his conception of Marxist dialectic. This has helped me to locate my own position philosophically. He has done this while paying compliments across our disagreements which have been very sustaining. Elizabeth Bott Spillius was kind enough to make extensive – sometimes highly appreciative and sometimes highly critical – and very detailed comments on essays on psychotic anxieties and on projective identification which have been sources for this text. I have pondered her comments and taken account of all which did not violate my own sense of what I am about.

Jeanne Magagna has encouraged me to believe that my psychoanalytic ideas may be of interest to clinicians and has made a number of useful suggestions about the literature, as well as supportive comments on the manuscript. I have benefited from Arthur Hyatt Williams' supervision of my clinical work in ways which I believe suffuse my writing, and he has also made helpful suggestions about specific chapters. I have also benefited from the supervision of Judith Jackson, Alex Tarnopolsky and Renata LiCausi, all of whom also encouraged my sense of professional identity as a psychotherapist. Ann Scott has helped considerably with the ideas, editorially and with the problem of keeping going.

A number of friends and colleagues provided comments and criticisms on all or part of an earlier draft of the book, and I thank them for their support and candour: Isabel Menzies Lyth, Eric Rayner, Dilys Daws, Barry Richards, Eric Rhode,

Paul Gordon, Margot Waddell, David Armstrong, Nicola Worledge, Kirsty Hall, Jane Kitto. I have reflected on all of their suggestions and have followed most of them, but I have sometimes found no alternative to what I'd originally tried to capture, for fear of losing the flavour of an idea. All of those who have given help will, I trust, appreciate that form of stubborn attempt to find my own voice, even at the expense of some inelegances. I accept that I may have got some things wrong, even badly wrong. If that turns out to be so, in spite of all my efforts to be accurate and to take good advice, I will console myself with the thought that my attempts to achieve clarity for myself and for others will have served a worthwhile purpose. Truth emerges more readily from error than from mere confusion

Em Farrell has given unstinting support.

I also wish to thank my patients and my students, with whom I seek to learn from shared experience.

I should like to acknowledge with thanks to Sigmund Freud Copyrights and Mark Patterson Associates for permission to quote from the works of Sigmund Freud and D. W. Winnicott and to Free Association Books for permission to quote from the works of Isabel Menzies Lyth and Tom Main. Although I have been careful to remain within the conventions of fair dealing, I am also grateful to the authors, copyright holders and publishers of all of the works I have quoted, especially the writings of Alfred North Whitehead, Edwin Arthur Burtt, Helen Keller, Joseph Lash, Wilfred Bion, Melanie Klein, Joan Riviere, Susan Isaacs, Paula Heimann, Elliott Jaques, Harold Searles, Margaret Little, Roger Money Kyrle, Joel Kovel, Victor Wolfenstein, Donald Meltzer, Hanna Segal, Elizabeth Spillius, Irma Brenman Pick, Herbert Rosenfeld, John Steiner, Joseph Berke, R. D. Hinshelwood, Richard Rorty, Philip Larkin, Willie Nelson. A large number of the writings I have quoted have been published by the Melanie Klein Trust, the Hogarth Press, Tavistock, Routledge, Jason Aronson, the London Institute of Psycho-Analysis, The International Psycho-Analytical Library, The New Library of Psychoanalysis and the *International Journal of Psycho-Analysis*, and Free Association Books. I am grateful to all of them. I want particularly to acknowledge my debt as a patient, therapist and writer to these organisations and to the individuals whose writings, clinical work and contributions to the work of the relevant institutions have meant so much to me and to many, many others throughout the world.

1   HUMAN NATURE AND SPATIAL NATURE

This is where the theory of object-relations may stem from

How can we 'place' psychoanalysis in the broader framework of modern thought? In the closely interrelated set of changes associated with the Scientific, Capitalist and Protestant Revolutions, a definition of knowledge was put forward. It defined real knowledge as concerned with spatiality or extension, in the sense that what could be scientifically known was restricted to what we loosely call 'things' that can be seen (perhaps with help from instruments) and measured. The world was divided into 'thinking substances' – the phenomena of mind – and 'extended substances' – the phenomena of bodies or matter, with extension, shape and dimensions. This formulation is called 'Cartesian mind-body dualism' and was formulated by René Descartes in his *Discourse on Method* (1637), which is often described as the founding document of modern thought. The spatio-temporal became coextensive with Nature.

The reason this book is about space is that I want to locate psychoanalysis in culture, and, conversely, the place of culture in psychoanalysis. Yet reliable knowledge is said to be spatial, and it is hard to work out the sense in which it is appropriate to think about the inner world in spatial terms. Most attempts to do so have tried to treat the mind *as if* it was a special sort of matter – by analogy. I think this has had very baleful consequences for the ways we think about ourselves and how we treat one another – often like objects or things.

This may seem a terribly abstruse project, but it has all sorts of practical consequences. For example, we find it puzzling when we try to think about physical disorders caused by emotional problems – notably ulcers or hysterical paralyses. These get a hyphenated designation: psychosomatic. We do not have a coherent language for thinking about them or for thinking through treatment regimes to alleviate the suffering they cause. The unclear location of psychoanalysis in conceptual terms means that those who divide the world into departments for administrative purposes don't know where to put it. This problem of classification reflects one of philosophy and cultural location. Is psychoanalysis arts, science, hermeneutics (the science of meaning)? Is it dialectical or didactic; is it about subjects and objects? Is it exclusively about the inner world? What is a 'real event' in psychoanalysis? It is no accident that psychoanalysis has no secure home in the departmental structure of universities and the grant-giving categories of research councils. Its object of study is ineffable. The psychologists don't want it; nor do the social scientists or the biologists or the medics – not even the psychiatrists. Indeed, one of the most heated controversies in early psychoanalysis concerned whether or not one should be a medical doctor in order to be a psychoanalyst. The Americans said yes; the British said not necessarily; Freud (1926) said no; a recent lawsuit in America has said no. Some of this was about status in a professional sense; some of it was about the conceptual status of psychoanalytic objects in an epistemological sense. It's a conceptual Flying Dutchman. I hope I can shed some light on the philosophical and conceptual bases for the lack of a clear location for psychoanalysis in the broader culture and offer some quite simple suggestions for clarifying its place.

This search for a framework of ideas within which we can locate psychoanalysis is part of a larger project concerned with the question: How is it appropriate to think about ourselves? What language, what rhetoric, what conceptual framework makes sense for the understanding of human nature? I've been at this for over forty years. I spent a long time studying philosophy and went on to investigate work on the nervous system, trying to root the understanding of the emotions that seem to make us human in the scientific study of the organism. The point, as it then seemed to me, was to find a way of testing our ideas about human nature and human frailty in something that could be measured and tested by the canons of the most reliable form of enquiry available to us: natural science. In the course of writing a book about the history of ideas about how mind relates to brain (Young, 1970, 1990), I began to wonder whence come the questions we ask the brain. The question moved from 'How are the functions of the brain localised?' to 'Where did we get the questions we ask the brain?' This is just another way of asking where the categories of psychology come from. Is there a natural classification of aspects of human nature which is in some way analogous to the classifications of the taxonomists in biology or the table of elements or fundamental particles in chemistry and physics? For reasons I shall go into, I think the answer is no.

This line of enquiry took me into the History and Philosophy of Science and the history of ideas in psychology and about (what the Victorians called) 'man's place in nature'. This led, with the help of the work of people like David Ingleby, Karl Figlio and Donna Haraway to questions about what sets of values bring people to ask the questions they do in science and medicine. Those scholars have done pioneering work on the forces in society that evoke or constitute or set agendas for scientific enquiry. Ingleby looked into the ideological forces at work in psychiatry (1972); Figlio studied the social determinants of disease categories on the boundary between the somatic and the psychic (1978, 1985); Haraway explored the boundary between the human and the animal – how the ways we think about primates serve as pedigrees for what we want to say about human families and societies (1989, 1990, 1992).

My own enquiries into these matters began with psychoanalysis (Young, 1960), and my subsequent research added a series of expanding contexts and deeper levels. I returned to thinking primarily about psychoanalysis as a result of my own analysis and a growing sense that analytic work is the last refuge of those who would wish to change the world but have learned that to change oneself and perhaps a few others is quite a lot to be getting on with, while not losing sight of the grander goal.

Modern thought has – at least officially – only one answer to the question of how we should think about ourselves. If we want reliable knowledge, we should think about ourselves in scientific terms. And real knowledge is about matter, motion and number. It is cast in spatial terms. There was a profound change in ways of thinking about natural knowledge and about humans in the revolutions of the sixteenth and seventeenth centuries. The Protestant Revolution focused on the individual as a centre of moral accountability. The Capitalist Revolution isolated an individual's labour power as a commodity which could be split off and sold, and was deemed to be separable from that person's social relations, moral essence and welfare. The Scientific Revolution separated out the moral, purposive and evaluative dimensions of the world and shoved them into the conceptually separable realm of thinking substances, the mind. What was left could be treated as material bodies in motion, whose formal features were to be represented in purely physical terms – as forms in space ('extended substances') and by formulas which could be mathematically specified and manipulated.

This piece of cosmic surgery raised at least as many problems as it was supposed to have solved. Having designated as science that which pertains to bodies, how were we supposed to think about mind? Mind was negatively defined as that which does not pertain to bodies or matter. That definition left the representation of mind with no language of its own. As I've already said, mind was always spoken of *by analogy* to the ways we speak of matter. Some analogies have come from physics (the mental atomism of the association of ideas), others from chemistry (mental elements and compounds), more recent ones from biology and physiology (structures, functions, sensory-motor theory and conditioning) and metaphors drawn from or linked to biology, functionalism and systems theory. This has proved very awkward for the official account of the history of science which describes it as an advancing edge of objectivity, whereby physical explanations progressed from celestial physics to terrestrial physics to the chemical elements to the history of the earth to that of life and on to society and mind (see Young, 1979a). The three great blows to human arrogance went from heaven to earth to humankind. We learned that our planet was not the centre of the heavens, that our species was not the pinnacle of special creation and – with Freud – that we do not even have direct access to the greater part of our own mental processes.

What is awkward for this official account is that it is only a small part of the story. Triumphalist accounts of the advance of materialist explanations have large components of lies and nonsense. The mendacity inheres in the fact that much that constituted admired explanations in science continued tacitly or surreptitiously to invoke the banished aspects of explanation which referred to purposes, goals or analogies to human intentions – anthropomorphism. This is true of such celebrated figures as William Harvey, whose account of the circulation of the blood was praised by Descartes as a triumph of materialist explanation, whereas Harvey saw it as purposive or teleological. The same can be said of the father of modern physiology, Albrecht von Haller, whose explanatory categories – 'irritability' and 'sensibility' – defied materialist reduction (Young, 1989). And Charles Darwin routinely employed analogies to human intention at the heart of his theory of evolution by natural selection (Young, 1985a, ch. 4). Thus, the great heroes of physiology and biology were breaking the official rules of scientific explanation in their undoubtedly fundamental scientific discoveries. The official account of scientific progress left out important aspects and distorted what actually happens in some of the most significant scientific explanations (Young, 1989, 1993).

Aside from this economy with the truth, there was the sheer nonsense of the official account of the relations between body and mind. A philosophical scandal lies at the heart of modern thought. Cartesian dualism says that humans are made up of two utterly basically (ontologically) different kinds of substances: body and mind. Yet they are defined so that interaction between them is literally inconceivable. We cannot, in principle, explain how a thought can cause a muscular motion or how pressure on our skin or light impinging on our retinas can cause a sensation, much less a thought. At the heart of Cartesian dualism lies the mystery of interaction – how a mental event can cause a bodily event or a bodily event can cause a mental one (Young, 1990).

Freud's way around this was a form of agnosticism: we don't know how these events are related, but we do know that they occur in parallel. Whenever there is a mental event, there is a bodily one, and certain bodily ones are paralleled by mental ones. This position is called 'psychophysical parallelism', and he adopted it in his first book, *On Aphasia* (1891; esp. Freud, 1891a), under the influence of the English neurologist, John Hughlings Jackson (Riese, 1958). Freud continued to maintain this position throughout his life and repeated it in his last book, *An Outline of Psychoanalysis* (1940), written in his last year.

But Freud left us with a bewildering legacy – a confused and inconsistent amalgam of nineteenth-century physicalist physiology projected onto an ambitious metaphorical anatomy and physiology of the mental apparatus. This was deployed alongside magnificent gifts as a story-teller. (It was not a Nobel Prize for science he won; it was the Goethe Prize for literary style.) To top it all off he added wonderfully moving accounts from great literature, most notably from Sophocles version of the Oedipus myth, and gripping accounts of speculative prehistory of civililzation. Add to this a delightful sense of the meaning to be wrung from jokes, events of the day and the dream as 'the royal road to the unconscious', and you have a fair jumble of languages and terms of reference (Young 1986b).

One of my main aims is to shed light on Freud's problems with language, but I have only been able to make some sense of his difficulties by seeing them in the context of a much wider and deeper set of issues involving the place of mind in nature and writings about the mess created for mind by the scientific revolution. I don't suppose many psychoanalytic practitioners would spontaneously go off and read a book entitled *The Metaphysical Foundations of Modern Physical Science,* but I promise you that it is well worth the effort – especially the last chapter. The author, E. A. Burtt, points out that the paradigm of explanation of modern science leads to a mess whenever you try to apply it outside its original context of the exact mathematical treatment of physical processes. He says, 'But when in the interest of clearing the field for exact mathematical analysis, we sweep out of the temporal and spatial realm all non-mathematical characteristics, concentrate them in a lobe of the brain, and pronounce the semi-real effects of atomic motions outside, they have performed a rather radical piece of cosmic surgery which deserves to be carefully examined' (Burtt, 1932, p. 202). A high price was paid for modern physical explanation: 'To get ahead confidently with their revolutionary achievements, they had to attribute absolute reality and independence to those entities in terms of which they were attempting to reduce the world. This once done, all the other features of their cosmology followed as naturally as you please. It has, no doubt, been worth the metaphysical barbarism of a few centuries to possess modern science' (p. 303).

Having shown why they created a mess, he turns to the consequences for the study of mind: 'But when it comes to the question of replacing this impossible doctrine by a positive theory of mind, there has been a radical diversity of opinion and a philosophy which will be fair to all the data and meet all the basic needs clamouring to guide their interpretation is yet to be invented' (p. 318). He mentions two approaches. The first seeks to know mind as an object of scientific study according to the canons of scientific research. It is first necessary to jettison the mind-body dualism and treat what was formerly considered to be mental as something bodily, i.e., materialist reductionism. The other alternative is to keep mind special and separate – idealism.

'To put ourselves briefly at the point of view of the former group, it does seem like strange perversity in these Newtonian scientists to further their own conquests of external nature by loading onto mind everything refractory to exact mathematical handling and thus rendering the latter still more difficult to study scientifically than it had been before. Did it never cross their minds that sooner or later people would appear who craved verifiable knowledge about mind in the same way they craved it about physical events and who might reasonably curse their elder scientific brethren for buying easier success in their own enterprise by throwing extra handicaps in the way of their successors in social science? Apparently not; mind was to them a convenient receptacle for the refuse, the chips and whittlings of science, rather than a possible object of scientific knowledge' (pp. 318–19).

An equally eloquent critique of the problems raised for the understanding of nature and humanity by the philosophical scheme of modern science was written by A. N. Whitehead in his Lowell Lectures, given at Harvard in 1925, *Science and the Modern World*. He focuses on the absurdity that what was regarded as real was only the primary qualities – spatio-temporal entities and relationships. What of the secondary qualities – sensations of colour, odor, taste, sight? These are seen as the qualities of the mind alone. The mind somehow projects them onto external nature. 'Thus the bodies are perceived as with qualities which in reality do not belong to them, qualities which in fact are purely the offspring of the mind. Thus nature gets credit which should in truth be reserved for ourselves: the rose for its scent: the nightingale for his song; and the sun for his radiance. The poets are entirely mistaken. They should address their lyrics to themselves, and should turn them into odes of self-congratulation on the excellency of the human mind. Nature is a dull affair, soundless, scentless, colourless; merely the hurrying of material, endlessly, meaninglessly' (Whitehead, 1925, pp. 68–9).

Whitehead grants that this is certainly an efficient system of concepts for scientific research. It reigns without a rival. 'And yet – it is quite unbelievable. This conception of the universe is surely framed in terms of high abstractions, and the paradox only arises because we have mistaken our abstractions for concrete realities . . . The seventeenth century had finally produced a scheme of scientific thought framed by mathematicians for the use of mathematicians' (pp. 69–70). Such abstractions are useful, as long as material processes are what you want to think about, but, as Burtt points out, there are other things to think about. Whitehead concludes: 'The enormous success of the scientific abstractions, yielding on the one hand *matter* with its *simple location* in space and time, on the other hand *mind,* perceiving, suffering, reasoning, but not interfering, has foisted onto philosophy the task of accepting them as the most concrete rendering of fact.

'Thereby, modern philosophy has been ruined. It has oscillated in a complex manner between three extremes. There are the dualists, who accept matter and mind as on equal basis, and the two varieties of monists, those who put mind inside matter, and those who put matter inside mind. But this juggling with abstractions can never overcome the inherent confusion introduced by the ascription of *misplaced concreteness* to the scientific scheme of the seventeenth century' (p. 70).

We are left with a metaphysical scheme of things which has proved successful in some ways but within which our humanity cannot be understood. I commend Burtt and Whitehead's books to you. I think they make sense of the metaphysical defensiveness and the insecure conceptual and cultural location of psychoanalysis. Surely there must be a better way. The only alternative, according to the official philosophical system of modern thought, is humanism, according to which categories appropriate to humanity are philosophically prior to and deeper than scientific categories. Some forms of humanism apply it to human nature, society, history and culture; others (and I am one) extend it to ideas of nature and all attempts to know it, even – especially – science (Young, 1973, 1977, 1979, 1981, 1981a, 1985b, 1992a). But if we accept that, we have to live with the uncertainties and forms of subjectivity and doubt that the scheme of modern scientific philosophy was designed to avoid. I shall argue as we go along that this is not only bearable but that we have paid a high price for some of the apparent certainties afforded by the scientific world view. To anticipate my conclusion, I shall end up by trying to make it plausible that those putative certainties are part of the Kleinian paranoid-schizoid position, while the uncertainties are part of the depressive position, but I mustn't get ahead of myself.

The connection of all of this to psychoanalysis is not far to seek. Freud trained as a neuroanatomist and physiologist in the school of physicalist physiology of Hermann von Helmholtz and Ernst Brücke (Amacher, 1965; Bernfeld, 1944, 1949, 1951; Kris, 1950). His first publications were detailed studies of the nervous system, and, as I have indicated, his first book was an attempt to localise functions in the brain. It was a close study of speech disorders, in the context of which he adopted a functional approach to the mind. But he was schooled in the discussion of mental matters in bodily terms.

He was so steeped in this tradition that his first attempted formulation of a theory of mental functioning was cast in strictly neurophysiological terms: 'Project for a Scientific Psychology' (1895), which begins: 'The intention is to furnish a psychology that shall be a natural science: that is, to represent psychical processes as quantitatively determinate states of specifiable material particles, thus making those processes perspicuous and free from contradiction' (Freud, 1895, p. 295). Here we find Freud setting out on the path which Burtt and Whitehead argue could only lead to confusion, and it is certainly true that he took this direction with decreasing conviction. Indeed, he asked that the manuscript of the 'Project' be destroyed, but he entrusted it to Marie Bonaparte, who rightly disobeyed him. In the text he set out in good heart to discuss satisfaction, pain, affects and wishes, the ego, primary and secondary processes, cognitive thought, remembering and judging, sleep and dreams, consciousness, and the topic which he was investigating in his clinical work as the key to the unconscious – hysteria.

Freud's attempt to express his proto-psychoanalytic ideas within the paradigm of explanation of modern physical science was not an aberration, and the appeal of this approach has remained for his followers, especially those who emigrated to America in the 1930s and came to be known as 'ego psychologists'. A succinct exposition of their attempts to treat the mind in metaphorically physicalist terms is 'The Points of View and Assumptions of Metapsychology' (1959) by David Rapaport and Merton Gill, which is an epitome of Rapaport's *The Structure of Psychoanalytic Theory: A Systematizing Attempt* (1959). The inner world is described according to five points of view: structural, topographic, economic, developmental and adaptive. Each has its physicalist concepts: mental structures, mental forces, mental energies, mental origins, mental adaptations (see below, pp. 43–4). We are here rooted in physics and biology. Indeed, an equally ambitions attempt was made by Frank Sulloway (1979) to claim that Freud was fundamentally a 'Biologist of the Mind' (the subtitle of his much-acclaimed book, which I have criticised in Young, 1986b).

I remind you that Cartesian dualism leaves us with no language for speaking about mind. Yet the overall project of psychoanalysis, in most of its manifestations, has been an attempt to think scientifically. The structuralist versions of psychoanalysis have tried to find formal systems and formal features without succumbing to the metaphorical physiology that represents ego psychology. My understanding of the work of Lacan is that it was an attempt to find formal structures – ways of making the mind correspond in some essential way to the requirements of the scientific revolution. The path of the ego psychologists' metaphorical physiology was anathema to Lacan, so he sought in the formal structure of language an equally reliable and rooted basis for mind.

As I said, there must be a better way. I think we can find it by attending to the aspects of psychoanalysis which defy scientific or linguistic normalisation. There is another side to Freud. There are the classics – the Oedipus complex, the primal horde, totem and taboo, Michaelangelo, dreams. Recalling his Goethe Prize, what he was really good at was telling a cracking good story. As my argument moves on, I shall offer narrative and storytelling as an alternative to scientistic and structural notions as a basis for psychoanalytic understanding. I learn most from those who can write evocatively about patients, for example, Freud's case studies,

Theodore Reik, Robert Lindner, D. W. Winnicott, Melanie Klein, W. R.
Bion, Harold Searles, André Green, Donald Meltzer, Nina Coltart.

I hope I have said enough to justify centring my reflections on ideas
of mental space. I want to conclude this introduction by mentioning
another dimension of space – between knower and known. The subject-
object distinction is as important at the mind-body dichotomy and related
to it. According to the theory of knowledge closely associated with
Cartesian dualism, the mind knows its objects for knowledge in a way
which creates an epistemological space between subject and object. This
is, in my opinion, as pernicious as mind-body dualism. It was formulated
by the philosophers of the scientific revolution in order to overcome
subjective bias. We operate with an implicitly spatial model. I, the subject,
am here, gazing across a metaphorical or physical space, at an object
which is in some sense out there. We can also imagine introspection in
these terms: the knowing subject viewing the known self as object.

Mind-body dualism and the subject-object distinction are basic to a list
of dichotomies which plague our sense of humanity and its place in nature.
I shall not deal with most of these in the following chapters, but I shall
list them here and suggest that those who may wish to explore the
connections or articulations of my argument to wider issues should pursue
some of the writings by Figlio, Haraway, Jordanova and me which are
listed in the bibliography:

science – arts

nature – culture

fact – value

science – morality

animal – human

mechanism – purpose

outer – inner

determined – free

(or, at least, responsible)

I shall argue that we can – and inescapably must – retain spatial ways
of thinking but that we need not treat what we know as alien from us,
like a thing – reified. The distinctions between mind and body and
between subject and object also lie at the heart of modern thought's
versions of the two most basic questions in philosophy. The first is the
study of what is ultimately real: ontology. The second is how we can know
it: epistemology. Both the mind which is 'in' the body and the subject

which knows objects 'out there' are capable of being conceived in very different ways. I think psychoanalysis has an important contribution to make to those reconceptualisations and that psychoanalytic theory and practice can greatly benefit from the resulting ways of thinking. Esoteric though some of my explorations may seem, my aim is to humanise our ways of thinking, so as to diminish the gap between thinking and feeling.

2   CULTURAL SPACE

The most capacious space within which we think about ourselves is called culture. Where is culture, and how did it come to be? What characterises it? It is a term one easily assumes one can define, but once you take thought it isn't so easy. I spent some time looking into definitions of culture. The *Dictionary of the History of Ideas* refers to 164 of them (Wiener, 1968–74, vol. 1. p. 614). I found a useful working description by Elvin Hatch in Adam and Jessica Kuper's *The Social Science Encyclopedia*. 'Culture is the way of life of a people. It consists of conventional patterns of thought and behaviour, including values, beliefs, rules of conduct, political organisation, economic activity, and the like, which are passed on from one generation to the next by learning – and not by biological inheritance. The concept of culture is an idea of signal importance, for it provides a set of principles for explaining and understanding human behaviour. It is one of the distinguishing elements of modern social thought, and may be one of the most important achievements of modern social science, and in particular of anthropology' (Hatch, 1985, p. 178).

A number of important points are made in this article. First, that culture is learned and depends on being brought up within a framework – a cultural space. Second, 'A large component of culture is below the level of conscious awareness'. Third, 'Cultural patterns structure both thought and perception' (*Ibid.*). In the past, cultures were often thought of in quite rationalistic ways as conscious creations. Similarly, there were more or less explicit rankings of cultures from the most primitive to (wait for it) ours. Modern thinking about culture is in some ways consistent with psychoanalytic ideas, especially with respect to the limited and subordinate role of intellect: 'With the development of the modern culture concept the intellect itself came to be viewed differently: instead of being the guiding principle behind culture, it was now seen to be largely constituted by culture. It was now understood that people acquire the ideas, beliefs, values, and the like, of their society, and that these cultural features provide the basic materials by which they think and perceive' (p. 179).

In recent years the domain and the resonances of the concept of culture have grown apace, so much so that I'm beginning to feel that it bids fair to become a universal solvent. The trouble with a universal solvent is that everything dissolves in it, so things end up undifferentiated, and nothing can be contained, since any potential vessel gets dissolved, too. When I was a boy, 'culture' definitely referred to what rich people did – opera, symphony, art exhibitions. This idea of 'high culture' coexisted with the subject matter of the *National Geographic*, – 'primitive culture'. No one told me that movies, jazz, dirty bop and fashion were culture, so it was still possible to have fun with them.

Then, in the 1960s, I slowly became aware of the growth of an academic discipline called 'cultural studies', whose main proponents in Britain were Raymond Williams at Cambridge and Richard Hoggart and Stuart Hall at a newly-created Centre for Contemporary Cultural Studies at Birmingham. Hoggart had pioneered cultural studies with his *The Uses of Literacy* (1957), and a number of volumes by Williams set out a broad domain in the popular arts, in both historical and contemporary terms: *Culture and Society 1780–1850* (1958), *The Long Revolution* (1961), *Television: Technology and Cultural Form* (1974), *Keywords: A Vocabulary of Culture and Society* (1976), *Culture* (1981). He describes his own development in a series of interviews, *Politics and Letters* (1979; see also Dworkin and Roman, 1993).

During and since the 1960s, research in cultural studies has burgeoned, so much so that it would be folly to try to list the main writings. The work of the Birmingham centre and its *Working Papers in Cultural Studies* led to a series of collections and monographs, a number of other centres have grown up, and there is no end to it in Britain and North America. A convenient way to canvass this literature would be to work through the journal *Theory, Culture & Society*, but there are many other periodicals, with associated academic and publishing programmes (the presses of the universities of Indiana and Minnesota are particularly prolific). I edit one such quarterly, *Science as Culture*, and as I write this book I find myself being consulted about a proposed series of collections and books under the rubric *Politics and Culture*. A collection of papers written for an international conference, *Cultural Studies*, provides a useful overview of the discipline in the early 1990s (Grossberg *et al.*, 1992; see also During, 1993).

It is in this framework that the debate about the fragmentation of modern life is being conducted: the loss of intellectual, moral and aesthetic coherence and the celebration of 'three minute culture' and architecture without rules of stylistic coherence – modernism *versus* postmodernism. See, for example, the monograph by David Harvey, *The Condition of Postmodernity: An Enquiry into the Origins of Cultural Change* (1980), a collection by Frederic Jameson, *Postmodernism or, The Cultural Logic of Late Capitalism* (1991), and two surveys: *Postmodernism* (Theory, Culture & Society, 1988) and *Postmodernism: ICA Documents* (Appignanesi, 1989). I list these writings to commend them to the reader. I do so, because I believe that psychoanalytic conceptions of culture sorely need broadening and deepening, and an alliance with cultural studies promises to facilitate this process.

What is important about the concept of culture which is being developed and cultivated in cultural studies is that culture is seen as lived values or ways of life. This broadens and democratises culture and directs attention to subcultures, so that is embraces the culture of the home, neighbourhood, school, street corner, factory, disco, soap opera, pub, street market, prison, shopping mall, office, profession, seminar or study group, psychoanalytic or psychotherapeutic training institution, country club, college, bingo parlour, transport cafe, cinema, industry, motorway shop and petrol station, singles bar, gay bar, swimming pool, ghetto, motorcycle gang, gym, yoga class, women's or men's group – wherever people congregate and act in ways associated with particular activities, values and social relations. Sensitive writers about these and other cultural settings have managed to evoke what is valued and expressed in particular groupings: their rituals, belief systems and the structures and dynamics of their social systems. This broadened sense of culture will come in handy in my concluding chapter.

Some would say that there already is a well-developed alliance between cultural studies and psychoanalysis, particularly in the realm of film studies. I acknowledge this but regret that until recently it has drawn almost exclusively on a particular version of Lacanian psychoanalysis at the expense approaches influences by other writers, e.g., Winnicott, Klein and Bion. Even so, there have been some attempts to juxtapose these debates in broader terms, but only a beginning has been made (see Finlay, 1989; Young, 1989a; Frosh, 1991). My point is a mixed one. Psychoanalysis needs cultural studies to help it overcome its narrow approach to culture, while cultural studies needs to broaden and deepen the uses it makes of psychoanalysis. If one looks at psychoanalytic theory and the literature, there is woefully little which touches on the broadened domain of culture which cultural studies has opened up. I think the reason for this lies in the narrowness of the classical Freudian model of culture.

Psychoanalytic writers have followed Freud in failing to make space for the diversity, the specificity and the historical development of various cultures or for the many intriguing sites in our culture mentioned above. The person whose writings about culture I have found most useful in this regard is Mary Douglas, whose short book, *Purity and Danger: An Analysis of the Concepts of Pollution and Taboo* (1966), cries out for integration with psychoanalytic ideas. She begins with the Biblical 'Abominations of Leviticus' and argues – against the received view – that the complex dietary prohibitions of the Hebrews had little or nothing to do with hygiene and everything to do with separating themselves off from the gentiles by means of their complex rules about preparing and serving particular foods, while eschewing others and maintaining firm boundaries between certain types of food. She interprets these rituals and taboos as part of the need to separate 'them' from 'us', the need for insiders and outsiders, for boundaries, for gaining identity through difference. Conventions are established for this purpose, and much of what is declared natural is, after all, conventional. Her ringing aphorism is most illuminating: 'Dirt is matter out of place' (p. 48). Definitions of things and the values placed on them are matters of convention, of social location. The laws of nature are framed to sanction moral codes (p. 13). Culture, including ideas of nature, health, disease and human nature, consists of a system of symbolic codes, specific to a given culture and its unique history. 'Any culture is a series of related structures which comprise social forms, values, cosmology, the whole of knowledge and through which all experience is mediated' (p. 153). By 'all experience' she means putatively objective knowledge, as well; this includes science (Douglas, 1975, pp. 210–48).

Mary Douglas' approach is available for integration with the claim on the part of psychoanalysis that all cultural phenomena have specific primitive meanings. The same can be said for aspects of the discussion of the history of the concept of culture itself in Raymond Williams' *Keywords*. He stresses the more resonant meanings: 'inhabit, cultivate, protect, honour with worship' (p. 77). Culture is not just a collection of artefacts. The term is 'a noun of process' which refers to nurturing, husbanding and cultivation of the traditions of arts and crafts, in the same way that 'to culture' can refer to growing yoghurt or a crop. To culture something is to look after it and help it develop. The nurturing resonances of the term bring it to the heart of the primitive processes considered by psycho-analysis and will come into their own when we examine the ideas of culture and of symbolism of Winnicott and Segal.

Williams also points out that in the eighteenth and nineteenth centuries, 'culture' was synonymous with 'civilization'. This was certainly true of Freud, who wrote, 'I scorn to distinguish between culture and civilization' (1927, p. 6). His main cultural writings are to be found under the heading of civilization, most notably *Civilization and Its Discontents* (1930), but also including *Totem and Taboo* (1912–13), *The Future of an Illusion* (1927), *Moses and Monotheism* (1939) and various essays, e.g., 'The Question of a *Weltanschauung*' (1933, pp. 158–82). *Group Psychology and the Analysis of the Ego* (1921) is not strictly about culture, but it is about social and political phenomena and thus relevant to an expanded conception of culture.

Before turning directly to Freud, I want to draw on another psycho-analytic writer's definition of culture and then to try to evoke what is uniquely human about cultural experience. Fairbairn says, 'cultural phenomena represent the symbolic and sublimated expression of re-pressed wishes of a primal character' (Fairbairn, 1952, p. 188). (I take up the concepts of symbolism and sublimation below.) He sees religion as the most important element in the development of culture, and it is certainly true that cultures characteristically associate their practices and artefacts with their beliefs and rituals around what they hold sacred. Fairbairn identifies two sources of the beliefs common to religion and culture. The first is the persistence of childhood attitudes toward parents and their displacement toward supernatural beings as a result of disappointment with the human parents – their failure to provide unlimited support. The second source is the persistence of Oedipal feelings and the need to obtain relief from the attendant guilt (pp. 188–89). On this account – and we will find it characteristic of Freud's notions – culture is less a celebration than a way of dealing with disappointment and unacceptable impulses by means of renunciation, sublimation and guilt, along with reparation.

What of the symbolic? The ability to experience symbols has been one of the main criteria for separating humans from other animals. It was thought for centuries that this demarcation was a firm dividing line – that animals were incapable of symbolic communication. I have no wish to review the history of this idea here (see Young, 1967) but should mention that it has proved difficult to find an unequivocal criterion for separating humans off from other animals: 'lower' animals have been taught true languages, just as they have been found to use tools, solve logical problems and break down innumerable barriers which humans have claimed separated them from human civility, such as it is (Taylor, 1964).

I don't often find myself thinking we are all that civil. We are a curious sort. We vacillate between idealising a state of nature as pastoral and seeing it as bestial. Somewhere between Rousseau's state of innocent nature and Social Darwinism's 'nature red in tooth and claw' we might find ourselves on our own terms, instead of trying to gain a definition of our humanity by writing pedigrees in our evolutionary past (Young, 1985; Haraway, 1989). It was once claimed that we were set off from lower forms by our intellect. But with the rise of cybernetics, computers and artificial intelligence, we seem to be falling back on our emotions and intuitions as that which makes us uniquely human.

Whether or not we share it with other species, there is no doubt that the ability to symbolise is generally considered to be the entrance to human culture. Patients who experience things concretely and equate the symbol with the thing are considered to be in a very primitive, regressed state. As we shall see in my concluding chapter, so are people under stress in groups and institutions. Writers on symbolism emphasise the boundary between signs and symbols as central to art and to shared meanings. Indeed, the role of the symbol in bearing meaning is what sets it off from mere signs or signals. Ernst Cassirer's *Philosophy of Symbolic Forms* (1953–57) is predicated on this distinction, as is Suzanne Langer's *Philosophy in a New Key* (1942), both of which have been found helpful by psychoanalysts attempting to understand the symbolic realm: signs indicate, while symbols *mean.*

The most striking and moving account I have ever read of the ability to inhabit the symbolic domain as the *sine qua non* of humanity is the story of Helen Keller's entry into language. As she tells it in *The Story of My Life* (Keller, 1903), she had become deaf and blind as a result of an illness when she was nineteen months old and was utterly unmanageable. Her parents were at their wits' end, when they employed a partially blind tutor, Annie Sullivan (movingly portrayed by Anne Bancroft in the film, 'The Miracle Worker'), who was determined to get through to the wild girl. She arrived three months before Helen's seventh birthday. I shall quote at length, both because I find the text so affecting and because of what it shows about the connection between symbolism and civility.

'The morning after my teacher came she led me into her room and gave me a doll. The little blind children at the Perkins Institution had sent it and Laura Bridgman [a famous blind woman and campaigner for the rights of the handicapped] had dressed it; but I did not know this until afterward. When I had played with it a little while. Miss Sullivan slowly spelled into my hand the word "d-o-l-l". I was at once interested in this finger play and tried to imitate it. When I finally succeeded in making the letters correctly, I was flushed with childish pleasure and pride. Running downstairs to my mother I held up my hand and made the letters for doll. I did not know that I was spelling a word or even that words existed; I was simply making my fingers go in monkey-like imitation. In the days that followed, I learned to spell in this uncomprehending way a great many words, among them *pin, hat, cup*, and a few verbs like *sit, stand,* and *walk*. But my teacher had been with me several weeks before I understood that everything has a name.

'One day when I was playing with my new doll, Miss Sullivan put my big rag doll into my lap also, spelled "d-o-l-l" and tried to make me understand that "d-o-l-l" applied to both. Earlier in the day we had had a tussle over the words "m-u-g" and "w-a-t-e-r". Miss Sullivan had tried to impress it upon me that "m-u-g" is *mug* and that "w-a-t-e-r" is *water*, but I persisted in confounding the two. In despair she had dropped the subject for the time, only to renew it at the first opportunity. I became impatient at her repeated attempts and, seizing the new doll, I dashed it upon the floor. I was keenly delighted when I felt the fragments of the broken doll at my feet. Neither sorrow nor regret followed my passionate outburst. I had not loved the doll. In the still, dark world in which I lived there was no strong sentiment of tenderness. I felt my teacher sweep the fragments to one side of the hearth, and I had a sense of satisfaction that the cause of my discomfort was removed. She brought me my hat, and I knew I was going out into the warm sunshine. This thought, if a wordless sensation may be called a thought, made me hop and skip with pleasure.

'We walked down the path to the well-house, attracted by the fragrance of the honeysuckle with which it was covered. Some one was drawing water and my teacher placed my hand under the spout. As the cool stream gushed over one hand she spelled into the other the word *water*, first slowly, then rapidly. I stood still, my whole attention fixed upon the motions of her fingers. Suddenly I felt a misty consciousness as of something forgotten – a thrill of returning thought; and somehow the mystery of language was revealed to me. I knew then that "w-a-t-e-r" meant the wonderful cool something that was flowing over my hand. That living word awakened my soul, gave it light, hope, joy, set it free! There were barriers still, it is true, but barriers that in time could be swept away.

'I left the well-house eager to learn. Everything had a name, and each name gave birth to a new thought. As we returned to the house every object which I touched seemed to quiver with life. That was because I saw everything with the strange, new sight that had come to me. On entering the door I remembered the doll I had broken. I felt my way to the hearth and picked up the pieces. I tried vainly to put them together. Then my eyes filled with tears; for I realised what I had done, and for the first time I felt repentance and sorrow' (Keller, 1903, pp. 33–5). Hanna Segal comments on the connection between Helen's entry into the world of symbolic language and her ability to experience remorse or depressive feelings. (In doing so she gets the sequence of events backward, but it is the connection that is important: Segal, 1981, pp. 63–4.) This is of some relevance to the notions of culture which are wider than those of Freud, which I shall discuss below.

Their biographer continues, 'In Annie's letter to Mrs. Hopkins about the "miracle," she wrote: "She has learned that everything has a name and that the manual alphabet is the key to everything she wants to know . . . Helen got up this morning like a radiant fairy. She has flitted from object to object, asking the name of everything and kissing me for very gladness. Last night when I got into my bed, she stole into my arms of her own accord and kissed me for the first time, and I thought my heart would burst, so full was it of joy"' (Lash, 1981, pp. 57–8).

Having tried by means of Helen Keller's extraordinary experience to convey the meaning of the symbolic realm, which is itself the realm of meaning, I now want to spell out Freud's ideas about culture. He says that 'civilization describes the whole sum of achievements and the regulations which distinguish our lives from those of our animal ancestors and which serve two purposes – namely to protect men against nature and to adjust their mutual relations' (Freud, 1930, p. 89). He suggests that the first civilized act may have been refraining from pissing on a small fire and putting it out. He considers this great cultural conquest – the gift of fire – as a reward for the renunciation of the instinctual wish to control or destroy (p. 90). (Lest this be dismissed as a passing thought, he returns to it and expands the idea at Freud, 1932, pp. 185–87). Another move toward civilization which involved basic bodily functions was the change in emphasis from the olfactory to the visual (Freud, 1930, p. 99n).

At the heart of his theory of culture was the belief that there is an irreducible antagonism between the demands of instincts and the restrictions of civilization. But succumbing to those restrictions does not free humankind from distress, since Freud also believed that civilization was the cause of neurasthenia (p. 60). Every aspect of civilization depends on sacrifice or renunciation of instinctual feelings (p. 95). Even the most rarefied aesthetic experience – the love of beauty – was derived from the inhibition of sexual feelings. (p. 83).

Instinctual renunciation provided energy through the mechanism of sublimation, the channelling of sexual energy into more socially acceptable activities: 'Sublimation of instinct is an especially conspicuous feature of cultural development; it is what makes it possible for higher psychical activities, scientific, artistic or ideological to play such an important part in civilized life' (p. 97). Putting the point bluntly, then, civilization *is* censorship (p. 136). He took a dim view of people: they are not nice. In consequence, civilization 'is perpetually threatened with disintegration' (p. 111).

The basis for all other acts of sublimation is the renunciation of rapacious sexual urges. The energy for cultural life is withdrawn from sexual life, which civilization tends perpetually to restrict (pp. 103–4). The foundation for all taboos and laws was the thwarting of the polymorphous sexuality of the primal patriarch. Overwhelming power is often accompanied by disinhibition of the urge to break sexual taboos. When people seek power, most settle for a modest amount and, on the whole, remain within the bounds of the conventions that set limits for our greedy and rapacious impulses. Indeed, middle class success is almost synonymous with respectability. But if one reads the biographies of *very* powerful men, sexual licence is a common theme – mistresses (lots of them), young girls, starlets. I am thinking, for example, of Howard Hughes; Jack, Bobby, and Edward Kennedy and their father, Joseph; H. L. Hunt (3 simultaneous families); James Goldsmith (two); Mafiosi and their whores; the high-rolling swindlers of Texas savings and loan associations and their whores (O'Shea, 1991); East European dictators and Chairman Mao, who had young women served up to them like bunches of grapes. In the film 'Prime Cut' (1972), orphan girls were hand-reared from childhood to puberty to meet the needs of the men who bought them at auction (on display in a barn, nude in the hay), to be kept drugged and used as sexual slaves, until Gene Hackman attacks the villains and saves Cissy Spacek and Shelly Duvall.

In my opinion the clearest filmic expression of this basic psychoanalytic truth is 'Chinatown' (1975), for which Robert Towne wrote the Oscar-winning screenplay to which the director, Roman Polanski, added additional perverse piquancy. Its genre is the 1940s detective thriller, in which the threading of a highly symbolic labyrinth leads to the perverse heart of capitalism: that with enough power one can with impunity break the incest taboo. In the last scene the detective, Jack Nicholson, is finally led away by sympathetic friends at the moment he discovers that he cannot prevent the patriarch, John Huston, from having his incestuous way.

The old man and his daughter, Faye Dunaway, had been lovers and had a daughter. The mother dies pointlessly, in spite of all of Nicholson's efforts to find out what was going on and prevent disaster. Huston gains custody of the progeny of the incestuous affair, his daughter/ granddaughter, Diane Ladd, because the corrupt and uncomprehending authorities defer to the man who is so rich and powerful. He has surreptitiously gained control over all the life-giving sources of water for the entire area surrounding the world's most opulent and sprawling metropolis, Los Angeles, in particular, the San Fernando and Owens Valleys, and thereby controls what became a veritable Eden of truck farming, much of which he bought up by using the names of innocent, trusting elderly pensioners. The psychoanalytic symbolism of water and rapacious power, of the relations between generations and of the dangers inherent in voyeuristically seeking to decipher the mysteries of the primal scene are evident throughout the film. Much of the story is based on historical truth involving one of the greatest engineering feats and one of the most audaciously corrupt land-grabbing and profiteering projects in history (See Dunne, 1982; Caughey, 1977, pp. 222–35, which includes a contemporary account entitled 'The Rape of Owens Valley'; Kahrl, 1982). Jack Nicholson lives on a road named after the key figure in the true history, Mulholland Drive. William Mulholland – Hollis Mulray in the film – was the architect of the vast scheme for diverting water to the San Fernando Valley and to Los Angeles. He is also famous for a terse speech at the ceremony when the aqueduct was turned over to the city. It symbolised the rapaciousness of those who profited from the corrupt land deals: 'There it is. Take it' (quoted in Caughey, p. 235). The author of the screenplay spent a number of years studying the history of this scandal.

At the moment of discovery, Dunaway says to the bewildered detective, who is slapping her between her utterances, 'She's my daughter.' 'She's my sister.' 'My sister.' 'My daughter.' 'She's my sister *and* my daughter. My father and I . . . Understand? Or is it too tough for you?' Nicholson asks, 'He raped you?' She shakes her head, and he begins to comprehend the polymorphous perversity at the heart of the mystery of the family and of capitalism. At the moment of disaster, as the mother dies and the sister/daughter is taken away by the triumphant patriarch, Nicholson's friends lead him away, saying, 'Forget it Jake; it's Chinatown' – inscrutable, impenetrable; there is nothing you can do to put things right. Prior to this tragic denouement, we have been told at various points in the film that his boyish epistemophilia had got him into trouble in Chinatown before. Someone had been hurt whom he had tried to protect, and his philosophy had become one of doing 'as little as possible', in fear of doing more harm. But his curiosity and Oedipal sarcasm always got the better of him – so much so that during a large portion of the film he wears a bandage on his nose as a result of its being cut with a switchblade, because he was too nosy. Always ready with a quip, he responds to one crook's question about what happened to his nose by saying, 'Your wife crossed her legs'. Sex, curiosity, patriarchy, power, corruption, incest and tragedy are the strands which make up the tangle he unravels.

The incest taboo is the foundation stone of civilization; all other taboos and laws were derived from this restraint (Freud, 1930, p. 100). 'Incest is anti-social and civilization consists of a progressive renunciation of it' (p. 60). *Consists.* The primal horde's restraint of the father was the basis of the totemic system, and this restriction is perpetually at risk and in need of reinforcement (pp. 100–01). This initially implausible claim has become increasingly credible, partly as a consequence of the growing exposure of the incidence of child sexual abuse and partly as the theme of 'Oedipus Rex' and 'Hamlet' have been seen as fundamental to the motivations and symbolism of civilization, for example, in Otto Rank's classical study of *The Incest Theme in Literature and Legend.* (1912; see also Jones, 1949; Rudnytsky, 1987; Young, 1993–94)

According to Freud, the act of murdering the rapacious father gave rise, not only to totemism and thereby to civilization but also to the basis of the Oedipus complex and the experience of guilt: 'We cannot get away from the assumption that man's sense of guilt springs from the Oedipus complex and was acquired at the killing of the father by the brothers banded together' (Freud, 1930, p. 131).

People are innately aggressive. 'Man is a wolf to other men' and hence must be tamed by institutions (p. 111; Gay, 1988, p. 546). The constitutional inclination to aggression is the greatest hindrance or impediment to civilization (Freud, 1930, pp. 129, 142). It is in this context that the space within which civilization occurs is described as bounded by the great opposition between love and destructiveness. 'Civilization is a process in the service of Eros, whose purpose is to combine single human individuals, and after that families, then races, peoples and nations, into one great unity, the unity of mankind . . . But man's aggressive instinct, the hostility of each against all and all against each, opposes this programme of civilization' (p. 122). The aggressive instinct is derivative of the death instinct. 'The history of civilization is the struggle between Eros and Death. It is what all life essentially consists of' (*Ibid.*).

This is a dour doctrine: life *consists of* – *is* – a struggle between love and destructiveness. Civilization *consists* of renunciation. He says elsewhere that 'love and necessity are the parents of civilization' (p. 101). We live our lives in a space between the two great meta-instincts, and the main forces at work are rapacious sexual and destructive instincts, guilt, renunciation and sublimation. Those who thought Klein's renderings of the Death Instinct too pessimistic did not read their *Civilization and Its Discontents*. She says that the interaction of the life and death instincts governs all of life (Klein, 1958, p. 245).

Once again, guilt is the means civilization employs to inhibit aggressiveness. The aggression is turned from external authority to internal prohibition and makes up the stern conscience or superego (Freud, 1930, p. 123). Freud sees 'the sense of guilt as the most important problem in the development of civilization' and claims 'that the price we pay for our advance in civilization is a loss of happiness through heightening of the sense of guilt'. He calls this 'the final conclusion of our investigation', thus making vivid the juxtaposition of civilization and discontent in his title (p.134). Peter Gay comments, 'Social institutions are many things for Freud, but above all they are dams against murder, rape, and incest' (Gay, 1988, p. 547).

I want to make a number of observations about Freud's theory of culture or civilization. First and foremost, it is mightily pessimistic and becomes the more so the more carefully one studies it. Peter Gay says, 'Freud's theory of civilization . . . views life in society as an imposed compromise and hence an essentially insoluble predicament' (p. 547). But, however hard Freud's view is, I must warn you that when we come to Bion's ideas on groups and institutions in chapters seven and eight we will find them even more so. My own reluctant conclusion is that neither Freud nor Bion is unduly pessimistic, but even if they were, it is extremely important to know not only that the veneer of civilization is thin but just how thin it is, lest we fall through it by dancing with too much gay abandon.

Putting this point another way, much of the libertarian optimism of the 1960s was based on the – essentially Reichian – belief that underneath our repressed selves lay a wonderfully Edenic innocence waiting to burst forth if we could only free ourselves from the repressive confines of authoritarian society. But what did burst forth when attempts were made to remove repression was the contents of Pandora's Box and a lot of bad behaviour which was aptly criticised as 'the tyranny of structurelessness' (Freeman, 1970). So I've arrived at a point where I'm quite happy to respect the need for boundaries and institutions, though they should not be more repressive than necessary. Care must be taken to distinguish authoritarianism, which it is as important as ever to oppose (and rather more so in some societies), from legitimate containment, which provides a precious framework for living, without which we are lost.

The space which Freud gives us for culture is not only fraught and precarious; it is not truly social. That is, his theory is based on a swingeing reductionism. There are no mediations between the inner world and the social and cultural worlds.

We have seen that the elimination of the primal father is the precondition and the source of energy for all of culture and that the Oedipus complex was the beginning of religion, morality, society and art (Gay, 1988, pp. 330, 332). Freud also argues that the development of civilization 'parallels the development of the individual and employs the same methods' (Freud, 1930, p. 144). The same dynamic sources account for individual behaviour and social phenomena (Gay, 1988, p. 312). For example, all of science grows from the child's search for the truth about the differences between the sexes and the mysteries of conception and birth (p. 314).

Freud said of *The Future of an Illusion* and *Civilization and Its Discontents*, 'I recognised ever more clearly that the events of human history, the interactions between human nature, cultural development, and the precipitates of primeval experience (as whose representative religion pushes to the fore) are only the reflection of the dynamic conflicts among ego, id, and superego, which psychoanalysis studies in the individual – the same events repeated on a wider stage' (quoted in Gay, p. 547). His biographer concludes, 'He could not have stated the essential unity of his thought any more forcefully' (*Ibid.*).

There is no place in Freud's thinking for what the social scientists call 'the autonomy of the social', that is, for social causes operating at a different level from the psychological and deriving from genuinely social forces, even though they are mediated through the individual psyche. There is not even *relative* autonomy. This is one reason why, when psychoanalysis is applied to other cultures, the result is so often wooden. The same can often be said of psychoanalytic renderings of aspects of our own culture – literature, painting, cinema, etc. Its use involves very basic, universal, explanatory factors which too often miss out the sensuous particularity of individual characters, nuances of plot or of light and shadow. It is rather like explaining the items in a chemist's shop by speaking only in terms of the fundamental particles of physics and chemistry – atoms, electrons, neutrons and protons – rather than referring to more phenomenal items like talcum powder, sun creme, athlete's foot medicine, condoms and perfume. There are objects, events and relationships in the everyday world which are entitled to their own level of discourse, and psychoanalysis needs to enrich its conceptual language to take account of them and – hopefully – to illuminate them.

The strictly Freudian model is not enough, but it is damned hard to specify what should be added. I am at present of two minds. I have felt for a long time that more was needed to help make sense of groups, institutions, historical events and other dynamics above the level of the family. I still think this and am engaged with others in trying to develop psychoanalytic ideas which are useful in 'the public sphere'. For example, I think that the concept of 'second nature' helps to bring unconscious phenomena into better contact with history. Second nature is deeply sedimented socialisation, but it is not biology, not inherited genetically. It is profoundly refractory but acquired in experience. It becomes a political project to analyse second nature and set about changing it (Young, 1988a). I shall sketch here some exemplary contributions to this project.

Herbert Marcuse and other people of, or influenced by, the Frankfurt School of Critical Theory have thought carefully about the articulation between the unconscious and historicity. It could be argued that much of the work of Theodor Adorno, Max Horkheimer and Erich Fromm (at least in the 1930s) was addressed to the boundary between nature and culture and the question of second nature. They were concerned, as Herbert Marcuse was more extensively, with 'the psychological obstacles in the path of meaningful social change' (Jay, 1973, p. 107), and Horkheimer was perfectly clear about the debt to Freud of the work of the Frankfurt Institute for Social Research: 'His thought is one of the foundation stones without which our own philosophy would not be what it is' (p. 102). Marcuse's *Eros and Civilization: A Philosophical Inquiry into Freud* (1955), was an attempt to examine the assumptions of *Civilization and Its Discontents* from the perspective of neo-Marxist ideas about human nature as a *relatively* social phenomenon, an ensemble of social relations. In this and other key writings – most notably *One Dimensional Man: The Ideology of Industrial Society* (1964), *An Essay on Liberation* (1969a) and *Five Lectures: Psychoanalysis, Politics and Utopia* (1970) – he provides a critique of psychology and social science which is, in my view, of unparalleled range and subtlety among the writers of the second half of the century, with respect to the problems of the human spirit in modern society. For my present purpose, however, it is not appropriate to provide an exposition of his overall argument. (For example, unlike many who drew on Freud for ideas in the social realm, Marcuse sought to give due weight to the death instinct, the destructive side of human nature.) I want to confine myself to an outline of those of his ideas which span psychoanalysis and historicity. In particular, Marcuse has offered a set of concepts which have two components (Marcuse, 1955, ch. 2). The first is universal in human nature, while the second is historically relative. At times he appears to say that the first is also historically relative on a much longer time scale, but this is left unresolved in his work.

At the first level, we have, for example, the reality principle, much as Freud would have it. But Marcuse adds another component, which changes over time and is the result of particular historical formations and contingencies. He calls this the 'performance principle', a measure of the requirement for productivity in education and at work which would change, for example, when the factory system replaced home labour or automation replaced earlier versions of the assembly line. In a more just and egalitarian society, in which competition for scarce resources was greatly reduced or eliminated, the 'performance' aspect would be radically diminished, perhaps to the vanishing point. As things stand, however, the powers that be seek to convince us that the necessity to bow to the requirements of super-exploitation is 'realistic'. Marcuse wants to grant the need for realism but to retain the right to envisage a better society, without allowing a sense of immutable inevitability to the present one. In the existing order of things, how hard people work is the result of a social and economic system which he abhors. The norms of production are determined by the profit motive. In a different system (not the ones which were until recently in operation in Eastern Europe, which he also abhorred), there could be much less alienated labour – less requirement to meet quotas, to perform on demand.

A second example of Marcuse's concepts which have both a universal and a historical component is concerned with repression, a basic mechanism with respect to the unconscious. He points out that the degree of repression is dramatically increased in certain societies, producing a requirement for 'surplus repression', which – like the performance principle – is historically relative. This was an important preoccupation of the Frankfurt School, since they were attempting to understand the psycho-social phenomena of Fascism in Europe, from which they went into exile, and of extreme conformism in America, to which they went for refuge and where Marcuse remained until his death in 1979. Powerful forces of authoritarianism and conformity were at work in both societies, though enforced by different sanctions. Moreover, Marcuse was a pioneer among leftists in mounting a critique of orthodox communism. His *Soviet Marxism* (1958) was, along with *Eros and Civilization* and *One Dimensional Man*, a key text for the student radicals and 'New Left' of the 1960s, who wished to revive the ideals of an unsullied vision of communism without having to embrace or defend Stalinism or even, in many cases, Leninism.

Marcuse was not, however, an advocate of the sort of 'let her rip' left libertarianism which many associated with that movement. He makes a point about sublimation and desublimation which was wise and cautionary and applied especially to the so-called 'sexual revolution' of that period. There was greater scope for promiscuity, nudity and soft pornography. But these forms of de-repression were alienated, ersatz and therefore, whatever their surface allure, fundamentally repressive. For this he coined the inelegant but accurate term 'repressive desublimation', to designate an historically relative, alienated sexual libertinism. The same critique was applied to many dimensions of political life and the 'consumer society'. He wrote a very influential essay on the ways in which nominally liberal political tolerance could, in fact, act as 'repressive tolerance' (Marcuse, 1969). With the vast growth of consumer goods and services, forms of comfort and leisure were being offered which diverted people's gaze from the absence of fundamental forms of freedom, fulfilment and self-expression: the society of the spectacle, the club and the lawn, ever more bizarre forms of dress and sexual licence – all of which sought to convert 'revolt into style'.

This same way of thinking led him to argue that in an age of extreme conformity and social authoritarianism, the traditional roles of the father and the family as sources and loci of the nurturing of values could be diminished so much that we would have to rethink aspects of traditional Freudianism with respect to family dynamics. For example, one of his *Five Lectures* was entitled 'The Obsolescence of the Freudian Concept of Man', in which he argued that 'the classical psychoanalytic model, in which the father and the father-dominated family was the agent of mental socialisation, is being invalidated by society's direct management of the nascent ego through the mass media, school and sport teams, gangs, etc.' (1970, p. 47).

Finally, he argued that at an even deeper level that 'the biologically given' is an elastic concept for human beings. He felt that *all* human needs have an historical character. They 'lie beyond the animal world. They are historically determined and are historically mutable (1970, pp. 62, 63, 65). Going further, he suggests in some places that the instinctual nature of humankind is malleable (1969a, p. 21; cf. on this equivocal point pp. 16, 17, 51, 63, 88, 91 and my discussion in Young, 1973, pp. 257–9 and, more generally, Jacoby, 1981; Jay, 1973, 1984; Young, 1988a).

Throughout his writings on psychoanalysis and society, Marcuse was attempting to remove Freud's ideas from the realm of universal humankind, to bring them inside history and put them at the disposal of those who wish to change human nature and society as they are found in particular societies and circumstances. At the same time, he was pointing out the politics *in* psychoanalytic concepts. He attempted 'to show the social and political content in basic psychoanalytic concepts . . . The psychoanalytic categories do not have to be "related" to social and political conditions – they are themselves social and political categories. Psychoanalysis could become an effective social and political instrument, positive as well as negative, in an administrative as well as critical function, because Freud had discovered the mechanisms of social and political control in the depth dimension of instinctual drives and satisfactions' (Marcuse, 1970, p. 44). I believe that there is much still to be learned from reflecting on his attempts to tease apart and challenge the levels of mutability and refractoriness in psychoanalytic concepts.

In the wake of Marcuse's and others' neo-Marxist writings, Victor Wolfenstein (to whose work on racism I shall return in chapter five) has set out to lay new groundwork for the relations between psychoanalysis and Marxism (Wolfenstein, 1993). He offers a thoroughgoing analysis of the dynamics of the socio-economic and historical, on the one hand, and the intrapsychic, on the other. The project of interrogating psychoanalysis with social and ideological questions, stoutly resisting reductionism and developing ideas adequate to a truly social and historical level of explanation, remains essential to my sense of mental space.

But while much of what I have written in these last pages is exemplary of the project of a social level of psychoanalytic thinking, it is a detour from my main purpose. I said (p. 25) I was of *two* minds. I have come simultaneously to hold the other point of view. I do so reluctantly and remain full of suspicion. Even so, as a result of my own analysis, clinical work and ongoing reflection, I have come to feel that there is more to be learned by looking even deeper into the unconscious, where we may perhaps find *socially* illuminating forces *beyond* and even *below reductionism,* as it were. In the remainder of this book I pursue this path while bracketing the more obviously social one.

I turn first to Donald Winnicott, whose writings on the primitive elements of culture strike me as among the most interesting in the psychoanalytic literature. The foregoing exposition of Freud's theory of culture notwithstanding, Winnicott argued that 'Freud did not have a place in his topography of the mind for the experience of things cultural. He gave new value to inner psychic reality, and from this came a new value for things that are actual and truly external. Freud used the word "sublimation" to point the way to a place where cultural experience is meaningful, but perhaps he did not get so far as to tell us where in the mind cultural experience is' (Winnicott, 1971, p. 112).

Winnicott seeks to rectify this omission with his concept of 'transitional phenomena'. I shall have much more to say about this in chapter six, but I want to offer a brief exposition here in the context of other psychoanalytic theories of culture. Winnicott says, 'I have used the term cultural experience as an extension of the idea of transitional phenomena and of play without being certain that I can define the word "culture". The accent needed is on experience. In using the word culture I am thinking of the inherited tradition. I am thinking of something that is in the common pool of humanity, into which individuals and groups of people contribute, and from which we may all draw *if we have somewhere to put what we find'* (p. 116). The place he offers is 'located is in the *potential space* between the individual and the environment' (p. 118). It 'is at the interplay between there being nothing but me and there being objects and phenomena outside omnipotent control' (*Ibid.*).

The notion of transitional phenomena is a generalisation of his concept of the transitional object, which he regards as 'both the child's first use of a symbol and its first experience of play' (p. 113). It is the first experience of a 'not-me' and fills the space of separateness between the mother and baby when the mother goes away for periods. It is neither subjective nor objective but partakes of both. It is both a deprivation of the mother and a symbol of union between mother and baby (pp. 115, 119). Typical examples are an infant's blanket (think of Linus' security blanket in the cartoon strip, 'Peanuts' – Schultz, 1976); it may be a piece of cloth or a teddy bear, the most famous example of which is Winnie the Pooh (Milne, 1926).

According to Winnicott, if the baby has no such controlled abandonment by the mother and recourse to transitional objects, it has no chance to use objects creatively, and there is no ability to play, no basis for cultural experience, no link with cultural inheritance and no basis for contributing to culture. This is his notion of a severely deprived child, unable to trust that the mother will return and therefore unable to risk playing, imagining or creating (Winnicott, 1971, p. 119). He calls the world of transitional objects, transitional phenomena and culture a 'third world' – neither inner reality nor the external world but transitional between them, a potential space that can partake of both and be filled with all the wonders of fun, art, religion, science and creativity (pp. 120–21).

The whole atmosphere of Winnicott's cultural space is positive and uplifting. What is awful is what happens if the controlled abandonment by the maternal figure does not occur at an appropriate rate. If it is too fast, there is no trust. If it is too slow, there is insufficient self-reliance and independence. But the tone of his writing about culture is far from the bitter struggle which is common to Freudian and most Kleinian cultural theory. This is not surprising, since Winnicott was unwilling to attach the significance to destructive or death wishes that Freud and Klein did (Winnicott, 1965, pp. 177, 178). His is an altogether more optimistic world view, not devoid of destructiveness and hate, but he does not make them half of human nature.

Winnicott grants that failure satisfactorily to make this developmental change to object relations in the transitional space can lead, in certain case, to 'a hypertrophy of intellectual processes related to a potential schizophrenic breakdown' (Winnicott, 1975, p. 225). He also granted the importance of what Klein called 'the depressive position' (wherein we relate to whole objects and can bear the mixture of good and bad in lovedones – see below, p. 78) and of reparation and listed the depressive position as Klein's most important contribution, which he ranked with Freud's concept of the Oedipus complex: 'the human individual cannot accept the destructive and aggressive ideas in his or her own nature without experience of reparation, and it is for this reason that the continued presence of the love object is necessary at this stage since only in this way is there opportunity for reparation' (Winnicott, 1965, p. 176).

I have stressed Winnicott's acknowledgement of the importance of the depressive position and reparation, which are central to Klein's notion of mental well-being, in order to make clear that though he grants much to her ideas in this area, he did *not* place these ideas at the centre of his explanation of cultural experience. Klein and Hanna Segal did. In a context that refers to the work of all artists, Segal says, 'all creation is really a re-creation of a once-loved and once whole, but now lost and ruined object, a ruined internal world and self. It is when the world within us is destroyed, when it is dead and loveless, when our loved ones are in fragments, and we ourselves in helpless despair – it is then that we must recreate our world anew, reassemble the pieces, infuse life into dead fragments, re-create life' (Segal, 1981, p. 190). In a postscript to this essay, 'A Psychoanalytic Approach to Aesthetics' (written almost thirty years later), she reiterates her main thesis 'that the essence of the aesthetic creation is a resolution of the central depressive situation and that the main factor in the aesthetic experience is the identification with this process' (p. 204). On this view, culture is a reparative process, mending a rent caused by the primitive self's own destructive impulses in the inner world. It is an attempt to move from the persecution and fragmentation of 'the paranoid-schizoid position' (see below, p. 78) to the depressive position, by means of reparation.

In his writings on aesthetic appreciation Donald Meltzer adopts a more positive tone, bordering on the mystical, and stresses the satisfying intimate 'fit' of the result. He refers to 'the essence of aesthetic appreciation through symbolic congruence: the "fitting" of the individual mind to the aesthetic object, in such a way that boundaries merge and yet the independent integrity of both partners in the drama – internal and external world – is affirmed and radiates significance . . . At the heart of aesthetic appreciation lies the problem of holding, recognising, the feel of the dream which is evoked between the dreamer and the aesthetic object (whatever form this may take). This is a diaphanous cloud of unknowing, which seems composed nevertheless of solid elements with shape and texture, awaiting capture into a symbolic correspondence' (Meltzer and Harris Williams, 1988, pp. 178, 179). Meltzer is exceptional among Kleinians in positing an ecstatic dimension to the aesthetic experience, a return to the bliss of the Garden of Eden of the first experience of the mother's beauty. (I shall be saying more about Meltzer's ideas about mental space in chapter three.)

I have canvassed a small number of psychoanalytic positions on cultural space. For Freud it is perpetually endangered, always operating on energy borrowed from the most rapacious and destructive impulses, inhabiting a force field between erotic and death-dealing impulses. For Winnicott it is rather more benign, conceived as a transitional world with rather a lot of potentially playful and creative space. With Segal we return to the fraught world of destructive feelings, with culture as an effort to make amends for our phantasy attacks on the mother's body. Meltzer, if I understand him, returns us to the bliss of Eden – perfect congruence between inner and outer – not a sublimation or reparation but a recurrent return to bliss.

None of these, it seems to me, provides a genuinely *social* cultural space. None transcends the reductionism of the intrapsychic which characterised Freud's account. Is this forevermore to characterise psychoanalytic accounts of culture? As I said above, this continues to concern me, but so does the hope of finding more if we probe deeper into the unconscious.

3   MENTAL SPACE

Having posed the problem of a space for mind in a world of bodies in chapter one and having surveyed ideas about culture – the largest space for exercising our humanity – in chapter two, I now want to turn directly to available ways of thinking about mental space. According to the paradigm of explanation of modern thought, all true and veridical explanations should be in terms of matter, motion and number or extension, figure and number.

As we saw in chapter one, the world is divided into extended substances and thinking substances, bodies and minds. Our humanity is a feature of ourselves as persons, an amalgam of minds and bodies, and we are thereby skewered or rent. We get treated to genuinely reductionist accounts, whereby mind is reduced to matter. Or we are metaphorically reduced so that mind is treated analogously to body. Or we are treated to a reductionism whereby we are considered in terms of a formal, science-like system, of which linguistics and structuralism are examples. Those are the scientific or science-like solutions. The more commonsensical one is that we get split into a mind in relation to a body. This is utterly odd, since who we are is all mixed up with how we feel about our bodies, yet we seem to live in our minds, while our feelings often get put into our bodies – 'somatized' – in ways that are odd, distressing and sometimes fatal, as in some psychosomatic (Menninger, 1938) and eating disorders (Kaufman and Heiman, 1964). Attempts to conceptualise the mind-body relationship have never got very far. It remains a mystery. Indeed, one of the main psychoanalytic texts on the subject is candidly entitled *On the Mysterious Leap from the Mind to the Body* (Deutsch, 1959).

According to science, finally and fundamentally, the spatio-temporal is thought to constitute nature. This leaves no reliable conceptual niche for the mental or the emotional. It is in the light of that broad issue that I am attempting to locate psychoanalysis. That is why 'mental space' is a problematic concept. According to Cartesian dualism, the reigning conceptualisation of our world view, if something is mental, it can't be spatial, and if it's spatial, it can't be mental.

How, then, is it appropriate to think *about* how we think, feel, picture? I am trying to draw a broad distinction between diagrammatic and schematic ways of thinking, on the one hand, and humanistic ones, on the other. I am not saying that there is a clear distinction between spatial and evocative explanations. I am trying to discover what kinds of explanations involving space – because all do – will be least likely to treat us as things: desiccated, reductionist, formalistic, mechanical, dead. The mind has always been conceived in some way that is spatial, but it can be statically spatial or dynamically so: picture thinking or movies, schemata or renderings of mental geography which encourage journeys of discovery, where one can learn from experience.

What I want to do in this chapter is not easy to convey. I shall say it at the start, do it and then take stock at the end. This has been the hardest chapter to write. I posed myself the problem: concepts of mental space. Then I drew on my own reading, thinking and clinical experience to address the question: what is in the mind? The more I thought, the more I didn't know. It took me the longest time to figure out that it's okay that I don't know, because it's concepts of mental space, not the contents of any particular mind, that I want to write about. The issue is not one of content but of capacity, not what is contained but that there should be a suitable container so that we can do for ourselves and our lovedones what a good analyst does: take things in; hold, ruminate and detoxify them; and, if seemly, let them out again in good time and good measure so that they can be of some constructive use in facilitating thought , feeling and constructively relating.

The history of thought about the mind and feelings is a terrible muddle. What I am seeking is a sense of the possibility of mental space, not what's in it. The goal of humanity and of psychoanalysis is the facilitation of a suitable space for containing, ruminating and making use of experience – not tipping it out, reprojecting it, mimicking it, batting it away, hoarding it, etc.

What's in the mind? How shall we think of it? The answers to those questions constitute the history of psychology, or, more broadly, the history of ideas of human nature. At other times and places a way into what was meant by human nature was characterised by a pantheon of gods. Every civilization has had its more or less complex complement of ideologies and gods. I will not now plunge into a history of ancient mythologies, but I will share one anecdote. An Indian woman, a psychoanalyst, came to me and offered to write a textbook of Kleinian ideas in terms of the gods of Hindu religion: Vishnu, the Destroyer, various sexualities and so on. It was immediately obvious to me that this would be a map of the way that culture thought about human nature, just as the Greek and Roman and other civilizations' gods are. The history of a civilization's views of that which o'erlooks its people is a reflections of its beliefs, hopes, fears and idealisations about itself. It is a map or a set of *dramatis personae* of its inner world, projected into the sky and underworld. This was the point of Freud's essay on religion, *The Future of an Illusion* (1927).

In our own cultural and intellectual tradition – by which I mean the Greco-Roman and Judeo-Christian traditions – the basic opposition in the history of theories about the inner world has been between that which is permanent, associated with the Greek pre-Socratic philosopher, Parminides, and that which is in flux, associated with Heraclitus. That which is permanent came to be thought of as Platonic, since Plato believed that what is most real is eternal – the formal features, forms or ideas. That which is in flux is traditionally associated with empiricism, whose most revered figure is the eighteenth-century Scottish philosopher, David Hume.

In recent thought, the abiding features in the mind have been referred to as *schemata*, the organising categories. The other element is the flux of life, the experiential and contingent. The problem of the orienting categories or universals came down to modern psychology as the question of faculties, traits or structural features of the mind. These are the framework for making sense of what we suffer in life – the day-to-day experiences, accidents, surprises, the raw material for learning. The question of how to classify – that in terms of which we think of mind – is the central issue for the psychology of personality. If there were no categories, no organising principles, no niches, we could not make sense of experience. Schemata without experience are empty; experiences without schemata are blind. They would not count as experience, since they would not be contained at all and would have no meaning. That is the point of conditioning in lower functions and symbolism in higher functions. The categories are given in the mind of the individual and – as we now think – have evolved during the history of the species.

There are many such classifications, some commensurable, some not,

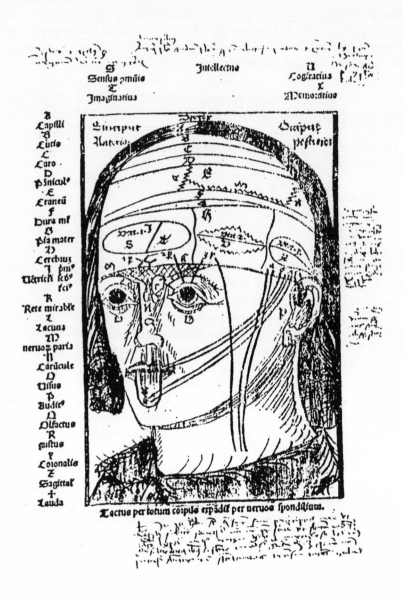

Illustration of ventricular localization from Magnus Hundt,
Anthropologicum, Leipzig, 1501 (see Pagel, 1958, facing p. 112).

some deep in folklore, some part of formal notions about human nature, some part of attempts at a science of mind. There are the five senses and the orienting sense, proprioception. These provide the raw materials for perception, which, in turn, on the empiricist account, add up to thoughts. There are various lists of passions. There are the seven deadly sins, a list of base passions. There is the major and basic opposition between good and evil, monitored by the moral sense. There are religions based on this. Manicheanism, a competitor with early Christianity, treated history as an eternal struggle between good and evil. I often think of this as the forerunner of Freud and Klein's idea of the great opposition between Eros and Thanatos.

Inside the recognisably scientific history of physiology and medicine, there is a long tradition of categorisation of mind. A typical list would include senses, intellect or reason, and memory. Many would list the senses separately and specify a place where they flowed together, the *sensorium commune*. These faculties were not always localised in the substance of the brain prior to the nineteenth century. They were frequently located in the ventricles of the brain, each with its own space, which was literally a cavity.

Throughout these classifications there was a wide divide between nature – the categories – and nurture or experience. From the seventeenth century onward, this took the form of a distinction between the flux of associations on the one hand and the larger units or categories on the other. This grand dichotomy was treated as analogous to the reigning theories in physics, called 'the mechanical philosophy': something akin to atoms and impacts. The atoms of physics became, by analogy, the particles of experience. How they banged into each other in order to build up experience, and not merely in a billiard ball way, became the problem of psychological theory. The reigning attempt to explain this was and is the association of ideas. There are elementary particles or sensa of experience. There are compounds and combinations – a whole metaphorical physics and chemistry. Thereby, mind was subjected to a reductionism, a metaphorical materialism.

The genealogy of the association of ideas or associationism, as the tradition came to be known, is not important to my present purpose, which is to examine its formal features in the context of notions of mental space. There are useful histories of associationism (Ribot, 1873; Warren, 1921), I have attempted to summarise the tradition (Young, 1968; 1970, chs. 2, 3, 5) and Rapaport, the chief codifier of ego psychology, has traced its history from Bacon to Kant (1974). The leading figures in the associationist tradition include the empiricist philosophers: Thomas Hobbes, John Locke, David Hume and John Stuart Mill. Others concentrated on the psychological aspects: John Gay, David Hartley (Young, 1972a), Étienne Bonnot de Condillac, James Mill, Alexander Bain (Young, 1970, ch. 3), Herbert Spencer (*Ibid.*, chs. 5, 6), David Ferrier (*Ibid.*, ch. 8) and Sigmund Freud.

Alongside this scientism lay various formalisms from folk psychology, with their own lists of passions, traits and faculties. These provided classifications, containers, ways of codifying raw experiences: form and content.

All of the above addressed themselves to the question of how the flow of experience leads to knowledge, character and personality. However, there are at least two divides. Many were more concerned with questions of epistemology – how can we know – than with questions of character and personality. The second divide had three branches. I have stressed associationism – a sort of mental atomism. Then there was the classification of mind according to reason, memory and other general, rather intellectualist, faculties. Finally, there was the more popular folk psychology of faculties or traits, which merges into folk tales and literature.

Various ideas about the structure of mind floated about in philosophy, debates about human nature and folk psychology for centuries, and some were speculatively linked to ideas about what is in the head. But serious empirical attempts to root conceptions of human nature in real science were not made until the turn of the nineteenth century, when systems for reading character from the visage, part of a long-standing tradition known as physiognomy, were connected to claims about the underlying brain, which came to be known as phrenology. Once again, I have no desire to tell stories at greater length than is relevant to my present purpose, especially since I have done it elsewhere (Young, 1968a, 1970, ch. 1).

What the phrenologists claimed was that there was a one-to-one correlation between features on the surface of the face and cranium, on the one hand, and underlying brain area, on the other. Each faculty or trait had its own localised area of brain, so that the functions of the brain *were* the faculties or traits. This was a tidy solution, since it raised no problem about relating the language of psychology to the language of physiology, thereby finessing an important aspect of the mind-body problem: mind-brain relations. The more important the faculty or trait, the larger the brain area and the corresponding protuberance on the surface of the skull. This theory was full of flaws. Indeed, it was nonsense at the empirical level, but it bore important conceptual fruits for the history of localisation of functions in the brain and theories of human nature. In particular, it stimulated research on cerebral anatomy and physiology. It also led to clinico-pathological correlations between neurological symptoms and studies of cerebral pathology. For our purpose this was notably true of Freud's neuropathological research on speech disorders due to brain damage, i.e., aphasia, the subject of his first book (1891), which provided the model for mind that he took over into *The Interpretation of Dreams* (1900). I'll return to this below.

Phrenology had a simple answer to the question: what is human nature? Human nature was the result of the combined action of the twenty-seven fundamental faculties (the list eventually grew to thirty-five), acting with the combined strengths of the particular combination in a given individual. If one looks at a list of phrenological faculties, they offer a fairly comprehensive list of attributes for thinking about human nature. There were debates about what should or should not be on the list, but the *approach* remained valid up to our own time, and the role of the founder of phrenology, Franz Joseph Gall, was recognised in modern personality theory, just as it is in the history of brain research (Young, 1972). A useful paper in the mid-1930s in a mainstream psychology journal, *Character and Personality,* was entitled 'Faculty versus Traits: Gall's Solution' (Spoerl, 1935–6), just as esteemed students of the nervous system could refer to important discoveries in the early twentieth century as the 'new phrenology', and a serious student of the history of research could write in *The Encyclopedia Britannica,* with credible licence, 'We are now all more or less phrenologists' (Anon., 1902, p. 710).

In addition to sketching the general problem of the categories of mental space, the dimension of all of this to which I want to draw particular attention is the role of the concept of 'function' in psychology and brain research. The concept of function and a theoretical tradition deriving from it – functionalism – loom large in the history of the human sciences in the late nineteenth and twentieth centuries, but it would take us out of our way to consider them (see Young, 1981a, for an account and bibliography). The concept of function and the adjective 'functional' brought comparative and developmental ideas into psychology and brought biological ideas of evolution and adaptation into theories of mind. These allowed theories of the dynamics of personality to move easily between the psychological, on the one hand, and the physiological and biological, on the other, without leaving the theory skewered or repeatedly jumping across a ghastly chasm between the mental and the bodily. 'Function' and 'functional' created common ground between the mental and the physiological. 'Functions' are exquisitely ambiguous between the categories of the mind and the body: 'mental functions', 'the functions of the brain', 'the functions of digestion and respiration' seem to inhabit a common space of integrated psychological and physiological concepts.

Freud took up this way of thinking from the English evolutionary associationist, Herbert Spencer, in his writings on aphasia, just as he took up the philosophical doctrine of psychophysical parallelism from John Hughlings Jackson in the same study. He learned to think in functional terms in the course of his attempts to classify forms of speech disorder neuropathologically (Riese, 1958).

You may feel that my argument is following a strange trajectory, but, as I mentioned above, I am heading in my own way toward *The Interpretation of Dreams* (1900) and the problematic nature of ideas of mental space in psychoanalysis. In the 'Project for a Scientific Psychology' (1895) Freud gave us five diagrams, one of them about the external world and stimuli (Freud, 1895, p. 313), one about how inhibition occurs (p. 324), one depicting the ego in neuronal terms (p. 324), one about the link between conscious and unconscious in dreams (p. 341). The final one, in his discussion of psychopathology, shows a different sort of link. It depicts a mixture of phenomenal matters – shop-assistants, clothes, shop – with psychological matters and biological ones – laughter, assault, flight, sexual release, being alone (p. 354). I think there is a progression here. He becomes increasingly comfortable about moving back and forth between the bodily and the mental and then represents the mental, the neuronal and the personal in a single frame of reference.

I now want to address how Freud wrote about mental spaces in *The Interpretation of Dreams*. I shall then compare his language with writings by Melanie Klein, Susan Isaacs, Wilfred Bion and Donald Meltzer. My aim is to explore ways of representing mental space. I believe that these writers move from picture thinking in Freud to writing about dimensionality in ways that place the spatial purely at the service of representing emotional dynamics. I think that psychoanalytic writing has moved from rather reductive picture thinking to representations of the problem of a space to think – capaciousness, container and contained.

Freud tells us early on about what a tangle dream thoughts are and refers to the dream's navel, about branching out and directions. This is metaphorical space. Then there is a very important passage where he provides diagrams (Freud, 1900, pp. 536–8). All are based on the reflex arc: stimulus-response. The way he is thinking about dreams is immersed in a functional model of mental and physiological, a physiological notion of the reflex and a neuroanatomical framework of localisation of functions.

Freud is discussing an idea of Fechner, 'that *the scene of action of dreams is different from that of waking intellectual life*' (p. 536). He comments, 'What is presented to us in these words is the idea of *psychical locality*. I shall entirely disregard the fact that the mental apparatus with which we are here concerned is also known to us in the form of an anatomical preparation, and I shall carefully avoid the temptation to determine psychical locality in any anatomical fashion', which he has been doing hitherto. 'I shall remain upon psychological ground, and I propose simply to follow the suggestion that we should picture the instrument which carries out our mental functions as resembling a compound microscope or a photographic apparatus, or something of the kind' (*Ibid.*) Here is the I-it notion of subject and object being viewed across epistemological space which I discussed in chapter one. 'On that basis, psychical locality will correspond to a point inside the apparatus at which one of the preliminary stages of an image comes into being. In the microscope and telescope, as we know, these occur in part at ideal points, regions in which no tangible component of the apparatus is situated. I see no necessity to apologise for the imperfections of this or any similar imagery. Analogies of this kind are only intended to assist us in our attempt to make the complications of mental functioning intelligible by dissecting the function and assigning its different constituents to different components of the apparatus. So far as I know, the experiment has not hitherto been made of using this method of dissection in order to investigate the way in which the mental instrument is put together, and I can see no harm in it . . .

'Accordingly, we will picture the mental apparatus as a compound instrument, to the components of which we will give the name of "agencies", or (for the sake of greater clarity) "systems". It is to be anticipated, in the next place, that these systems may perhaps stand in a regular spatial relation to one another, in the same kind of way in which the various systems of lenses in a telescope are arranged behind one another. Strictly speaking, there is no need for the hypothesis that the psychical systems are actually arranged in a *spatial* order. It would be sufficient if a fixed order were established by the fact that in a given psychical process the excitation passes thought he system in a particular *temporal* sequence.' Now we are falling back on the reflex arc as a model for thinking. 'The first thing that strikes us is that this apparatus, compounded of Y systems, has a sense of direction. All our psychical activity starts from stimuli (either internal or external) and ends in innervations. Accordingly, we shall ascribe a sensory and motor end to the apparatus. At the sensory end there lies a system which receives perceptions; at the motor end there lies another, which opens the gateway to motor activity. Psychical processes advance in general from the perceptual end to the motor end. Thus the most general schematic picture of the psychical apparatus may be represented thus:

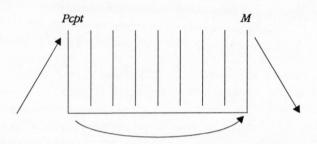

He concludes, 'This, however, does no more than fulfil a requirement with which we have long been familiar, namely that the psychical apparatus must be constructed like a reflex apparatus. Reflex processes remain the model of every psychical function' (pp. 536–8).

His spatial language is not always based on physiological space (but see p. 565); but it *is* always topographic. He speaks of dreams *located* in the unconscious, resistances *barring the path* to consciousness, wishes *finding their way*, things *slipping through, points of attachment, penetrating more deeply*, a *schematic picture*, a *psychological scaffolding, directions, paths,* ideas *covering* others, *localities in the mental apparatus*. Later on, we find him wishing to get away from notions of locality 'derived from a set of ideas relating to a struggle for a piece of ground' (p. 610). He says he would prefer to 'replace a topographic way of representing things by a dynamic one' (*Ibid.*). Ideas should 'never be localised in organic elements of the nervous system but, as one might say, *between* them', like a virtual image in a telescope (p. 611).

Nevertheless, he continues to use spatial analogies (p. 615) and to refer to the unconscious as a 'larger sphere', while the conscious is a 'smaller sphere' (pp. 612–13). He continues to use such images, although he is keen not to allow psychic reality to be confused with material reality (p. 620). If we look ahead to the structural hypothesis of id, ego and superego, these get represented spatially in relation to the topographic concepts of conscious, preconscious and unconscious in the famous egg diagram in *The Ego and the Id* (1923, p. 24), which is repeated in *The New Introductory Lectures* (1933, p. 78).

This schematic way of thinking, with topography and structure, employing terms without resonances in the language of everyday life and emotions, became defining characteristics of Freudian metapsychology. There is a continuity of rhetoric from Freud to latter-day Freudians, culminating in the systematic efforts of David Rapaport mentioned in chapter one, and summarized in his joint article with Merton Gill, 'The Points of View and Assumptions of Metapsychology' (1959), which I shall quote here in synoptic form:

'The *dynamic* point of view demands that the psycho-analytic explanation of any psychological phenomenon include propositions concerning the psychological forces involved in the phenomenon.

'(a) There are psychological forces.

'(b) Psychological forces are defined by their direction and magnitude.

'(c) The effect of simultaneously acting psychological forces may be the simple resultant of the work of each of these forces.

'(d) The effect of simultaneously acting psychological forces may not be the simple resultant of the work of each of these forces.

'The *economic* point of view demands that . . . psycho-analytic explanation . . . include propositions concerning the psychological energy involved in the phenomenon.

'(a) There are psychological energies.

'(b) Psychological energies follow a law of conservation.

'(c) Psychological energies are subject to a law of entropy.

'(d) Psychological energies are subject to transformations, which increase or decrease their entropic tendency.

'The *structural* point of view demands that . . . psycho-analytic explanation . . . include propositions concerning the abiding psychological configurations (structures) involved in the phenomenon.

'(a) There are psychological structures.

'(b) Structures are configurations of a slow rate of change.

'(c) Structures are configurations within which, between which, and by means of which mental processes take place.

'(d) Structures are hierarchically ordered.

'The *genetic* point of view demands that . . . psycho-analytic explanation . . . include propositions concerning its psychological origin and development.

'(a) All psychological phenomena have a psychological origin and development.

'(b) All psychological phenomena originate in innate givens, which mature according to an epigenetic groundplan.

'(c) The earlier forms of a psychological phenomenon, though superceded by later forms, remain potentially active.

'At each point of psychological history the totality of potentially active earlier forms codetermines all psychological phenomena.

'The *adaptive* point of view demands that . . . psycho-analytic explanation . . . include propositions concerning its relationship to the environment.

'(a) There exist psychological states of adaptedness and processes of adaptation at every point in life.

'(b) The processes of (autoplastic and/or alloplastic) adaptation maintain, restore, and improve the existing states of adaptedness and thereby ensure survival.

'(c) Man adapts to his society – both to the physical and human environments which are its products.

'(d) Adaptation relationships are mutual: man and environment adapt to each other' (Rapaport & Gill, 1959, pp. 8- 9).

The systematic spelling out of this way of thinking makes it painfully and irritatingly obvious that this rampant scientism drains the life and feeling out of experience. How's your epigenetic groundplan? Are you adapting enough to your society? Do you prefer to do so autoplastically or alloplastically? The authors grant that some of their assumptions may not pan out, but they suggest that the points of view 'should be accepted – for the time being – as the framework of psycho-analytic metapsychology' (p. 9). When I was taught psychoanalysis at a leading American medical school, it was presented in these terms, proudly rooted in biology.

There is warrant in Freud's corpus for each assertion in neo-Freudian metapsychology. What Rapaport and Gill did was to select the physicalist, biologistic and conformist elements and offer them as the whole. They were rightly criticised by Marcuse, Lacan and others for squeezing the life out of psychoanalysis and reducing it to a palliative, conservative pablum. The exercise of systematising psychoanalysis and filtering out the awkward and messy concepts is directly analogous to the fallacy of misplaced concreteness discussed in chapter one (p. 7). Our abstractions are allowed to be taken as the most concrete rendering of experience at the expense of a more mundane and every-day language which we experience as nearer to life itself, which somehow disappears. Nor is there a place in this scheme for un-worked-out theoretical concepts such as the ego ideal or cussed ontological ones like the death instinct. Heaven knows how this scheme would accommodate some of the more interesting ideas in non-Freudian psychoanalysis such as second skin, autistic cysts, false self, container/contained, claustrum, projective identification, paranoid-schizoid and depressive positions, transitional objects and phenomena, countertransference.

But there is more to Freud, as I've said, than physicalist scientism and picture thinking. There are two other major strands to his thinking. The first is the use of myth, the classics, dreams, poetry, literature, jokes and the phenomena of everyday life. The second is case studies, clinical material and the use he makes of autobiography: *stories.* In my opinion, Freud's writings are in tension between various versions of the language of extended substances, on the one hand, and a rich mixture of evocative and experiential accounts of the inner world, on the other. These are the scientific and the humanistic strands in his work. He is a mixture of picture thinking and functional/dynamic thinking.

In matters of this kind, there is no theory-neutral terrain. The very reading of texts is an interpretive activity. This is doubly true of Freud, since the text most people who are not fluent in German read is the translation into their own language, so what they read is filtered through the translators' way of thinking. The English translation is probably the one used most often. It has recently been pointed out that the translators of the so-called *Standard Edition of the Complete Psychological Works of Sigmund Freud* did their work while looking through neo-Freudian spectacles. It was translated under the general editorship of James Strachey, in collaboration with Anna Freud, assisted by Alix Strachey and Alan Tyson. They often chose words which were resonant with a scientistic rather than with a humanistic way of interpreting Freud's ideas. Bruno Bettleheim wrote an impassioned little book about this, *Freud and Man's Soul* (1983). His objection is not merely to the choice of terms but to a misrepresentation of the basic framework of Freud's thought, rendering it in objectivist terms. It could be argued that there is nothing to choose between the Strachey translation and the sort of reading proposed by Bettleheim, but the creation of a group devoted to bringing out a new translation makes it clear, at the very least, that the existing translation does not speak to how many people now interpret Freud's thinking. Karl Figlio (1984) has expanded this point into a wider debate about how we render the inner world psychoanalytically.

In my opinion there is everything to choose between the model of mind which characterises neo-Freudianism and other traditions in psycho-analysis, especially the Kleinian (I shall turn to Searles and Winnicott in subsequent chapters). Paradoxically, the sense of spatial knowledge in the work of the latter-day Freudians seems to me to be at the expense of an enabling sense of mental space – a space to think.

I want now to plunge straight into a very different, wholly human and experiential rhetoric, one which could not be more different from the formalistic language of extended substances, forces, and energies. The first point to be made about a different conception of mental space is the need for space itself. This calls for sweeping away the baggage of scientistic metapsychology. I am not claiming that what I am recommending that we put in its place is not metapsychological or even that it is mellifluous. What it is is experiential, albeit significantly unconsciously so.

The second point is the premise that all knowing and experiencing occur through primitive processes, through exploring, interacting with and coming to know the mother's body. The primitive is never transcended; it remains operative and determinant, no matter how abstract and abstruse the knowing involved. Experience is always alimentary. Primitive functions continue to be served. The whole basis of the Kleinian tradition stems from the single proposition that primitive emotionality is never gone beyond. The goal of therapy is not to enhance the so-called 'conflict-free sphere of the ego'. It is always to work on and through the primitive by means of the interpretation of primitive anxieties. Margaret Rustin defines the contents of the inner world as an 'inner picture of mother, father, siblings and so on, and at a more primitive level of the parts of the body – emotionally significant for the baby and small child – breast, nipple, eyes, arms, legs, penis etc. seen as alternatively benevolent and hostile' (Rustin, 1989, p. 312).

On this model, the first thought of the infant is of the absent object. The contents of the baby's mind are three things: the breast, being held and the copulating couple, i.e., the belief or sense that insofar as the parents are together, it is a threat, while maturation involves being able to believe that the mother and father could join together to enrich the baby rather then merely to exclude him' (Meltzer *et al.*, 1975, p. 96). The Oedipal relationship is not only a rite of passage on a developmental scheme which occurs between about three and a half years old and six; it is also a constellation, posing a recurrent triangulation to be borne and negotiated from birth and in every important situation one encounters along life's way (Britton, 1992; Young, 1993–94).

Klein writes in a consistently experiential way and employs an evocative language of feelings throughout. This does not mean that she eschews conceptual terms, but they are always in relation to the world of emotions: 'The first form of anxiety is of a persecutory nature. The working of the death instinct within – which according to Freud is directed against the organism – gives rise to the fear of annihilation, and this is the primordial cause of persecutory anxiety. Furthermore, from the beginning of post-natal life . . . destructive impulses against the object stir up fear of retaliation. These persecutory feelings from inner sources are intensified by painful external experience for, from the earliest days onwards frustration and discomfort arouse in the infant the feeling that he is being attacked by hostile forces. Therefore the sensations experienced by the infant at birth and the difficulties of adapting himself to entirely new conditions give rise to persecutory anxiety. The comfort and care given after birth, particularly the first feeding experiences, are felt to come from good forces. In speaking of "forces" I am using a rather adult word for what the young infant dimly conceives of as objects, either good or bad. The infant directs his feelings of gratification and love towards the "good" breast, and his destructive impulses and feelings of persecution towards what he feels to be frustrating, i.e., the "bad" breast. At this stage splitting processes are at their height and love and hatred as well as the good and bad aspects of the breast are largely kept apart from one another. The infant's relative security is based on turning the good object into an ideal one as a protection against the dangerous and persecuting object. These processes – that is to say splitting, denial, omnipotence and idealisation – are prevalent during the first three or four months of life (which I termed the "paranoid-schizoid position"). In these ways at a very early stage persecutory anxiety and its corollary, idealisation, fundamentally influence object relations' (Klein, 1952, pp. 48–9).

She turns next to the formation of the superego and to the depressive position. 'In my view . . . the introjection of the breast is the beginning of superego formation which extends over years. We have grounds for assuming that from the first feeding experience onwards the infant introjects the breast in various aspects. The core of the superego is thus the mother's breast, both good and bad . . . The ego's growing capacity for integration and synthesis leads more and more, even during these first few months, to states in which love and hatred, and correspondingly the good and bad aspects of objects, are being synthesised; and this gives rise to the second form of anxiety – depressive anxiety – for the infant's aggressive impulses and desires towards the bad breast (mother) are now felt to be a danger to the good breast (mother) as well.' The mother is increasingly perceived as a person, and the infant feels he is destroying a whole object, a loved person, with his greed and uncontrollable aggression. 'These anxieties and corresponding defences constitute the "depressive position", which comes to a head about the middle of the first year and whose essence is the anxiety and guilt relating to the destruction and loss of the loved internal and external objects' (pp. 49–50).

Since I am mounting a critique of objectivist terms and praising emotive language, I suppose that in order to be consistent, I ought to deplore some rather unresonant terms at the heart of Klein's otherwise personal and touching style. 'Paraniod-schizoid position' does convey fragmentation, persecution, craziness, but 'depressive position', which is her goal for mental well-being, is a rather astringent and stoical phrase, especially since it is supposed to convey concern for others and the ability to bear mixtures of good and bad, pleasure and pain.

I particularly regret another term at the heart of post-Freudian psychoanalysis, one which Klein, Winnicott and Fairbairn jointly introduced: 'object relations' (Greenberg and Mitchell, 1983). The idea behind this rather objectivist (pun intended) term is that we are always, from the first days, relating to other *people* as central to our psychic lives, for good and ill. Persons are not objects, and objects are not persons (Kohon, 1985). These are obvious but important points, especially when juxtaposing scientism and humanism. Even so, there it is. In the very act of transcending instinct-oriented ideas about people and placing us once and for all in an interpersonal world, highly-original psychoanalysts retain terminological vestiges of a reifying way of thinking. In this case, the vestige comes from classical libido theory, whereby every instinct has an aim and an object, as in the song: 'The object of my affection can turn my complexion from white to rosy red'. Objects, in the object relations sense, are the objects of our feelings and attachments. Klein says, 'The analysis of very young children has taught me that there is no instinctual urge, no anxiety situation, no mental process which does not involve objects, external or internal; in other words, object-relations are at the *centre* of emotional life. Furthermore, love and hatred, phantasies, anxieties, and defences are also operative from the beginning and are *ab initio* indivisibly linked with object-relations. This insight showed me many phenomena in a new light' (Klein, 1952, p. 53).

I said above that primitive processes are never transcended. Klein argues that the introjection of the breast lays the foundation and is the prototype for all internalisation (Klein, 1958, p. 238) and that the vicissitudes of the life and death instincts, as I have already mentioned, govern the whole of mental life (pp. 239, 245). Similarly, primitive phantasies are present throughout life: 'Phantasies – becoming more elaborate and referring to a wider variety of objects and situations – continue throughout development and accompany all activities; they never stop playing a great part in mental life. The influence of unconscious phantasy on art, on scientific work, and on the activities of everyday life cannot be overrated' (p. 251).

Susan Isaacs provides a vivid account of the richness of the unconscious inner world in her classical essay on 'The Nature and Function of Phantasy' (1952). 'We must assume that the incorporation of the breast is bound up with the earliest forms of the phantasy-life. This hallucination of the internal satisfying breast may, however, break down altogether if frustration continues and hunger is not satisfied, instinct tension proving too strong to be denied. Rage and violently aggressive feelings and phantasies will then dominate the mind, and necessitate some adaptation' (p. 86). The power of these phantasies great: 'The phantasies of incorporating (devouring, absorbing, etc.) loved and hated objects, persons or parts of persons, into ourselves are amongst the earliest and most deeply unconscious phantasies, fundamentally oral in character since they are the psychic representatives of the oral impulses . . . In our view, phantasy is the operative link between instinct and ego-mechanism . . . Although themselves psychic phenomena, phantasies are primarily about bodily aims, pains and pleasures, directed to objects of some kind' (p. 99). When we do turn our curiosity onto the external world and act upon it, 'the postponement of satisfaction and the suspense involved in the complicated learning and thinking about external reality which the child presently accomplishes – and for increasingly remote ends – can only be endured and sustained when it also satisfies instinctual urges, represented in phantasies, as well' (p. 108).

As we move from the most primitive phantasies to the domain of symbolism, Klein took up Ferenczi's view 'that primary identification, which is the forerunner of symbolism, "arises out of the baby's endeavour to rediscover in every object its own organs and their functioning"' and Jones' notion that the pleasure principle is at the heart of the equations basic to symbolism (pp. 110–11). Klein showed, 'by means of illuminating clinical material, how the primary symbolic function of external objects enables phantasy to be elaborated by the ego, allows sublimations to develop in play and manipulation and builds a bridge from the inner world to interest in the outer world and knowledge of physical objects and events. His pleasurable interest in his body, his discoveries and experiments in this direction, are clearly shown in the play of an infant of three or four months. In this play he manifests (among other mechanisms) this process of symbol-formation, bound up with those phantasies which we will later discover in analysis to have been operating at the time. *The external physical world is in fact libidinalized largely through the process of symbol-formation'* (p. 110). And so on to the world, but the primitive is never transcended.

Donald Meltzer's depiction of mental space builds directly on the notion of phantasy described above and provides a lovely account of the nature and benefits of successive dimensions, showing by example that spatial concepts are not inevitably reifying and scientistic. But well before providing his account of dimensionality, he gives a poignant account of an autistic child with no capaciousness, no space to reflect upon and ruminate experience: 'For months he had drawn doors and gates, usually with complex wrought-iron grills. Then gradually rather Victorian gothic houses took shape. One day he painstakingly drew an ornate house seen from the front on one side of the page, a house in Northwood, while on the other side he drew a back view of a pub in Southend. Thus the child demonstrated his experience of a two-dimensional object; when you enter by the front door you simultaneously exit by the rear door of a different object. It is in effect an object without an inside' (Meltzer *et al.*, 1975, p. 18). For this child 'the distinction between inside and outside is not a fact' (p. 19). He has 'a paper-thin object without a delineated inside. This produces a primal failure of the containing function of the external object, and thus of the formation of the concept of self as a container . . . This deficiency of containment related to internal spacelessness of the self . . . ' (pp. 19–20).

Meltzer turns, at the end of the *Explorations in Autism,* undertaken with four co-workers, to an account of 'Dimensionality as a Parameter of Mental Functioning . . . ' which I have found helpful in thinking about the meaning of mental space. He begins, 'It is our view that , insofar as an organism can be said to have a mental life and not merely to exist in a system of neurophysiological responses to the stimuli coming to it from internal and external sources, it lives in "the world" and this world may be variously structured. One has perhaps become accustomed to think of "the world" as four-dimensional and constituting the "life space" (K. Lewin) of the organism. From the psycho-analytical viewpoint this life-space may be said to comprise the various compartments of the "geography of phantasy" (Meltzer) moving on [in?] the dimension of time. This geography is ordinarily organised into four compartments inside the self; outside the self; inside internal objects; inside external objects; and to these may sometimes, perhaps always, be added the fifth compartment, the "nowhere" of the delusional system, outside the gravitational pull of good objects. The dimension of time on the other hand can be recognised to have a development from circularity to oscillation and finally to the linear time of "life-time" for the individual, from conception to death' (p. 223).

He then characterises the dimensions, one by one. 'Freud's original systematic theory as expressed in the "Project", the VIIth chapter of the "Traumdeutung" or the "Three Essays" is essentially a description of one-dimensionality: source, aim and object of neurophysiologically and genetically determined drive patterns. A linear relationship of time-distance between self and object would give rise to a "world" which had a fixed centre in the self and a system of radiating lines having direction and distance to objects which were conceived as potentially attractive or repellent . . . It is not a world conducive to emotionality except of the simplest polarised sort. Gratification and fusion with the object would be undifferentiated . . . a one-dimensional world, which we have characterised as substantially mindless, consisting of a series of events mot available for memory or thought' (pp. 224–5).

A two-dimensional world is that of the boy with the paper-thin object. He knows surfaces and 'may be marvellously intelligent in the perception and appreciation of the surface qualities of objects, but its aim will necessarily be curtailed by an impoverished imagination, as it will have no means for constructing in thought objects or events different from those it has actually experienced. In the language of Bion, it would have no means for distinguishing between an absent good-object and the presence of a persecuting absent-object. The reason for this limitation of thought and imagination would reside in the lack of an internal space within the mind in which phantasy as trial action, and therefore as experimental thought, could take place' (p. 225). The two-dimensional personality is the limiting case of shallowness (p. 235). The self would also be impaired in memory, desire, foresight. Threats to the integrity of this world would be experienced as 'break-down of the surfaces – cracking, tearing, suppuration, dissolution, lichenification or ichthyotic desensitizing, freezing numbness, or a diffuse, meaningless, and therefore tormenting sensation such as itching' (pp. 225–6).

Three-dimensionality introduces the notion of 'orifices in object and self' and the self as containing potential spaces. 'The potentiality of a space, and thus the potentiality of a container, can only be realised once a sphincter-function has become effective. The feeling 'of being adequately

contained is a precondition for the experience of being as continent
container . . . ' (p. 226).

In order to achieve four-dimensionality and thereby to embark on the
process of development, projective identification must be relinquished, a
struggle against narcissism must be mounted, and introjective identification must begin to replace a narcissistic one.

The details of Meltzer's account – though I find them appealing – are
incidental to my purpose, which is to find a way of treating mental space
as available for containment, a place where one can bear experience, hold
it and be able to ruminate it, metabolise it, reflect upon it, savour it. The
meaningfulness of experience is always under threat. It may be batted
away or used to locate, amplify and feed madness and then be reprojected
or reduced to cliché or collapsed into despair. The point of capaciousness
is that it should serve as a container for thought, and the point of thought
is to keep emotion alive. Without living emotion there are no viable
relationships, and without relationships there is no world. The greater the
pressure of primitive anxieties on the dimensionality of mind, the less able
we are to symbolise and to participate in culture. In the following chapters
I will explore some Kleinian concepts, along with one of Winnicott's,
which strike me as bearing on our capacity to be containers of experience
and to act on the world of personal and other objects in a worthwhile
way. I believe that these concepts provide the parameters of the restriction
and enhancement of mental space.

4   ANALYTIC SPACE: COUNTERTRANSFERENCE

The analytic space is the mental space within which psychoanalysis and psychotherapy occur. It is a space shared between patient and therapist. In this chapter I shall characterise the two main processes which occur in the analytic space – transference and countertransference. While doing so I shall carry further my philosophical reflections on the relations between psychoanalysis and the modern world view. I wish to begin with an important distinction – that between didactic and evocative knowledge. Didactic knowledge is imparted, while evocative knowledge is elicited or brought forth.

Everything with which I am concerned in this chapter comes from what may at first glance appear to be a relatively trivial technical problem in psychoanalysis: the unconscious feelings stirred up in the therapist by the patient. I wish to argue, however, that it leads to the very heart of the analytic process and, beyond that, to our conception of human nature and how we may fruitfully think about how we come to know – the theory of knowledge or epistemology. This is a considerable weight to place on the concept of countertransference, but I shall try to argue that it can bear it. My story has a nicely linear plot, taking us from the simple to the complex and on to the interactive and the dialectical.

I want to start with the traditional stance of the therapist in the analytic session – that of neutrality, holding up a mirror to the patient. But in offering the image of a mirror Freud did not mean that one should not be human. He was not urging the therapist to be inanimate glass and silver nitrate; he was saying that one should not tell about oneself. There was a tendency among the early psychoanalysts to be self-revealing. The mirror was an image in the service of the rule of abstinence: speak to the patient only about himself or herself and about characters who inhabit the patient's inner world.

Before turning to countertransference, we must consider transference. Freud said, 'What are transferences? They are the new editions or facsimiles of the impulses and phantasies which are aroused and made conscious during the progress of the analysis; but they have this peculiarity, which is characteristic for their species, that they replace some earlier person by the person of the physician. To put it another way: a whole series of psychological experiences are revived, not as belonging to the past, but as applying to the person of the physician at the present moment' (Freud, 1905, p. 116). In a way, then, transference is a mistake, and, as Freud was to learn, the analytic process is based on this mistake – that the patient experiences the analyst as someone else. The patient, according to Racker, '"displaces" or "transfers" infantile and internal conflicts to current situations and objects which are out of place and inappropriate' (Racker, 1968, p. 15). A transference interpretation is basically pointing this out to the patient. Fenichel said, 'The process that requires demonstrating to patients the same thing again and again at different times or in various connections, is called, following Freud, "working through . . . Again and again the patient must in analysis re-experience 'there too' and 'there again'"' (Fenichel, 1941, pp. 78–80, quoted in Searles, 1978–9, p. 176). Fenichel's view of the task in working through is this: 'An analyst giving a transference interpretation says, schematically: "It is not I toward whom your feelings are directed; you really mean your father." But there are many patients who know about transference and defend themselves against emerging emotional excitement by referring to its transference nature. In such instances the "reversed transference interpretation" is necessary; "You are aroused at this moment not about your father but about me"' (Fenichel, 1945, p. 522, quoted in Searles, 1978–9, p. 176).

All of this seems relatively straightforward, even mechanical. The concept of transference became increasingly enriched, however, so that it was eventually perceived that what is transferred is the total situation, a relationship or objects in a context, and not merely an individual. Moreover, the objects transferred are not external ones but internal objects (Klein, 1952; Joseph, 1983). As a consequence, ideas of the transference became broadened into a wider context and deepened into the object relations of the inner world.

Turning to countertransference, you may think of it as an arcane topic; it is certainly an unwieldy word, one which conjures up the most abstract of latter-day metapsychological conceptualisations. In fact, it arose very early and was very immediate: it is why Freud's first collaborator, Joseph Breuer, gave up. He ran away from Anna O because she aroused him. If transference is projection, countertransference is projective identification – something elicited by the patient in the therapist: evocative knowledge. Anna O elicited in Breuer a sexual excitement which he found unacceptable and was unbearable to himself and his wife, so he abandoned the work (Gay, 1988, pp. 63–9).

For Freud the transference went from being an annoying interference to an instrument of great value to the main battlefield of the analysis. An analogous story can be told about the countertransference, but it is a story with profound implications. Now, to define countertransference. Freud rarely discussed the topic; he saw countertransference as the patient's influence on the analyst's unconscious. He said that no analyst could go farther than he or she had progressed in their own analysis, so the analyst's analysis was all-important. He first mentions the concept in 1910: 'We have become aware of the "countertransference", which arises in [the analyst] as a result of the patient's influence on his unconscious feelings, and we are almost inclined to insist that he shall recognise this countertransference in himself and overcome it. Now that a considerable number of people are practising psychoanalysis and exchanging their observations with one another, we have noticed that no psychoanalyst goes further than his own complexes and internal resistances permit; and we consequently require that he shall begin his activity with a self-analysis and continually carry it deeper while he is making his own observations on his patients. Anyone who fails to produce results in a self-analysis of this kind may at once give up any idea of being able to treat patients by analysis' (Freud, 1910, pp. 144–5). Later, of course, Freud also insisted on a training analysis conducted by a suitable analyst.

It is often thought that Freud held a limited view of countertransference, and he certainly had little to say on the topic. Even so, I would argue that the following quotation, properly contemplated and making due allowance for the technological imagery of his day, contains all we need to know: 'To put it into a formula: [the analyst] must turn his own unconscious like a receptive organ toward the transmitting unconscious of the patient. He must adjust himself to the patient as a telephone receiver is adjusted to the transmitting microphone. Just as the receiver converts back into sound waves the electric oscillations in the telephone line which were set up by sound waves, so the doctor's unconscious is able, from the derivatives of the unconscious which are communicated to him, to reconstruct that unconscious, which has determined the patient's free associations' (Freud, 1912, pp. 115–6). This quotation takes us much deeper; it is much more resonant and in touch with primitive processes than the previous one, even though it was penned only two years later.

With respect to the subsequent history of ideas about counter-transference, Laplanche and Pontalis trace three successive positions on the subject, which I shall characterise in my own terms: (1) Get rid of it by means of one's own analysis, and concentrate on the patient's transference. (2) Exploit it in a controlled way, using the therapist's unconscious as an instrument for fathoming the patient's unconscious. (3) Go with it, treating the resonances from unconscious to unconscious as the only authentically psychoanalytic form of communication (Laplanche and Pontalis, 1983, pp. 92–3).

Before embarking on that history, I want to say something about projective identification, since we will need this concept as we go along. I shall discuss this concept at length in chapters six and seven, but for the present I want to point out that countertransference is an aspect of projective identification. In the countertransference relationship, the patient puts something into the therapist which the therapist experiences as his or her own. That's not a bad definition of one of the forms of projective identification, in which the patient splits off an unacceptable or undesirable (or otherwise uncontainable) part of the self and puts it into another person. That person must have, if only to a very small degree, the potential to identify with and express that feeling. It rises up from the general repertoire of that person's potential feelings and gets exaggerated and expressed. The projector can then feel: 'It's not me; it's him', while the process of identification in the recipient may yield a bewildering feeling, reaction or act (Hinshelwood, 1991, pp. 179–208). In an attentive therapist, interrogating the countertransference leads to a fruitful interpretation.

We can now see this congruence in action in a passage where Freud is quite explicit about a concept usually seen as originating with Klein. He is talking about the projections of jealous and persecuted paranoiacs, of whom it is said that they project onto others that which they do not wish to recognise in themselves. He continues, 'Certainly they do this; but they do not project it into the blue, so to speak, where there is nothing of the sort already. They let themselves be guided by their knowledge of the unconscious, and displace to the unconscious minds of others the attention which they have withdrawn from their own. Our jealous husband perceived his wife's unfaithfulness instead of his own; by becoming conscious of hers and magnifying it enormously he succeeded in keeping his own unconscious' (Freud, 1922, p. 226).

Fenichel writes in the same vein: 'It is interesting to note that the hatred is never projected at random but is felt usually in connection with something that has a basis in reality. Patients with persecutory ideas are extremely sensitive to criticism and use the awareness of actual insignificant criticisms as the reality basis for their delusions. This basis has, of course, to be extremely exaggerated and distorted in order to be made available for this purpose . . . The paranoid individual is particularly sensitised to perceive the unconscious of others, where such perceptions can be utilised to rationalise his tendency toward projection' (Fenichel, 1945, p. 428, quoted in Searles, 1978–9, p. 177).

Anyone who has ever worked in a mental hospital will recognise this instantly. Paranoids are geniuses at getting under the skin and ferreting out latent tendencies in others, especially staff. But, of course, this is only a relatively apparent exaggeration of the norm, as any of us can attest from our experiences of how much can get tangled up in a moment during telephone calls with prospective patients, and in relations with lovers or one's own children. Projection, introjection, exaggeration, reprojection – these are norms of social interaction. It is all a matter of degree. Nevertheless, as in the rest of life, everything can depend on matters of degree. Projective identification is a normal mechanism, but when employed excessively or virulently, it lies at the heart of paranoid processes, racism, narcissism, and innumerable other pathological conditions (see below, ch. 7). When employed excessively, it is also central to pathological conformism and ruthless ambition and acts as a defence against schizophrenic breakdown (Meltzer, 1992). Relinquishing its excessive use is essential to becoming a decent person.

There is a rich history of ideas of countertransference, some phases of which I will not spell out except to list familiar names, since the relevant papers are competently reviewed in a collection edited by Edmund Slakter (1987): Stern (1924); Deutsch (1926); Glover (1927); Sharpe (1930); Hann-Kende (1933); W. Reich (1933); Strachey (1934); Low (1935). There are other overviews, for example, by Kohon (1986) and Orr (1988), a collection of *Essential Papers on Countertransference* (Wolstein, 1988) and a growing number of monographs and papers, which has brought forth the inevitable *Beyond Countertransference* (Natterson, 1991; *cf.* Alexandris and Vaslamatzis, 1993).

I want to begin my own story of recent work with a paper by Winnicott, startlingly entitled 'Hate in the Counter-transference' (1947). I am re-entering the history of ideas at the point where the transition is occurring between countertransference as 'that which is to be got rid of', to 'that which is to be made something of' or exploited. Winnicott said that to feel hate, when it has been projected into you and evoked by the patient, is part of the therapist's proper responsiveness. When the patient seeks the therapist's hate, the therapist must be able to make contact with it, to bear it without retaliating and to contain it; otherwise the analysis fails.

Two years after Winnicott made this point, Paula Heimann took up the topic and began with the traditional view: 'I have been struck by the widespread belief amongst candidates that the countertransference is nothing but a source of trouble' (Heimann, 1949–50, p. 73). She takes a contrary position: 'My thesis is that the analyst's emotional response to his patient within the analytic situation represents one of the most important tools for his work. The analyst's countertransference is an instrument of research into the patient's unconscious' (p. 74). 'Our basic assumption is that the analyst's unconscious understands that of his patient' (p. 75). She claims that 'the analyst's countertransference is not only part and parcel of the analytic relationship, but it is the patient's *creation,* it is a part of the patient's personality' (p. 77).

Winnicott was writing about psychotics and borderline personalities; Heimann extended the point to include work with all patients. However, when she returns to the topic a decade later, she reflects at length on how to handle countertransference material and takes up a cautious position, eschewing self-revelation. But in her conclusion, she reverts to the early view of Freud. In so doing, it seems to me, she fails to see the larger potential of the concept. She says, in her last paragraph, 'In conclusion, Freud's injunction that the countertransference must be recognised and overcome is as valid today as it was fifty years ago. When it occurs, it must be turned to some useful purpose. Continued self-analysis and self-training will help to decrease incidents of countertransference' (p. 160). For her, countertransference was still a hot potato – something to learn from when it occurs but preferably to be got rid of. Putting the point at its starkest, we will see below that to 'reduce the incidents of countertransference' is no longer a goal among many therapists.

Another writer in this period, Roger Money Kyrle, takes up a position that acknowledges that countertransference can be both useful and a serious impediment. As his title implies, countertransference was coming to be seen as a normal part of the analytic process: 'Normal Counter-transference and Some of its Deviations' (1956). He draws our attention to the fine texture of the process, whereby something is put into the analyst, reprojected in an interpretation and then taken in by the patient. If the receiving parts of the analyst are intact, what gets reprojected is likely to be helpful, but if the projection falls afoul of unresolved issues in the analyst's unconscious, a mess can be created. Everyone would be happy if 'normal countertransference' was all there was. 'Unfortunately, it is normal only in the sense of being an ideal. It depends for its continuity on the analyst's continuous understanding. But he is not omniscient. In particular, his understanding fails whenever the patient corresponds too closely with some aspect of himself which he has not yet learnt to understand' (Money-Kyrle, 1956, p. 361). In such cases, what ensues is a reprojection of something which is not helpful, not congruent with the patient's needs. The analyst may recover then or in the next session, but the patient is not simply waiting for him to get it right. He or she may well have moved on and be relating to the analyst as a damaged object as a result of the distorted interpretation. The result will take some sorting out. What is attractive about Money-Kyrle's reflections is the light they shed on the process – the minute details – of these interrelations.

A sense that countertransference was, in the 1950s and 1960s, still basically seen as something to be wary of has been driven home for me by a revealing incident in the publishing history of the work of Margaret Little. In 1950, she wrote a paper on 'Countertransference and the Patient's Response to It'. It was duly reprinted in a collection of her writings, *Transference Neurosis and Transference Psychosis* in 1981. But when the book came out in a paperback edition five years later, she added an intriguing footnote: 'I read this paper in 1950, almost exactly three years after my analyst's death. I could not then give the true account, but disguised it as best I could. (That version has rightly been questioned.) I have given *this* account in chapter 21 [a dialogue between her and Robert Langs], and also in my paper 'Winnicott Working in Areas where Psychotic Anxieties Prevail: A Personal Record' in *Free Associations* (1985) 3:9–42' (Little, 1986, p. 33n). The last-mentioned article had been submitted to a journal and rejected with the suggestion that it should be put in a vault until a suitable date well in the future. One of the referees told me that he had urged its sequestration because it revealed that a practising training analyst continued to work while she was very ill, that her analyst, Donald Winnicott, permitted this and had broken various boundaries with respect to the analytic frame, and that knowledge of this would be too distressing to her former patients, including some analysts still in practice whose training analyst she had been. When, after the most careful consideration, the article was published in *Free Associations*, Margaret Little received a gracious note from the editor of the rejecting Journal, saying how pleased he was that the article had been sufficiently modified so as to make it suitable for publication. Yet not a word had been altered from her original submission.

My justification for telling this rather gossipy tale about the context of publishing these pieces is that it nicely illustrates that when we are dealing with the complex, subtle and primitive processes which occur in transference and countertransference, we are moving about on a very perilous terrain, one which puts at risk the boundaries of the analytic frame, the maintenance of which are essential to the successful conduct of psychoanalytic work. One view of the analytic frame is that it contains the psychotic parts of the relationship, thus allowing the work to proceed (Blejer, 1966). Taking full account of countertransference – and not confining attention to transference, keeping the therapist's unconscious processes out of the question – means that the analytic frame is constantly at risk of being violated. Many feel that the relations between Margaret Little and D. W. Winnicott went beyond the appropriate boundaries. I believe the debate about the relationship between countertransference and the analytic frame has an important bearing on how we do analytic work and how we conceptualise the maintenance of analytic integrity.

Margaret Little has stressed in these and subsequent writings (1957, 1987, 1989, 1990) that the relations between analyst and patient are much more complex and interactive, both consciously and unconsciously, than is acknowledged by orthodox models of the therapeutic process. A strong reaction against her views came from an orthodox Freudian, Annie Reich (1951), who argued that countertransference was not a therapeutic tool and was not useful for understanding or communicating with the patient. Slakter comments that Annie Reich was defending a conception of psychoanalysis as the analysis of the ego's defences and rejecting 'the seductive, regressive pull of id psychology' (Slakter, 1987, p. 23).

At this point I want to interrupt my narrative of the history of countertransference and to broaden the terms of reference to revert to the philosophical issues raised in chapter three about the ways we *picture* the mind. I suggest that in the history of psychoanalysis there has been a subtle tension between 'picture thinking', on the one hand, and personal, evocative, story-telling accounts, on the other. We've seen that these two ways of representing things are intermingled in two of the classic texts, 'Project for a Scientific Psychology' (1895) and *The Interpretation of Dreams* (1900), and one can almost feel Freud's relief when he abandons the imagery of the telescope and the diagram and replaces them with *stories.* After chapter seven of *The Interpretation of Dreams* spatial representations and pictorial diagrams are rare, e.g., the rendering of the structural point of view in *The Ego and the Id* (Freud, 1923, p. 24) and the oval diagram in Lecture XXXI of *The New Introductory Lectures* (Freud, 1933, p. 78), and when they do appear, they are rather more metaphorical than truly spatial.

As we have seen, in the traditional pictorial approach the knowing subject is at one end of an investigative instrument – typically a telescope or microscope. What is essential about this way of representing the mind and the process of knowing is the spatial gap. The subject is at one end, while the object is at the other end or 'out there'. The subject is the knower; the object is to be known. The object is open to scrutiny, and the subject is not. I now want to tell a story in which this representation of the problem of knowing within and between people is increasingly complicated, starting with the picture-thinking view and moving on to an interactive and then to a dialectical one.

I am a subject. You are an object. I am here; my essence is in here. You are there – out there, across a physical and epistemological space. I can infer that you are also a subject – by eye contact, by tone of voice, by analogy to my own experience and by other cues – but you easily revert to being experienced as an object, and I may easily lapse into treating you as one – as someone who does not touch me: alien. You may sense this and be alienated from me.

But the situation can be seen as much, much more complicated. I may experience myself as alienated from myself – as a thing, as a bug, as ugly, as dead. This is of the essence of the concept of alienation, where a person or a worker can experience himself or herself as alienated from the product, the means or instruments of production, from fellow workers and from one's own humanity (or 'species being'). Alienation is the subjective moment of the objective condition of exploitation at work, just as an analogous estrangement can occur in bad human relationships or in psychotic moments or states. Rather than experience yourself as dead, you may put that feeling into me by projection, and if I take up the projection (unconsciously) and display it, a successful projective identification is in being between us. There are other forms of projective identification which do not depend on what I feel or display, so that you can be in projective identification with me in other ways, depending on your inner state and mine.

As we enrich the model, mental and interpersonal space lose the quality of a picture with simple locations. There are no simple spaces in this enriched account, one which can be called interactive, phenomenological or dialectical, depending on how mutually constitutive the relationships are conceived as being. In an interaction things get batted back and forth. In a phenomenological description you are no longer an 'it' but a 'thou', a person with whom I can identify and empathise, as I am for you. (It could be argued that the concept of 'thou' only makes sense in the light of at least a tacit understanding of projective identification.) In a dialectical account, there are many layers and reverberations. I am here and there at once, as you are. You are in me. I can expel a part of myself. You can take it in and re-expel it, and I can experience it as you, while, in another part of my mind, knowing where that part came from. (It should be obvious that I am not listing the permutations systematically. I only want to make the point that interpersonal relationships are much richer and multi-layered than the subject-object 'picture' account allows.)

Moving on to related expressions: I enter you. You withdraw. Or you may contain my distress. I push through your defences. We become one and then separate but feel love, hatred or ambivalence or frequent oscillations among these at many levels: a relationship. If we move on further to part-object relationships and on still further to tenderness, envy, spite and reparation, it soon becomes obvious that the simple subject-object model is a *reductio ad absurdum* of human relationships.

Returning to my main theme, I suggest that the history of ideas if countertransference is a progressive closing of the spatial gap between therapist and patient. It is a turning away from pictorial models toward story-telling ones, in which knowledge is not seeing but evocation. I offer two longish examples to drive my point home.

The first is from Tom Main's essay on 'Some Psychodynamics of Large Groups': 'Although projective processes are primitive attempts to relieve internal pains by externalising them, assigning or requiring another to contain aspects of the self, the price can be high: for the self is left not only less aware of its whole but, in the case of projective identification, is deplenished [sic] by the projective loss of important aspects of itself. Massive projective identification of – for instance – feared aggressive parts of the self leaves the remaining self felt only to be weak and unaggressive. Thereafter, the weakened individual will remain in terror about being overwhelmed by frightening aggressive strength, but this will now be felt only as belonging to the other. Depending on the range of this projective fantasy the results will vary from terrified flight, appeasement, wariness and specific anxieties about the other, even psychotic delusions about his intentions.

'The above instance concerns only the projector's side of the projective relationship: but projective processes often have a further significance. What about the person on the receiving end of the projection? In simple projection (a mental mechanism) the receiver may notice that he is not being treated as himself but as an aggressive other. In projective identification (an unconscious fantasy) this other may find himself forced by the projector actually to feel his own projected aggressive qualities and impulses which are otherwise alien to him. He will feel strange and uncomfortable and may resent what is happening, but in the face of the projector's weakness and cowardice it may be doubly difficult to resist the feelings of superiority and aggressive power steadily forced into him. Such disturbances affect all pair relationships more or less. A wife, for instance, may force her husband to own feared and unwanted dominating aspects of herself and will then fear and respect him. He in turn may come to feel aggressive and dominating toward her, not only because of his own resources but because of hers, which are forced into him. But more: for reasons of his own he may despise and disown certain timid aspects of his personality and by projective identification force these into his wife and despise her accordingly. She may thus be left not only with timid unaggressive parts of herself but having in addition to contain his. Certain pairs come to live in such locked systems, dominated by mutual projective fantasies with each not truly married to a person, but rather to unwanted, split off and projected parts of themselves. Both the husband, dominant and cruel, and the wife, stupidly timid and respectful, may be miserably unhappy with themselves and with each other, yet such marriages although turbulent are stable, because each partner needs the other for pathologically narcissistic purposes. Forcible projective processes, and especially projective identification, are thus more than an individual matter: they are object-related, and the other will always be affected more or less' (Main, 1975, pp. 100–01). This is an excellent exposition of some of the complexities of unconscious processes at work in everyday life. I trust that the analogy to transference and countertransference is obvious. In case it is not, I want to follow this example with a lovely account of the power of countertransference and the use that can be made of it in a clinical setting.

I shall excerpt the relevant passage from a dense and illuminating account of a clinical case of Margaret Rustin's, which, for reasons of confidentiality, I do not wish to quote in detail. What is of interest in the present context comes out very clearly in the therapist's reflections, which is the point at which I shall begin quoting: 'There is much to explore in these associations, but I now want to add an important fact about this session which I was not able to make use of at the time. I myself was having two experiences in addition to the conversation I have reported. I was struggling with a frustrating conviction that I could not properly get hold of the transference situation in the session . . . Much more uncomfortable than this intellectual frustration was a state of irritable anxiety which was building up, particularly focused on an urgent desire to suck or bite my fingers. Trying to understand these feelings and impulses is the process required of the therapist to work through the countertransference. I am here using the term countertransference to refer not to the neurotic response of analyst to patient, but to the broader current conception of countertransference which pays close attention to the feelings stirred up in the analyst by the patient's material.

'In the following session, the meaning of this projection began to emerge.' There follows more material in which alcoholism and stealing drink loom large. Rustin continues, 'I found myself plagued by similar surges of anxious discomfort to those of last week's session . . . ' Then more clinical material, including the alcoholic's sitting there with thumb in mouth saying how delicious the stolen drink was, which enraged and overwhelmed the patient. The account continues, 'At this moment, I felt the relief of illumination. The image of X with . . . thumb in . . . mouth linked with my impulse to suck and chew my fingers during these last two sessions, an impulse which I felt was being irresistibly projected into me. Now I knew where this was coming from. So I gathered together the threads I could now follow . . . ' (Rustin, 1989, p. 315). The author's account makes admirably clear the central importance of the countertransference to the interpretation and its evident usefulness to the patient.

There is an equally graphic – and, in this case, excruciating – account of projective identification and countertransference, in which the therapist found herself unaccustomedly an unaccountably buying and cooking squid, only to find to her chagrin and amusement, as she contemplated the cut up pieces frying in oil, that she was retaliating against a particularly murderous 'prick' of a suicidal patient (Eigner, 1986).

I have chosen the foregoing examples to convey the power of the projective processes involved in countertransference. The person who has looked into these most extensively is Harold Searles. The collection of his papers on *Countertransference and Related Topics* (1979) contains what I regard as two profound essays on the subject, while the dialogue between Searles and Robert Langs explores in a very illuminating way the details of the interrelations between analyst and patient (Langs and Searles, 1980).

In 1949 – just when Winnicott and Little were challenging the orthodoxy in Britain – Harold Searles, an American psychoanalyst of remarkably independent spirit and originality, sought to publish a paper which significantly broadened the clinical importance of the countertransference, but it was rejected by both of the psychoanalytic journals to which he submitted it. It was only published in the wake of his achievements as an analyst of schizophrenics. In it he anticipates much of his subsequent work on the real basis, in the analyst's personality, for transference phenomena, phenomena which appropriately evoke the countertransference. He summarises his article as follows: ' . . . transference phenomena constitute projections, and . . . all projective manifestations – including transference reactions – have some *real* basis in the analyst's behavior and represent, therefore, distortions in degree only. The latter of these two suggestions implies a degree of emotional participation by the analyst which is not adequately described by the classical view of him as manifesting sympathetic interest, and nothing else, toward the patient. It has been the writer's experience that the analyst actually does feel, and manifests in various ways, a great variety of emotions during the analytic hour' (Searles, 1978–9, p. 165).

In his papers on 'The Patient as Therapist to His Analyst' (1975) and 'Transitional Phenomena and Therapeutic Symbiosis' (1976), as well as in his dialogue with Langs, Searles drives home again and again the centrality, the normality, the basic and essential utility of countertransference. Langs grants its ubiquity, but – if I read him aright – still wants to master and minimise it (e.g., Langs and Searles, 1980, pp. 96–7). Searles glories in its omnipresence and rich potential.

One of the affinities of his ideas is the interpersonal psychiatry of Harry Stack Sullivan, but the main source is his extensive psychoanalytic work with schizophrenics (he has worked with one woman for more than thirty years). He also makes alliances with the (independently developed) ideas of Winnicott and Little. I commend his cornucopia of examples to the reader. After reflecting upon them I would be surprised if anyone could retain the traditional view of the analyst as mirror or as a subject looking at the patient across physical or metaphorical space at an object to be known by peering, as it were, through some sort of technological instrument. (I have written at some length about Searles' insights – Young, 1992).

I now have to draw breath and speak about the analytic frame. You will recall that this topic was raised in the context of discussing Margaret Little's work with Winnicott and Annie Reich's orthodox objections.

Lurking around my whole account has been a whiff of scandal – a suspicion that if we get too involved with the countertransference, there's no telling where it will all end. Annie Reich feared that it would end in the id, not in the ego, where she seemed to assume that all good analytic work is done. It is noteworthy, then, that the writers who have set out to broaden and deepen the concept of countertransference have been people who were exploring primitive, psychotic processes: Winnicott on borderline and schizophrenic patients, Little on her own psychotic illness and Searles, who has worked a great deal with schizophrenics and borderlines.

The analytic space is bounded by the analytic frame; it is the emotional environment in which it is seemly and safe enough to conduct the therapeutic alliance. It is a container, and containment is its essence. It is made up of a set of conventions, quite mundane ones, but they are under constant threat. The session starts and ends on time; confidentiality is total; you never take notes (though many do); no interruptions are permitted; no personal information about the therapist should be made available (or discernible in the paraphenalia in the room); accounts should be presented on the same day of the month; there should be due warning for breaks; other missed sessions should be minimised and announced well in advance; patients should not be touched. (My analyst shook hands at the end of each term. I emulated him until two patients missed menstrual periods after I shook hands with them.)

Others would extend this list in various ways. Practically all would say that social relations between therapist and patient should be taboo, and most would say that those with ex-patients should be minimised. Sexual relations are strictly taboo. Others would make a distinction between current patients, recent ex-patients and ex-patients some years later (I would not).

These aspects of the frame are important, but the essence is an attitude of abstinence and containment. If that is right, and if the essence is internalised, it is silly to make a long list of prohibitions. As the cellist Tortellier was fond of saying, one must be pure but not pur*iste*. The frame must provide a bounded space in which it is bearable to do the work – for the patient to be safe enough to explore what is unsafe, that is, defences built up and maintained over a lifetime. Praising, blaming, encouraging – all such dimensions of normal social relations are eschewed in a strict interpretation of the analytic frame. What is on offer is interpretation, the understanding that the patient can take away and treat as food for thought. In their dialogue, one point on which Langs and Searles agree is that 'the therapist's appropriate love is expressed by maintaining the boundaries'

(Langs and Searles, 1980, p. 130). Langs' view is that as soon as you modify the frame, the likelihood of a misalliance or pathological symbiosis is greatly increased (pp. 44, 127). As he says, 'frame' is 'a nonhuman term for a very human set of tenets and functions. It serves to hold and to contain, to establish boundaries and conditions of relatedness and communication' (p. 179).

There are those who advocate occasional suspension of what can be seen as rigid or strict maintenance of the boundaries of the frame – what Christopher Bollas has called 'Expressive Uses of the Countertransference' (Bollas, 1987, ch. 12). Related views have been expressed by Symington (1986), Little (see above) and – perhaps most notoriously – by Nina Coltart, in a lovely essay entitled '"Slouching Toward Bethlehem" . . . or Thinking the Unthinkable in Psychoanalysis' (1986), in which she tells a gripping tale, the denouement of which is shouting at her patient to what appears to be good effect. Symington and Bollas tell similar stories. Indeed, Bollas tells us that on one occasion he quite deliberately and temperately said to a patient, 'You know, *you* are a monster' (Bollas, 1989, p. 38), and it turns out that she did know and in due course professed to be relieved that he could say so and that the relationship could survive his acknowledging the fact. Searles also owns up to revealing, at selected moments, aspects of his subjective feelings toward patients, though much more often with schizophrenics than with others (Langs and Searles, 1980, pp. 123–4).

As I mentioned above, Paula Heimann counselled against such self-revelations and criticised Margaret Little for advocating them (Heimann, 1959–60, p. 156). Rayner (1991) reports that the approaches of Coltart and Bollas are widespread among members of the Independent or Middle Group in the British Psycho-Analytical Society, while it is usual among Kleinians to eschew such self-revelations. Among the authors I have mentioned, however, it is common ground that such practices are open to abuse, and great care must be taken to avoid 'acting out in the countertransference' (Heimann, 1959–60, p. 157).

While there are important differences in the degree to which various practitioners may be willing to express their countertransference, it is my impression that there is a growing consensus that being closely attuned to it is a, if not *the,* basis for knowing what is going on and for making interpretations. I want to leave this issue open, while making clear that my own bias is against expressive uses of the countertransference (which is not to say that I have never done it and never will). The tendency to 'get rid of it' is certainly waning among the writers whom I am examining, while more and more is being made of it. My best experiences in supervision have resulted from the supervisor asking me what I was feeling at a particular moment – usually a moment when I felt I did not understand the material. I would go so far as to say that this has never failed to provide at least some enlightenment. Interrogating the countertransference must not be seen as seeking a fact which is available on the surface of the mind. Countertransference is as unconscious as transference is. Understanding it is an interpretive *task*.

I want now to move to the third of Laplanche and Pontalis' renderings of the countertransference: the injunction, not merely to exploit it but to 'go with it'. The experience of countertransference is, in the first instance, apprehensible but not comprehensible. What is occurring between patient and therapist is not merely interactive; it is interpenetrative or dialectical. Much, often most, of what goes on in an analytic session is non-verbal and atmospheric, and one could not say how it is imparted. The atmosphere may be soporific, tense, comforting, assaultive, arousing.

I had a patient who spoke so horribly and in such a sustained way in one session that she filled the room with her (symbolic) vomit and had to flee, since, if she opened her mouth again, she would have to take in some of her own spew. I was able to make an interpretation in these terms, because I was feeling nauseous. I had another patient who spent many sessions at the beginning of our work standing on the threshold of the room. He had panic attacks. It took me the longest time to figure out that he was imparting to me the cliff-hanging feeling that was characteristic of his attacks. One reason I could not figure it out, by the way, was because he was a training patient, and I was in a panic that I might lose him or that colleagues might see him hovering there. When I belatedly made the interpretation, fruitful work began.

Another patient would come to a session, never looked at me, would speak one or two sentences and often remain silent for the rest of the period. It eventually dawned on me that she unconsciously wanted me to feel starved the way her mother had made her feel. I *had* been feeling that way, but it took some time to convert that sense into a thought. When I did make that interpretation, she slowly began to give more, though she remained likely to revert to sullenness and withholding. Yet underneath this mean exterior was a longing and warmth and gratitude that no camera could detect but which I came to know and to find sustaining in innumerable bleak sessions.

A patient can rob one of the ability to think. Indeed, there was one in a group I conducted who was able to project her sexuality so powerfully that, on occasion, no one in the group, including me, could think of anything but her breasts and legs. As Bion said, 'Refuge is sure to be sought in mindlessnsess, sexualization, acting out and degrees of stupor' (Bion, 1970, p. 126).

A paper by Irma Brenman Pick takes the normality of counter-transference to its logical extreme, without a trace of seeing it as something to be got rid of. She carefully considers is as the basis of understanding throughout the session: 'Constant projecting by the patient into the analyst is the essence of analysis; every interpretation aims at a move from the paraniod/schizoid to the depressive position' (Brenman-Pick, 1985, p. 158). She makes great play of the tone, the mood and the resonances of the process: 'I think that the extent to which we succeed or fail in this task will be reflected not only in the words we choose, but in our voice and other demeanour in the act of giving an interpretation . . . ' (p. 161). Most importantly, she emphasises the power of the projections and what they evoke countertansferentially: 'I have been trying to show that the issue is not a simple one; the patient does not just project into an analyst, but instead patients are quite skilled at projecting into particular aspects of the analyst. Thus, I have tried to show, for example, that the patient projects into the analyst's wish to be a mother, the wish to be all-knowing or to deny unpleasant knowledge, into the analyst's instinctual sadism, or into his defences against it. And above all, he projects into the analyst's guilt, or into the analyst's internal objects.

'Thus, patients touch off in the analyst deep issues and anxieties related to the need to be loved and the fear of catastrophic consequences in the face of defects, i.e., primitive persecutory or superego anxiety' (p. 161). As I see it, the approach adopted by Brenman Pick takes it as read and as normal that these powerful feelings are moving from patient to analyst and back again, through the processes of projection, evocation, reflection, interpretation and assimilation. Moving on from the more limited formulations of an earlier period in the writings of Winnicott, Heimann and even Money-Kyrle, these feelings are all normal, as it were, in the processes of analysis. More than that, as she puts it, they are the essence.

Kleinians have not always taken this view of countertransference. Klein had begged Heimann not to deliver her first paper on countertransference and told Tom Hayley in the late 1950s that she thought countertransference interferes with analysis and should be the subject of lightning self-analysis (Grosskurth, 1985, p. 378). According to Spillius, 'Klein thought that such extension would open the door to claims by analysts that their own deficiencies were caused by their patients' (Spillius, 1992, p. 61). Having said this, it is important not to be too literal about the use of the term 'countertransference'. Klein's subtle interpretations of her patients' inner worlds – especially their preverbal feelings and ideas – only make sense in the light of her ability to be resonant with their most primitive feelings, and Bion's injunction to 'abandon memory and desire' is made in the name of countertransference, whatever term we attach to the process. Indeed, it can be said that his writings are about little else.

Implicit in the way I have been writing about the phenomena of countertransference is a model for knowledge – that the way we really learn is from the Other's response to what we convey. We learn by evoking and provoking. We do not learn by imparting but by re-experiencing what we have projected and has then been passed through another human being (though that person may be held in imagination). We learn by putting something out and finding out what comes back. Our relationship with the world is a phenomenological 'I-thou', not a scientistic 'I-it'. It is evocative knowledge.

It may be thought that this model for knowledge is appropriate to relations between people (and perhaps pets) but that it in no way applies to knowledge of the external world. Some such distinction would seem to be common sense. However, it does not take into account recent thinking in the history, philosophy and social studies of science which argues that we project onto nature particular versions of reality and frame it according to the prevailing value systems and preoccupations – the 'world view' or *weltangschauung* of a period or subculture or discipline. What is true for a particular version of the world is also true for the individuals who inhabit it. Jerome Bruner (1951) has shown this with respect to children's perceptions of ordinary objects: what they see – even the size of coins – is dependent on their social location. M. L. J. Abercrombie (1960) has shown it for the anatomical and scientific perceptions of medical students: the most mundane observations only make sense in the light of unconscious forces. Donna Haraway (1989, 1991) has shown it for various fields of scientific research, particularly the social construction of primatology, providing a pedigree for our humanity (see Young, 1992a). Other versions of this position are now commonplace among students of scientific thought, e.g., Figlio, 1978, 1979, 1985, 1990; Hesse, 1980; Young, 1977, 1981, 1985, 1990, 1994, 1994a-d).

In the clinical realm, Searles' first book was a major study of how schizophrenics projectively perceive and treat the external environment (1960). This provides an interesting link between views of the inner world and ideas of the outer one: both worlds are highly interpretative. Karl

Figlio (1990) has generalised this view to nature as projectively experienced by nuclear disarmers and members of the peace movement. These 'friends of the earth' relate to the planet as a significant Other – a thou. Moving beyond our culture, we have seen that the history of social anthropology can be seen as a case study of my thesis, as the work of Mary Douglas exemplifies (above, ch. 2). Similarly, philosophers now argue that truth is made, not found (Rorty, 1980, 1982, 1989). Those who reflect on the philosophical implications of the belief systems of different epochs, tribes and disciplines point out that each of these social groups has its own cosmology, which articulates more or less well with that of other tribes (Horton, 1967, Bloor, 1976; Douglas, 1975). Ordinary, didactic imparting of knowledge and learning from teachers and from the media do not thereby cease to occur; they become special, limited cases of a richer model for the process of knowing.

The integration of psychoanalytic theory with developments such as those outlined here is, in my opinion, an important desideratum. What I have provided here is the barest sketch, in the hope that it will make attractive the project of bringing together a social, and cultural account of ways of knowing (epistemology) with the philosophical bearings of recent developments in psychoanalysis. Aspects of the work of Winnicott, Klein, Bion, and Meltzer seem to me to lie at the centre of this project. I have in mind, in particular, the concept of transitional space (chapter 6) and the notion that all experience is mediated through primitive processes and known through the mother's body (chapters 3, 7; cf. Young, 1986a, 1989c).

Returning to the psychoanalytic sphere, the weight I have put on the concept of countertransference need not be borne by that concept alone; it can be shared by ways of thinking across a broad range of disciplines. In the analytic relationship, it turns out that the real justification for the free-floating attention that is characteristic of psychoanalysis is that it makes our minds available for the patient's projections and facilitates their search for the resonances in us for what they feel. Freud said, 'He should simply listen, and not bother about whether he is keeping anything in mind' (Freud, 1912a, p. 112). Bion put it poetically in his injunction that the analyst should 'impose upon himself the positive discipline of eschewing memory and desire. I do not mean that "forgetting" is enough: what is required is a positive act of refraining from memory and desire' (Bion, 1970, p. 31).

If this sounds a bit mystical, so be it. Racker shares an appropriately Oriental parable: One day an old Chinese sage lost his pearls. 'He therefore sent his eyes to search for his pearls, but his eyes did not find them. Next he sent his ears to search for the pearls, but his ears did not find them either. Then he sent his hands to search for the pearls, but neither did his hands find them. And so he sent all of his senses to search for his pearls but none found them. Finally he sent his *not-search* to look for his pearls. *And his not-search found them.* '(Racker, 1968, p. 17).

Once one is in this state, one is open to the patient's unconscious and to the injunction that 'Constant projecting by the patient into the analyst is the essence of analysis' (Brenman Pick, 1985, p. 158). And at the other end of the analysis lies the ability of the patient to take back the projections. This is an important criterion of improvement. Bearing projections is the whole basis of containment: the therapist can bear to take in and contain the projections, to hold them and give them back, in due course, in the form of accessible interpretations.

I am suggesting that countertransference – as an aspect of projective identification – is not only the basis for analytic work but central to the basic process in all human communication and knowing. We only know what is happening because we are moved from within by what we have taken in and responded to from our own deep feelings. The space between people is filled – when it is and to the extent it is – by what we evoke in one another.

5   PRIMITIVE SPACE: PSYCHOTIC ANXIETIES

In this and the two chapters which follow I shall examine the forces at work in the inner world which militate against the existence, maintenance and creative use of congenial mental space. Why do we feel hemmed in, haunted, unable to think and to pursue our better impulses to fruitful results? What makes life so unsafe from the inside, as well as from the outside? They are topics it is hard to think about, partly because they are so primitive and pre-verbal, partly because they are so distressing. I believe that the fact that they have been rendered more explicitly by Kleinians than by other psychoanalytic writers is due in no small measure to the fact that for the most part Kleinians eschew the physicalist and scientistic language of neo-Freudian metapsychology and employ terms which are more resonant with experience as people suffer it. The same can be said of many writers in the Independent tradition, but they are less prone than Kleinians to explore the most primitive dimensions of human nature.

It has been said that Klein wrote more about the positive, loving and hopeful side of human nature in her later writings than in her earlier ones. I grant this, but it is her stress on the primitive, distressed and destructive side of humanity which was so startling for her contemporaries and which strikes me as her most original contribution. I also believe that this side of her thinking is closest to Freud's mature thinking, when he stressed the role of Thanatos and reflected on society and civilization. My comment to those who think I may unduly stress her more sombre thoughts is that plenty of people have offered optimistic – even palliative – renderings of psychoanalysis. I am very struck by the bleak side of human nature on the hoof, in particular, the rampant inhumanities which have followed the nominal ending of the Cold War. Klein and those who have pursued her steady gaze into human distress seem to me to give the best guidance on what we are up against. If we do not take the full measure of the consequences of human anxieties and defences, we will not be sufficiently stoical or prepared for the long haul of staying with humanity in the determined pursuit of better interpersonal and social relations.

One of the illuminating distinctions that Kleinian psychoanalysis has given us is that between knowing and knowing about. In psychoanalysis, knowing about something often operates as a defence against knowing it in a deeper, emotional sense. I well recall my first, greatly-valued supervisor, Bob Hinshelwood, saying once in an ironic way that if you don't understand what the patient is on about in the session, you make a clever interpretation, and if you aren't in touch with the patient at all, you can always write a paper. It is fairly easy to know about psychotic anxieties and projective mechanisms, but knowing them in an inward and sustained way is very difficult, indeed.

Of course, what one comes to know one knew all along, as I shall illustrate, and knowing about it can be as much a barrier as a catalyst to being able to *think* about that tacit knowledge. At the unconscious level we all know about the normality and ubiquity of psychotic anxieties, but it is quite another matter to be able to reflect upon some of the consequences of the omnipresence of these primitive unconscious phantasies for life, culture, politics and the theory of knowledge.

Having completed a reconsideration of the literature on psychotic anxieties, I will address two tasks. The first is to try to describe and give some emotional meaning to the kinds of phantasies against which we – as individuals and in groups and institutions – spend so much of our energy defending ourselves. Second, I want to gather together and draw attention to the implications of Kleinian ideas for how we think of human nature, by which I mean, with respect to individuals and all other levels of culture and civilisation. It turns out that defence against psychotic anxieties is offered by Kleinians as a deeper explanation than the incest taboo for the basis of that thin and all too easily breached veneer that constitutes civility and stands between what passes for the social order, on the one hand, and chaos (or the fear of it), on the other. This turns out to be a mixed blessing, since our defences against psychotic anxieties act as a powerful brake on institutional and social change toward less rigid and more generous relations between individuals and groups. They diminish mental space; put differently, they fill one with disabling feelings and make it hard to the point of impossibility to think.

As we saw in chapter two, Freud's theory of civilisation drew attention to the taboo against violent sexual competitiveness and rapaciousness as the corner-stone of civilisation. The polymorphously perversely sexual patriarch was said to have been killed by the primal horde, thus establishing the incest taboo, the basis for all other taboos and the system of custom and legality that gave birth to civilisation and culture. Freud constantly emphasised that man is a wolf to other men, that the veneer of civilisation is thin and under threat from moment to moment and that all of life is a constant struggle conducted in the fraught space between erotic and destructive instincts. For Freud the basic conflicts occurred at this level of the psyche. As Meltzer describes it, Freud's world is 'a world of higher animals', 'creatures seeking surcease from the constant bombardment of stimuli from inside and out'. He contrasts Klein's world as 'one of holy babes in holy families plagued by the devils of split off death instinct' (Meltzer, 1978, part III, pp. 115–16). One is a world of animals as scientific objects reacting to stimuli, the other a world of human subjects haunted by demons. One emphasises the relations with the environment, the other relations with the inner world of phantasy.

This is not merely a difference of emphasis. Matters which may appear on the surface be about common sense or adult relationships or genital sexuality may also turn out to be about much more primitive psychological levels of distress. Similarly, the difference between the worlds of Freud and Klein may be described as one of *level* of explanation and of causality. Bion put the point clearly in the conclusion to his essay, 'Group Dynamics – A Re-view', Bion says, 'Freud's view of the dynamics of the group seems to me to require supplementing rather than correction' (Bion, 1961, p. 187). He accepts Freud's claim that the family group is the basis for all groups but adds that 'I would go further; I think that the central position in group dynamics is occupied by the more primitive mechanisms that Melanie Klein has described as peculiar to the paranoid-schizoid and depressive positions. In other words, I feel . . . that it is not simply a matter of the incompleteness of the illumination provided by Freud's discovery of the family group as the prototype of all groups, but the fact that this incompleteness leaves out the source of the main emotional drives of the group' (p. 188). He then summarises the notions of 'work group' and the 'basic assumptions' that assail them – 'dependence', 'pairing', 'fight-flight' (which I characterise below, p. 157–8) – and suggests that these may have a common link or may be different aspects of each other. 'Further investigation shows that each basic assumption contains features that correspond so closely with extremely primitive part objects that sooner or later psychotic anxiety, appertaining to these primitive relationships, is released. These anxieties, and the mechanisms peculiar to them, have already been displayed in psychoanalysis by Melanie Klein, and her descriptions tally well with the emotional states' of the basic assumption group. Such groups have aims 'far different either from the overt task of the group or even from the tasks that would appear to be appropriate to Freud's view of the group as based on the family group. But approached from the angle of psychotic anxiety, associated with phantasies of primitive part object relationships . . . the basic assumption phenomena appear far more to have the characteristics of defensive reactions to psychotic anxiety, and to be not so much at variance with Freud's views as supplementary to them. In my view, it is necessary to work through both the stresses that appertain to family patterns and the still more primitive anxieties of part object relationships. In fact I consider the latter to contain the ultimate sources of all group behaviour' (p. 189). In Bion's view, then, what matters in individual and group behaviour is more primitive than the Freudian level of explanation. The ultimate sources of our distress are psychotic anxieties, and much of what happens in individuals and groups is a result of defences erected *against* psychotic anxieties, so that we do not have to endure them consciously.

I'll say something about the term 'psychotic' and then turn to the concept of phantasy and the anxieties which primitive phantasies generate. To most of us 'psychotic' refers to psychosis, a primary disturbance of relations with reality, and psychotic symptoms are an attempt to restore the link with objects (Laplanche & Pontalis, 1983, p. 370). When I was trained as a psychiatric aide in a state mental hospital in the 1950s, we were taught a small number of things about psychosis, and they seemed adequate in those pre-Laing (1960; Young, 1966a) and pre-Goffman (1961) times. Psychotics were 'out of contact with reality' for much or all of the time. They heard and saw things that were not there – hallucinations – and wildly distorted things that were – delusions. The notion of 'psychotic' was safely restricted to people designated as 'mad'. Their likely diagnoses were schizophrenia (four varieties: catatonic, paranoid, hebephrenic, simple); true paranoia; manic-depressive psychosis; psychotic depression; organic psychosis. The categories of dementia praecox or schizophrenia and of manic-depressive psychosis have been in existence for less then a century and are more recent than Freud and Breuer's *Studies on Hysteria*. Emil Kraepelin coined the term 'dementia praecox' in 1896.

What we now call psychosis has always had a special place in practically all cultures, although that place has varied from divine, to diabolical, to providing special insight, to links with witchcraft and

enviable freedom from social (though not always physical) restraints.
Think of the 'Ship of Fools' and the depictions and expressions of the mad
by Bosch, Breughel, Goya and van Gogh, Magritte and Man Ray, as well
as the manifestos of the Surrealists and Dadaists. In their very different
ways, they all celebrated illumination coming from the most primitive
levels of the unconscious. Like the critiques of the categories of psychiatry
written by Foucault (1967), Laing (1960) and Cooper (1972), these artists
pointed to madness as offering a basis for making critiques of the
repressions, sublimations and alienation of conventional society and put
one in touch with something truer and in some senses better (see also
Gordon, 1990). These notions remain widespread. In a BBC2 television
film in a series on 'Madness', Jonathan Miller referred to ideas of the mad
as childlike, as direct beneficiaries of God and to the beatific association
between poverty and lunacy, while that morning's *Observer* (13 October
1991) alluded to 'the sixties argument that the mad are truly sane'. I am
not analysing or assessing these claims, only noting their currency.

I want to turn now to the mechanisms in question and their evolution
from the asylum to the nursery. Klein described schizoid mechanisms as
occurring 'in the baby's development in the first year of life characteristically . . . the infant suffered from states of mind that were in all their
essentials equivalent to the adult psychoses, taken as regressive states in
Freud's sense' (Meltzer, 1978, part III, p. 22). Klein says in the third
paragraph of her 'Notes on Some Schizoid Mechanisms' (1946), 'In early
infancy anxieties characteristic of psychosis arise which drive the ego to
develop specific defence-mechanisms. In this period the fixation-points
for all psychotic disorders are to be found. This has led some people to
believe that I regard all infants as psychotic; but I have already dealt
sufficiently with this misunderstanding on other occasions' (Klein, 1946,
p. 1). Meltzer comments that 'Although she denied that this was
tantamount to saying that babies are psychotic, it is difficult to see how
this implication could be escaped' (Meltzer, 1978, part III, p. 22).

Kleinian thinking evolved in three stages. As in the above quotation,
Klein saw schizoid mechanisms and the paranoid-schizoid position as
fixation points, respectively, for schizophrenia and paranoid psychosis the
depressive position as the fixation point for manic-depressive psychosis.
Then the paranoid-schizoid and depressive positions became developmental stages. Her terminology included 'psychotic phases, 'psychotic
positions' and then 'positions' (Klein, 1935, pp. 275n–276n, 279). Thirdly,
in the work of Bion and other post-Kleinians, these became economic
principles and part of the moment-to-moment vicissitudes of everyday life.

The notations 'ps' and 'd' were connected with a double-headed arrow –
ps↔d – to indicate how easily and frequently our inner states oscillate
from the paranoid-schizoid to the depressive position and back again
(Meltzer, 1978, part III, p. 22). In Bion's writings on schizophrenia an
ambiguity remained as to whether or not the psychotic part of the
personality is ubiquitous or only present in schizophrenics, but Meltzer
concludes his exposition of Bion's schizophrenia papers by referring to
the existence of these phenomena in patients of every degree of
disturbance, even 'healthy' candidates in training to be therapists (p. 28).
Going further, he and colleagues have drawn on the inner world of autistic
patients to illuminate the norm; Frances Tustin (1986) has essayed on
autistic phenomena in neurotic patients, while Sydney Klein (1980) has
described 'autistic cysts' in neurotic patients.

I offer here John Steiner's brief characterisations of the two positions
which have come to be seen as the basic modes of feeling between which
people oscillate: 'As a brief summary: in the paranoid-schizoid position
anxieties of a primitive nature threaten the immature ego and lead to a
mobilisation of primitive defences. Splitting, idealisation and projective
identification operate to create rudimentary structures made up of
idealised good objects kept far apart from persecuting bad ones. The
individual's own impulses are similarly split and he directs all his love
towards the good object and all his hatred against the bad one. As a
consequence of the projection, the leading anxiety is paranoid, and the
preoccupation is with survival of the self. Thinking is concrete because of
the confusion between self and object which is one of the consequences
of projective identification (Segal, 1957).

'The depressive position represents an important developmental
advance in which whole objects begin to be recognised and ambivalent
impulses become directed towards the primary object. These changes
result from an increased capacity to integrate experiences and lead to a
shift in primary concern from the survival of the self to a concern for the
object upon which the individual depends. Destructive impulses lead to
feelings of loss and guilt which can be more fully experienced and which
consequently enable mourning to take place. The consequences include
a development of symbolic function and the emergence of reparative
capacities which become possible when thinking no longer has to remain
concrete' (Steiner, 1987, pp. 69–70; see also Steiner, 1993, pp. 26–34).

So much for bringing 'psychotic' into the realm of the normal and
neurotic. Turning now to 'phantasy' I'll begin by pointing out that a full
page of the *index* to *Developments in Psychoanalysis* (Klein *et al.*, 1952)

is devoted to this single term, and the entry fills half a page in the historical account of *The Freud-Klein Controversies 1941–1945* (King and Steiner, 1991). The essays in *Developments in Psychoanalysis* are versions of the papers which formed the Kleinian texts in that controversy. Many things were at stake, but at the heart of it, in my opinion, was the question of the primacy of the inner world, as opposed to the more interactive, adaptive framework of ideas which came to be associated with ego psychology and, more recently, so-called 'contemporary Freudianism'. Anna Freud rebuts the claim that she 'has an inveterate prejudice in favour of the modes of external reality . . . and of conscious mental processes' (King and Steiner, 1991, p. 328), but I think that the relative weights assigned to inner and outer worlds provides a legitimate demarcation between Kleinian and Freudian orientations. The contrast became even more marked between Klein and her successors, on the one hand, and developments in America, on the other: the school of ego psychology developed by Hartmann (1958), Kris (1950a), Lowenstein (1963; *cf.* Hartmann, Kris and Lowenstein, 1946) and the American school epitomised by the systematising work of David Rapaport (1967). Ego psychology is probably the majority point of view in Continental and American psychoanalysis (Tyson and Tyson, 1990), but it is in a minority position in Britain, where it is associated with the Hampstead Child-Therapy Clinic (now called The Anna Freud Centre) and the contemporary Freudian or 'B Group' at the Institute of Psycho-Analysis, where its best-known exponents are Joseph Sandler (1987, 1989), Anne-Marie Sandler (1978) and Peter Fonagy.

As a part of the issue over the primacy of the inner world, I believe that people were genuinely shocked by what they thought was sheer craziness and nastiness of the child's unconscious as described by Klein and her supporters. Indeed, there is a protest along these lines by Michael Balint, who dryly comments in the discussion of Susan Isaacs' fundamentally important paper (to which I shall turn next) that 'perhaps Mrs Klein is laying undue emphasis on the role of hatred, frustration and aggression in the infant' (King and Steiner, 1991, p. 347). Fairbairn, in contrast, seemed to feel (at least at that time) that Kleinian accounts of phantasy were so successfully descriptive of the inner world that he proposed dropping 'phantasy' in favour of 'inner reality' (p. 359).

I begin with the elementary point that '*phantasy*' refers to 'predominantly or entirely unconscious phantasies', as distinct from the sort of conscious *fantasies* or imaginings we associate with daydreams or idle imaginings (Isaacs, 1952, pp. 80–81). Joan Riviere appeals to Freud's hypothesis that the psyche is always interpreting the reality of its experiences – 'or rather, *mis*interpreting them – in a subjective manner that increases its pleasure and preserves it from pain' (Riviere, 1952a, p. 41). Freud calls this process 'hallucination; and it forms the foundation of what we mean by *phantasy-life*. The phantasy-life of the individual is thus the form in which the real internal and external sensations and perceptions are interpreted and represented to himself in his mind under the influence of the pleasure-pain principle'. Riviere adds that 'this primitive and elementary function of his psyche – to misinterpret his perceptions for his own satisfaction – still retains the upper hand in the minds of the great majority of even civilised adults' (p. 41).

I suggest – and this lies at the heart of my overall argument – that *this point about misinterpreting the reality of the psyche's experience as normal and basic and hallucinatory is the essential point – the ur-fact – about human nature. It is also the essential basis for the theory of knowledge and out hopes for better human relations in couples, families, groups, institutions, communities and nations. It provides the potential space within which we can re-evaluate, ruminate and reconsider our relations with the world. It is the point of origin of mental space.*

This general function for phantasy is repeated in Susan Isaacs' definition. The '"mental expression" of instinct *is* unconscious phantasy . . . There is no impulse, no instinctual urge or response which is not experienced as unconscious phantasy' (Isaacs, 1952, p. 83). 'The first mental processes . . . are to be regarded as the earliest beginnings of phantasies. In the mental development of the infant, however, phantasy soon becomes also a means of defence against anxieties, a means of inhibiting and controlling instinctual urges and an expression of reparative wishes as well . . . All impulses, all feelings, all modes of defence are experienced in phantasies which give them *mental* life and show their direction and purpose' (*ibid.*).

When we turn to the content of the phantasies a problem of communication arises: 'they are apt to produce a strong impression of unreality and untruth' (Riviere, 1952, p. 20). This is because when we write or speak about them we are clothing preverbal and very primitive mental processes in the language of words in dictionaries. My way round this is to share some images and experience from my own clinical and personal experience. Phantasies are rendered by patients as black holes, nameless dread, part objects, offal, shit, urine, dreams of wet cinders or barren desert mindscapes, pus, slime, feelings of being overwhelmed, engulfed, disintegrated, in pieces, devoured, falling through empty space, spiders, bugs, snakes. Language drawn from work with autistic patients includes dread of falling apart, falling infinitely, spilling away, exploding away, threat of total annihilation, unintegration (as distinct from the *dis*integration of schizophrenia), experiencing a missing person as a hole (rather than 'missing' them as not present).

When I cannot find a piece of paper or go to a room and cannot recall why, I don't just think of age and preoccupation. The fabric of reality is momentarily rent asunder, and in that moment I feel in imminent danger of dying, of disintegration, of unendurable panic. When I was a boy there was a nearby grand house, set in large grounds in a gully, with walls and a gate with a heavy chain and a wrought iron sign: '*DRIVERDALE*'. I could not go near it without intense anxiety. (It was a feat of my adolescence to drive my motor-bike at high speed through the grounds.) The same intense terror was experienced with respect to a green house we had to pass on the way to the swimming pool, and we called the woman who lived there 'The Green Witch'. I believed in and feared the Bogeyman and could not go to sleep unless the door of my wardrobe was shut. I was mortally afraid of the Frankenstein monster and the Mummy (of 'The Mummy's Curse'), and until I went away to university I could not go into the kitchen without first reaching round the door jamb and turning on the fluorescent light, which took an age to go on. I was similarly wary of the darkened back porch, while going into the back garden after dusk was simply out of the question. My childhood and adolescence were filled with terrors, imaginings, fantasies and some activities about which I would blush to tell – all tearing the fabric of civilised society. Prominent among the terrors was the sheer horror of hearing the word 'Terrell', the name of the nearby state mental hospital. I cannot recall a time when this word did not conjure up an unpicturable hell, into which my depressed mother and I were in imminent danger of being tossed as a result of my transgressions, in particular, my inability to behave with sufficient respect and deference toward my father. A version of this terror still overcomes me when I am in the grip of an argument and cannot let up. Behind these conscious experiences, I now know, lay psychotic anxieties.

I offer these reports as my version of what Klein calls 'a cave full of dangerous monsters' (Klein, 1935, p. 272). My general point is that if you ask the question, 'What is a psychotic anxiety when it's at home and not in the pages of an implausible and nearly unfathomable text by Melanie Klein?', you'll be able to be less sceptical if you interrogate the fringes of your own memories and distressing experiences and, of course, dreams. Elizabeth Spillius points out that 'unconscious phantasies are somewhat more accessible in early childhood; in adulthood the path to them is indirect, through dreams, in imaginative constructions, sometimes in group behaviour, in symptoms, parapraxes, etc., though always in disguised form' (personal communication).

I shall offer more illustrations anon, but for the present I want to assert that psychotic anxieties are ubiquitous, underlie all thought, provide the rationale for all culture and institutions and, in particular cases, help us to make sense of especially galling ways of being. I have in mind Meltzer's idea of the claustrum, wherein dwell ultra-ambitious and survivalist conformists who *live in* projective identification, which he takes to mean that their dwelling place in the inner world is just inside the rectum, thus confirming the colloquial description of such people as 'arseholes'. His analysis shows that this degree of use of projective identification is a defence against schizophrenic breakdown. This suggests that many of our chief executives and leaders live perpetually on the verge of madness. No wonder that they absolutely *must* get their way (Meltzer, 1991, 1992).

Klein's views on these matters are based on Freud and Abraham's notions of oral libido and fantasies of cannibalism (Gedo, 1986, p. 94). She refers to sadistic impulses against the mother's breast and inside her body, wanting to scoop out, devour, cut to pieces, poison and destroy by every means sadism suggests (Klein, 1935, p. 262). Once again, the projective and introjective mechanisms of the first months and year give rise to anxiety situations and defences against them, 'the content of which is comparable to that of the psychoses in adults' (*Ibid.*).

Orality is everywhere, for example, in the 'gnawing of conscience' (p. 268). Riviere says that 'such helplessness against destructive forces within constitutes the greatest psychical danger-situation known to the human organism; and that this helplessness is the deepest source of anxiety in human beings' (Riviere, 1952a, p. 43). It is the ultimate source of all neurosis. At this early stage of development, sadism is at its height and is followed by the discovery that loved objects are in a state of disintegration, in bits or in dissolution, leading to despair, remorse and anxiety, which underlie numerous anxiety situations. Klein concludes, 'Anxiety situations of this kind I have found to be at the bottom not only of depression, but of all inhibitions of work' (Klein, 1935, p. 270).

It should be recalled that these are pre-linguistic experiences developmentally, and sub-linguistic in adults. As I have said, it is a characteristic of the world view of Kleinians that the primitive is never transcended and that all experiences continue to be mediated through the mother's body. Similarly, there is a persistence of primitive phantasies of body parts and ·

bodily functions, especially biting, eating, tearing, spitting out, urine and urinating, faeces and defecating, mucus, genitals.

Having said that, I shall offer an example of undiluted Klein. She is in the middle of an exposition of the part which the paranoid, depressive and manic positions play in normal development (p. 279) and offers two illustrative dreams, which I shall not quote. (I should emphasise that I am drawing on a passage from the middle of an exposition and interpretation which is six pages long.) I want to convey the flavour of the primitive phantasies which I have been discussing. Here is part of the interpretation: 'The urination in the dream led on to early aggressive phantasies of the patient towards his parents, especially directed against their sexual intercourse. He had phantasied biting them and eating them up, and among other attacks, urinating on and into his father's penis, in order to skin and burn it and to make his father set his mother's inside on fire in their intercourse (the torturing with hot oil). These phantasies extended to babies inside his mother's body, which were to be killed (burnt). The kidney burnt alive stood both for his father's penis – equated with faeces – and for the babies inside his mother's body (the stove which he did not open). Castration of the father was expressed by the associations about beheading. Appropriation of the father's penis was shown by the feeling that his penis was so large and that he urinated both for himself and for his father (phantasies of having his father's penis inside his own or joined on to his own had come out a great deal in his analysis). The patient's urinating into the bowl meant also his sexual intercourse with his mother (whereby the bowl and the mother in the dream represented her both as a real and as an internalised figure). The impotent and castrated father was made to look on at the patient's intercourse with his mother – the reverse of the situation the patient had gone through in phantasy in his childhood. The wish to humiliate his father is expressed by his feeling that he ought not to do so' (Klein, 1935, p. 281). And so on for another half page. A similarly daunting example could be drawn from Meltzer's account of the dream materials which can be attributed to unconscious phantasies of anal masturbation (Meltzer, 1966, esp. pp. 104, 106–7).

This is veritably hard to bear, hard to credit, hard to follow. Klein is operating – well and truly – in the most primitive parts of the inner world, where dream symbolism meets up with primitive bodily functions and body parts. Her way of describing these phantasies is easy to caricature and becomes wooden when adopted in a parrot-like fashion by inexperienced acolytes. In the subsequent history of Kleinian psycho-analysis, however, her outlook on unconscious phantasy has continued to prevail. Elizabeth Spillius reports that this is one of Klein's concepts which has been 'very little altered' by subsequent Kleinians (Spillius, 1988, vol. 1, p. 2).

However, many Kleinians (though not all, for example, Donald Meltzer) have altered their language and have become more likely to make interpretations in terms of functions rather than anatomical part objects. Edna O'Shaughnessy has suggested the notion of 'psychological part objects' as an analogy to bodily part objects. Spillius takes this up and argues 'that we relate to psychological part objects . . . to the functions of the part object rather than primarily to its physical structure. It is the capacities for seeing, touching, tasting, hearing, smelling, remembering, feeling, judging, and thinking, active as well as passive, that are attributed to and perceived in relation to part objects'. Spillius concludes her remarks on this change in emphasis in technique by relating it to Klein's concept of projective identification. The functions 'are frequently understood as aspects of the self which are projected into part objects' (pp. 2–5; cf. vol. 2, pp. 8–9).

Klein was untroubled by being called an 'id psychologist' (Gedo, 1986, p. 91). She unrepentantly conceived the analyst's task to be to confront the patient with the content of the unconscious. She eschewed 'corrective emotional experience', did not encourage regression and the reliving of infantile experiences (nor did she avoid them when they occurred), or explicit educational or moral influences, and kept 'to the psycho-analytic procedure only, which, to put it in a nutshell, consists in understanding the patient's mind and in conveying to him what goes on in it' (Klein, 1955, p. 129). She felt that confidently articulating interpretations of very primitive material in the face of resistance diminishes the patient's anxiety and opens the door to the unconscious. Nor did she shy away from such deep interpretations or transference interpretations from the beginning of analytic work with a patient (Klein, 1975, vol. 2, pp. 22–24; Gedo, 1986, p. 92).

Why is all this such an innovation? Riviere points out that anxiety was of great significance to Freud, but that much of his rhetoric was scientific, especially physiological. He did not concern himself with the psychological *content* of phantasies. Indeed, he and many of his 'Freudian' followers have tended to use scientistic analogies instead of conveying human distress in evocative language. By contrast, 'Anxiety, with the defences against it, has from the beginning been Mrs Klein's approach to psycho-analytical problems. It was from this angle that she discovered the existence and importance of aggressive elements in children's emotional life . . . and [it] enabled her to bring much of the known phenomena of mental disorders into line with the basic principles of analysis' (Riviere, 1952, pp. 8–9).

This contrast between Freud and Klein takes us back to one of the major themes of my argument – the issues raised in chapters one to three. I am referring to the need to break away from describing the inner world in terms drawn from a metapsychology based on analogies drawn from physics and biology. I am advocating, instead, the bold use of terms drawn from the language of everyday life and the employment of any way of representing primitive processes that comes to hand. This involves a move from the didactic and objectivist language of natural science and the epistemologies which kow-tow to it and toward evocative and phenomenological ways of attempting to convey the inner meaning of experience. Mental space need not be reduced to the realm of extended substances; it can be filled and populated by whatever helps us to keep feeling alive. Rather than defer to the canons of Cartesian dualism, our criterion should be whether or not a given account resonates with the dialectic of experience.

Kleinians have consistently written in a language which eschews physicalist scientism, albeit Klein did retain a notion of instinct, even though this was largely redundant as a result of her object relations perspective. They went on to propose elements of a general psychology, including the claim that there is 'an unconscious phantasy behind every thought and every act' (Riviere, 1952, p. 16). That is, the mental expression of primitive processes '*is* unconscious phantasy' (*Ibid.*). It is not only a background hum, as it were. Isaacs claims that 'Reality thinking cannot operate without concurrent and supporting unconscious phantasies' (Isaacs, 1952, p. 109). And again: 'phantasies are the primary content of unconscious mental processes' (pp. 82, 112). 'There is no impulse, no instinctual urge or response which is not experienced as unconscious phantasy' (p. 83). 'Phantasies have both psychic and bodily effects, e. g., in conversion symptoms, bodily qualities, character and personality, neurotic symptoms, inhibitions and sublimations' (p. 112). They even determine the minutiae of body language (p. 100). The role of unconscious phantasy extends from the first to the most abstract thought. The infant's first thought of the existence of the external world comes from sadistic attacks on the mother's body (Klein, 1935, p. 276; 1946 p. 5). 'Phantasies – becoming more elaborate and referring to a wider variety of objects and situations – continue throughout development and accompany all activities; they never stop playing a great part in mental life. The influence of unconscious phantasy on art, on scientific work, and on the activities of everyday life cannot be overrated' (Klein, 1959, p. 251; cf. p. 262).

These anxieties are not only ubiquitous: they interact in complicated ways. As Riviere points out, 'It is impossible to do any justice here to the complexity and variety of the anxiety-situations and the defences against them dominating the psyche during these early years. The factors involved are so numerous and the combinations and interchanges so variable. The internal objects are employed against external, and external against internal, both for satisfaction and for security; desire is employed against hate and destructiveness; omnipotence against impotence, and even impotence (dependence) against destructive omnipotence; phantasy against reality and reality against phantasy. Moreover, hate and destruction are employed as measures to avert the dangers of desire and even of love. Gradually a progressive development takes place . . . by means of the interplay of these and other factors, and of them with external influences, out of which the child's ego, his object-relations, his sexual development, his super-ego, his character and capacities are formed' (Riviere, 1952a, pp. 59–60).

Turning, as I promised to do at the end of chapter three, to the bearings of these ideas on groups and institutions, I want to begin with two points. The first is that the move is a simple one. Bion says, 'My impression is that the group approximates too closely, in the minds of the individuals composing it, to very primitive phantasies about the contents of the mother's body. The attempt to make a rational investigation of the dynamics of the group is therefore perturbed by fears, and mechanisms for dealing with them, which are characteristic of the paranoid-schizoid position. The investigation cannot be carried out without the stimulation and activation of those levels . . . the elements of the emotional situation are so closely allied to phantasies of the earliest anxieties that the group is compelled, whenever the pressure of anxiety becomes too great, to take defensive action' (Bion, 1961, p. 163). The psychotic anxieties in question involve splitting and projective identification and are characteristic of the paranoid-schizoid and depressive positions, now as group processes (p. 164). The move from the individual to the group does not raise new issues about explanation. He says a little further on, 'The apparent difference between group psychology and individual psychology is an illusion produced by the fact that the group brings into prominence phenomena which appear alien to an observer unaccustomed to using the group' (p. 169).

My second point is that those of us who have tried to change institutions, and have learned that there are things that'll knock you down that you didn't see coming, will be relieved to have this illumination and to be better informed about what we are up against. I remember with some chagrin the occasion when a senior colleague insisted that I train in group therapy and go to a two-week residential Leicester Conference on group relations (Miller, 1990). I was offended by his saying I'd had no experience of groups, since I'd spent my Sixties and Seventies in all sorts of collectives, co-ops and even a commune. Looking back from the vantage point of a number of years of conducting and being supervised on group therapy, trying to assimilate the experience of a Leicester Conference (which all acknowledge takes years) and being a member of staff at group relations events, I am persuaded that unless we understand the psychotic anxieties Bion is on about, we will never know what we are up against in human nature and in trying to change things. Bion says that falling into the forms of basic assumption functioning which he describes is instinctive, involuntary, automatic, instantaneous and inevitable (Bion, 1961, pp. 153, 165). However much experience one may have of groups and institutions, group relations events provide a unique setting for reflection about the primitive processes at work in them.

Elliott Jaques and Isabel Menzies Lyth are also very sober and stoical in their assessments of the barriers to change. Jaques begins his essay on 'Social Systems as a Defence against Persecutory and Depressive Anxiety' (1955) by reiterating that 'social phenomena show a striking correspondence with psychotic processes in individuals', that 'institutions are used by their individual members to reinforce individual mechanisms of defence against anxiety', and 'that the mechanisms of projective and introjective identification operate in linking individual and social behaviour'. He argues the thesis that 'the primary cohesive elements binding individuals into institutionalised human association is that of defence against psychotic anxiety' (Jaques, 1955, pp. 478–9). He points out that the projective and introjective processes he is investigating are basic to even the most complex social processes (p. 481, cf. 481n).

His conclusion is cautionary and points out the conservative – even reactionary – consequences of our psychotic anxieties and our group and institutional defences against them. He suggests that as a result of these reflections on human nature 'it may become more clear why social change is so difficult to achieve, and why many social problems are so intractable. From the point of view here elaborated, changes in social relationships and procedures call for a restructuring of relationships at the phantasy level, with a consequent demand upon individuals to accept and tolerate changes in their existing patterns of defences against psychotic anxiety. Effective social change is likely to require analysis of the common anxieties and unconscious collusions underlying the social defences determining phantasy social relationships' (p. 498).

I turn now to the investigator who, in my opinion, has made the most of this perspective, Isabel Menzies Lyth, who built her research on the shoulders of Bion and Jaques. She has investigated a number of fraught settings, but the piece of research which has deservedly made her world-famous is described in a report entitled 'The Functioning of Social Systems as a Defence against Anxiety' (1959). It is a particularly poignant document, which addresses the question why people of good will and idealistic motives do not do what they intend, that is, in this study, why nurses find themselves, to an astonishing degree, not caring for patients as they had originally wished to do and leaving the nursing service in droves. It would be repetitious to review the mechanisms she describes. They are the ones discussed above. What is so distressing is that they operate overwhelmingly in a setting which has as its very reason for existence the provision of sensitivity and care. Yet that setting is full of threats to life itself and arouses the psychotic anxieties I have outlined. She says, 'The objective situation confronting the nurse bears a striking resemblance to the phantasy situations that exist in every individual in the deepest and most primitive levels of the mind. The intensity and complexity of the nurse's anxieties are to be attributed primarily to the peculiar capacity of the objective features of her work situation to stimulate afresh those early situations and their accompanying emotions' (Menzies Lyth, 1959, pp. 46–7).

The result is the evolution of socially structured defence mechanisms which take the form of routines and division of tasks which effectively preclude the nurse relating as a whole person to the patient as a whole person. 'The implicit aim of such devices, which operate both structurally and culturally, may be described as a kind of depersonalisation or elimination of individual distinctiveness in both nurse and patient' (pp. 51–2). She lists and discusses the reifying devices which reduce everyone involved to part-objects, including insight into why nurses mechanically follow orders in ways that defy common sense (p. 69). There is a whole system of overlapping ways of evading the full force of the anxieties associated with death, the ones which lie at the heart of the mechanisms which Klein described (pp. 63–64; cf. Riviere, 1952a, p. 43).

Menzies Lyth draws a cautionary conclusion rather like Jaques': 'In general, it may be postulated that resistance to social change is likely to be greatest in institutions whose social defence systems are dominated by primitive psychic defence mechanisms, those which have been collectively described by Melanie Klein as the paranoid-schizoid defences' (Lyth, 1959, p. 79). In recent reflections on her work and that of her colleagues, she has reiterated just how refractory to change institutions are (Lyth, 1988, pp. 1–42, and personal communications).

The Leicester Conferences on group and organisational behaviour, with particular emphasis on authority and leadership, have been held at least once a year since 1957. They are heir to the traditions discussed above, especially the work of Klein, Bion, Jaques and Menzies Lyth. (Other influences are mentioned in Miller, 1990, pp. 165–69.) One among several interrelated ways of characterising the two-week residential conferences is that they are so arranged as to facilitate experiential learning about the ways in which group processes can generate psychotic anxieties and institutional defences against them (p. 171). The struggles that ensue in the members' minds between individuation and incorporation, as a result of the conference group events, is hard to credit by anyone who has not taken part in a Leicester Conference or related 'mini-Leicester' events. Similarly, descriptions of events and feelings are likely to seem odd to anyone not familiar with the sorts of events around which the conferences are structured. I believe, however, that the relevant emotional points will be sufficiently clear without a (necessarily) long description of the conference rubric.

My own experience involved feeling continually on the edge of disintegration as a result of behaviour in the various group events (ranging in size from a dozen to more than a hunderd people) which I found appalling and from which there seemed no escape, while efforts to persuade people to behave well produced flight, sadism collusive lowering of the stakes or denial. The potential of the group for uniting around (what was called on occasion) 'cheap reconciliation' or for cruelty, brought me to the point of leaving on several occasions, and I frequently had the experience of having to use all my resources to hold myself together against forces which I experienced as profoundly immoral, amoral or pathetically conformist. No appeal to standards of group decency was of much avail.

I ended up forming a group in my mind which consisted of all the people I admired in history and in my lifetime, e.g., Socrates, Lincoln, Gandhi, King, Bonhoeffer, Marcuse, Mandela, who had stood up to intolerable social forces without quitting the field or having their spirits broken. I dubbed this 'The PS↔D Solidarity Group' and, armed with their mandate (bestowed by one part of my mind onto another), managed to talk my way into a meeting with the staff, for the purpose of mounting a critique of the rubric of the exercise. I felt contained by the inner solidarity provided by my imagined group, while I was, in truth, actually on my own in the phenomenal context of the conference events. I had blown out of a group in considerable distress, because it had utterly failed to live up to its self-designation of advocating and practising decency and civility among its members and urging such standards on the larger group of conference members.

Just as I was on the point of sitting down to confront the staff group in the name of my inner world group (vainly hoping they would show some interest in its name, membership and values), a representative of the group I had left appeared and bestowed 'plenipotentiary powers' (the highest of the designated forms of delegation of authority) on me, freeing me from the dreaded status of 'singleton'. A singleton is a person with no role status in he large group (see Miller, 1990, p. 179 and Turquet, 1975, where the plight of the singleton is insightfully and poignantly described). I had felt unutterably alone, almost totally in the grip of paranoid persecutions, holding on for dear life to my hallucinated historical group. The bestowal of my conference group's trust reincorporated me into the social whole on terms I could accept.

My confrontation with the staff group, acting in this exercise as 'Management', was – predictably – without issue, but I went away feeling that I had spoken my piece without suffering the humiliation that many others had experienced. I had offered my analysis of the situation and their role in it, one dimension of which was that they *would* – as a part of the point of the exercise – continue to behave as they were doing, i.e., act as an immovable object onto which the groups would project their phantasies about authority and (hopefully) begin to take responsibility for themselves. I felt that I had done that and negotiated my own rite of passage – just.

Having gone some way toward resolving my own temporary insanity (though not my omnipotence) I was only able to bask pleasantly in group membership for a few minutes before members of another group, who had sought refuge in being regressed and silly (they had all been to previous conferences and might have been expected to be street wise, but they took refuge in regression and called themselves 'The Potty Training Group'), stormed into the room where the staff/Management group were holding court. The person whom I had considered to be the mildest member of that group physically attacked a German member of staff with shouts of 'fascist' and other violent epithets. He was aided and cheered on by other members of his group, until one, a woman I felt sure was a Jew but I now recollect was probably not but was a German, broke down sobbing and shouted for all this to stop, which it did.

The descent from work or task-oriented groups to groups in the thrall of psychotic basic assumptions is, as Bion pointed out, spontaneous and inevitable (Bion, 1961, p. 165), even in a situation which all concerned know to be temporary and 'artificial'. I continue to find this profoundly sobering. I also continue to ruminate it and am far from having digested the experience, though I have found it increasingly helpful in my work and related activities.

After canvassing the literature on psychotic anxieties and reflecting on it and my own personal and clinical experience, I am left with a daunting sense of the power of the inner world and an awesome awareness of how very deep, primitive, abiding and alarming its nether regions are. I shall try to say something more about the articulation between these anxieties and wider social and ideological forces. But notice this: my argument moved from individual to group phenomena with some ease. The principles which apply to the inner world of the individual also help to illuminate the inner world of the group. The group is at work in the inner world of the individual, and the most primitive level of the individual has its grip on the group. The anxieties I have attempted to outline (and, to a degree, evoke), exist throughout human nature – in all of life from the cradle (some say earlier) to the grave, in all of play and culture, and act as a brake on benignity and social change which it is hard to imagine releasing, even notch by notch. I shall return to this problem in the next two chapters, where the role of projective processes will be examined.

The history of psychoanalysis has left us with a small number of ideas about the veneer of civilisation. Freud said it was thin and constantly under threat. One reading of those who still speak in his name and quote his slogan: 'Where id was, there ego shall be. It is a work of culture – not unlike the draining of the Zuider Zee' (Freud, 1933, p. 80), takes this to mean that the result can be dry, flowering land, i. e., that there can be a 'conflict-free sphere of the ego'. A second, rather disparate, group proffer a continuum extending from Wilhelm Reich's advocacy of desublimation and a promise of a return to Eden, to the Winnicottian position that eschews Klein's undoubted stress on the power of destructive forces, and sees rather more decency and hope in liberal society.

I dare say that Klein said rather less about the other side of human nature – the constructive or erotic impulses – because she found herself in mutually critical dialogue with colleagues whom she felt over-emphasised those aspects. Finding the twig bent, as she thought, too far one way, she bent it the other way, perhaps to leave it straight for those that followed. It is my impression that some of her followers are embarrassed about this and want to emphasise her more optimistic ideas. I find this odd and inconsistent with her courage to know the worst in the service of a better world. A third group are orthodox Kleinians who recall that the veneer of civilisation is very thin indeed and that the maelstrom beneath is perpetually and rather pathetically defended against. It can be argued that this provides the basis for an optimism of the will, coupled with a pessimism of the intellect and a belief that it is essential to know what is bubbling away underneath the surface if we are to have any hope of cooling some of the crust. I also believe that this position is consistent with a careful reading of Freud's *Civilisation and Its Discontents,* written half way through his sixteen-year struggle with cancer. It is worth recalling that he says there that the history of civilisation is 'the struggle between Eros and Death, between the instinct of life and the instinct of destruction, as it works itself out in the human species. This struggle is what all life essentially consists of . . . And it is this battle of the giants that our nurse-maids try to appease with their lullaby about Heaven' (Freud, 1930, p. 122).

Human nature turns out to be far more ambivalent and refractory at a much deeper level that we ever imagined when we embarked on making the world suit our desires. The nurse-maid told us that, too, in the deeper levels of the fairy-tales she recited and which we avidly requested. I find myself thinking increasingly of Sisyphus, whom Albert Camus (1955) urged us to imagine as happy. Perhaps he comforts himself with the stoical maxim: 'It is not given to you to complete the task, yet you may not give it up'.

6 PROJECTIVE SPACE: THE RACIAL OTHER

The analytic space is designed to be containing and enabling, but much of life is not so constructive and safe. Racism and associated forms of institutionalised hatred – nationalism, certain forms of virulent tribalism – strike me as the most obvious areas of the internal worlds of humans which do not seem amenable to the forces of enlightenment. Alas, although psychoanalysis has addressed itself to other forms of being less than fully and constructively human – for example, psychosis, psychopathy, autism, mental handicap – the psychoanalytic literature is relatively silent on the subject of racism. My aim in this chapter is to explore the issues and the literature as something of a 'worst-case' study of what we are up against in the understanding of human nature and the horrid, destructive aspects of a distressingly large portion of most people's mental space. The psychological characteristics of racism are splitting, violent projective identification, stereotyping and scapegoating. I will attempt to bring these psychoanalytic categories to bear on the contingencies of the social, historical, economic and ideological phenomena of organised hatred.

I want to begin with two quotations. The first is from a U.N.E.S.C.O. publication entitled *The Race Question in Modern Science:* ' . . . among the Dakota Sioux Indians in the state of South Dakota it is regarded as incorrect to answer a question in the presence of others who do not know the answer; this might be interpreted as showing off, or as bringing shame to others, and is consequently condemned by the whole group' (quoted in Levidow, 1978 , p. 29). Is it surprising, then, that these people don't do well on IQ tests?

The second quotation is from an eminent scientist, C. D. Darlington, Fellow of the Royal Society and a Professor of Genetics at Oxford. In his book on *The Evolution of Man and Society*, he wrote, 'All advanced societies, as we have seen, arise from a stratification of social classes whose genetic differences and mutual dependence are the permanent foundation of their advance.' (Darlington, 1969, p. 366). 'Indeed, class differences ultimately all derive from genetic and, usually, racial differences' (p. 547). Colonised and genetically stratified societies are, as always, advancing faster than the uncolonized or decolonized and unstratified societies (e. g., p. 675). 'In short, racial discrimination has a genetic basis with a large instinctive and irrational component. Its action may be modified by education or by economic processes. But it cannot be suppressed by law' (p. 606).

According to Darlington, who turns out to be both a racist and a Social Darwinist, science tells us that segregation and apartheid are not to be lightly dismissed. The principle of subordinating one racial group to another 'has governed the evolution of all advancing societies since soon after the beginning of agriculture. And it has been the means of their advancement' (p. 607). Similarly, 'All the great races of man differ in smell; they dislike one another's smell and are kept apart by it. But in the nostrils of all other races the pygmies positively stink. It is a property which has arisen from their genetic and ecological isolation' (p. 645). The Irish, the working class and black people do not fare much better in Darlington's account, though their supposed genetic deficiencies are different ones.

I began with those quotations – one rather touching and edifying, showing why the Sioux consider IQ tests impolite, the other obviously racist, even though written by an authoritative scientist – to illustrate a premise of what I want to say: that there are, in truth, very striking cultural differences, ones which are likely to evoke strong reactions between different identifiable groups, and experts who write about them can do so in progressive and reactionary ways.

All the differences which lead to racialist oppression are not based on obvious and easily observable features. I am told that the untouchables of Japan are simply not physically identifiable as different from other Japanese, yet they are banished from polite society and are confined to certain areas and certain trades, especially work with leather. When there *are* identifiable differences, there are forms of discrimination *within* so-called races. Garveyism in the West Indies and United States had as its first battle the need to fight the hierarchy extending from light-skinned to dark-skinned blacks, before it could address the problem of black/white racism. It remains true in both countries that light skin is widely admired, and light-skinned leaders have predominated in the West Indies. Similarly, the (East) Indian caste system is a powerful racist structure within a larger culture, a culture which is in some other contexts perceived as a relatively homogeneous racial minority which merits a uniform degree of racial oppression. Franz Fanon (1967) makes a similar point about shades of black as perceived by blacks themselves. In South Africa, blacks resent Indians, their role as small shopkeepers as oppressive and stereotype them as cheats.

It should be obvious by now that I could easily – or fairly easily – so muddle up the putatively natural or ethnic basis of concepts of race that it won't wash to try to base racism on any clear-cut real or biological types. Indeed, there is a large and sophisticated literature in the social sciences which has sought to delineate the concept of race from those of class and nation. This literature has been critically canvassed by Floya Anthias in 'Race and Class Revisited – Conceptualising Race and Racism' (1990). She sees nationhood and ethnicity 'as central organising principles of social relations in the modern era' and locates the concept of race in relation to those notions (p. 38). However, as Benedict Anderson has eloquently shown, nationhood is itself an historically contingent social construct; a nation is an 'imagined community' with no natural basis and, in most cases, a rather arbitrary and recent origin (1983).

Anthias' summary is terminologically dense but provides a useful reminder of the complexity of the terrain of race: 'Race has no analytical validity in its own right but is a social construction with its own representational, organisational and experiential forms linking it ontologically to the wider category of ethnos which provides its analytical axis. Race denotes a particular way in which communal or collective differences come to be constructed and understood. Its placement within the category of ethnos, that is nation and ethnicity, is not in terms of cultures of difference but in terms of the specific positing of boundaries. These involve mechanisms of both inclusion and exclusion of individuals on the basis of the categorisation of human subjects into those that can belong and those that cannot. From this point of view, race is a particular articulation of where and how the boundary is to be constructed. In this case it is on the basis of an immutable fixed biologically or physiognomically based difference. This may be seen to be expressed in culture or life-style but is always grounded in some notion of stock, involving the collective heredity of traits' (p. 22).

Fortunately, the putative biological difference, the notion of 'stock' and 'the collective heredity of traits' have not stood up to scientific scrutiny. The close study of blood groups has shown a continuum, not a clear boundary, at the points where racial differentiation is claimed by the racists. Claimed racial differences are not natural; they are natural*ised*. Some close students of the issue have argued that *no* serious natural phenomenon can be identified as 'race' and relegate the term to being merely a 'category of everyday life' (p. 32). If that is taken to mean that it is an ideological rather than a natural category, I would agree. However, like all ideological categories, it is certainly real and deeply embedded in human psychology – more deeply and intractably than we often suppose, as I shall attempt to show. For the moment, my point is that we have here a psychological and ideological phenomenon which is firmly rooted in the society. It is not a disease to be identified, diagnosed and treated. Rather, it is a mediation of an amalgam of economic, ethnic, class and nationalist forces which engender splitting off taboo or feared aspects of the self; projection of them onto the Other, who usually reprojects a version of them; scapegoating and stereotyping a particular social group. The mechanisms are primitive and universal, but their deployment is learned in tacit ways, imbibed with the culture, expressed as second nature, without deliberation.

My second point takes us to the loud silence in the psychoanalytic literature. Joel Kovel says somewhere that the main barrier to getting the psychoanalytic community to address social, much less radical, issues lies in the social location of its practitioners. An allied observation – my own – is that a racist society will have a racist science (Young, 1987a). The problem of racism and psychoanalysis is a special case of a issue in recent studies in the social construction of knowledge, i.e., that groups seek legitimacy in nature, including the allegedly biologically 'given', for their social views and beliefs. The social process of scientific research and writing involves natural*isation*, the embodiment of belief systems in the agendas and 'findings' of science. I have argued above that there is a growing consensus among those who think about science as a social and cultural process that conceptions of nature, including human nature, are made, not found. Once such naturalisations get legitimated, they find their way into individuals and are deeply – unconsciously – sedimented and become routine: second nature (Young, 1981a, 1988a).

The unbearable and unacceptable parts of the group and the individual may be wishes, fears, idealisations, denigrations. When they get split off and projected into others, anxiety in the self and the group is diminished. When the others take them up and behave according to the stereotype, the projection is vindicated: in the 'lazy nigger', the 'cunning yid', the 'crazy Indian', the 'fanatical Arab'. Both sides then live on in a set of mutual projections and reprojections, rather like those I described in chapter four with respect to the members of a couple. Those involved in racism are among the most virulent in human nature. They rank with, and often combine with, torture, murder, foetocide, genocide – the most violent and snarling expressions of spite, perversity and cruel depravity. I am thinking of rape, castration, bayoneting. lynching, gassing, extermination and related forms of behaviour toward inferior*ised* peoples such as blacks, Tamils, Jews, Indians, Palestinians, Protestants, Catholics, Kurds, Armenians, Bosnians, Muslims, Croatians.

These are not facts about correctable biases in society or in the literature on human nature; they are facts about the sociology of knowledge and of the unconscious. The culture's values and a professional group's values will determine the value systems that get lived out in history and the questions that get asked, what counts as an acceptable answer, what research is prestigious, what work gets funded and published or – as the fundamental particle physicists say – what is 'sexy'. In this and the previous paragraphs I have juxtaposed the virulence and ubiquity of racism with the blinkered social location of those who ponder and write and edit and publish in the psychoanalytic world. There is a loud silence in the psychoanalytic literature about racism. Why? Because it is not a topic affecting the institutions, the careers, the prestige, the patronage networks and the incomes of by far the majority of psychoanalysts and psychotherapists. Ask yourself how many black patients get treated or even heard of or how many black or brown psychotherapists or psychoanalysts you know or know about. I can think of only a handful and know of only a small number of inquiries which are attempting to understand the gap between blacks and Asians in the population and the number of patients and therapists from these minority groups in Britain (Ilahi, 1988).

Of course, black/white racism is not the only kind. This explains the small amount of literature which I *have* found in the psychoanalytic journals. It is about anti-semitism, with particular reference to the Holocaust and work with survivors of Hitler's camps (Kren, 1987; Faimberg, 1988; Kogan, 1989). It would be silly to think that psychoanalysis is free from racism, and I don't only mean anti-gentile attitudes. I recently read the autobiography of an eminent psychoanalyst who has held the highest offices in his profession, and it was patently anti-semitic. I asked him about this in the presence of his Jewish (actually his second Jewish) wife, and he acknowledged that it was so. He said, rather wistfully, that they just feel somehow alien to him. Lest it be thought that I am making a cheap shot here, read on to the end of the chapter, where the near-inevitability of something like his – and my – racism will be made apparent.

There are, of course, some notable exceptions to this bleak picture, this loud silence – the writings of Fanon, Kovel and Wolfenstein – and I shall revert to these. Even so, given the role of racism in the various societies where the largest number of psychoanalysts and psychoanalytic psycho-therapists live and work, the silence is resounding. As I was writing this chapter, I read a review by the eminent socialist historian, Gwyn Williams, in which he said that a good historian learns how to listen for the silences. I'd like to think I am a good historian, and I want to make a noise about this silence. It's not acceptable.

In the period with which my own historical research has been mainly concerned there is a readily apparent truism which also applies to the present, as I shall argue below. People of good will, people of great intelligence and liberality, people (I am referring to the mid-nineteenth century) who were deeply opposed to slavery, could nevertheless be straightforwardly and profoundly racist. Charles Darwin and T. H. Huxley – pre-eminent in their age for shining the light of science and fighting superstition, prejudice and obscurantism – are striking examples. Here is Huxley from an essay entitled 'Emancipation: Black and White', written in 1865: 'It may be quite true that some negroes are better that some white men; but no rational man, cognizant of the facts, believes that the average negro is the equal, still less the superior, of the average white man. And, if this be true, it is simply incredible that, when all his disabilities are removed, and our prognathous [projecting jaw] relative has a fair field and no favour, as well as no oppressor, he will be able to compete successfully with his bigger-brained and smaller-jawed rival, in a contest which is to be carried on by thoughts and not by bites. The highest places in the hierarchy of civilisation will assuredly not be within the reach of our dusky cousins, though it is by no means necessary that they should be restricted to the lowest. But whatever the position of stable equilibrium into which the laws of social gravitation may bring the negro, all responsibility for the result will henceforward lie between nature and him. The white man may wash his hands of it, and the Caucasian conscience be void of reproach for evermore. And this, if we look to the bottom of the matter, is the real justification for the abolition policy' (Huxley, 1865, pp. 17–18).

Huxley's argument then turns to the subject of women, who receive the same treatment: it is illiberal to add social inequality to their obvious biological inferiority. He concludes with respect to both sorts of inferior creatures: 'The duty of man is to see that not a grain is piled upon that load beyond what nature imposes; that injustice is not added to inequality' (p. 23).

In *The Descent of Man*, Darwin's second most important book and the one in which he spelled out the implications of his theory of evolution for humankind, he wrote, 'But the inheritance of property by itself is very far from evil; for without the accumulation of capital the arts could not progress; and it is chiefly through their power that the civilised races have extended and are now everywhere extending their range, so as to take the place of the lower races' (Darwin, 1874, p. 135; see also Young, 1985, 1994d).

It could be argued that these men were not directly enough concerned with the race question to be subjected to this scrutiny. In fact, both were seriously involved in the abolitionist movement. Even so, let's look at Abraham Lincoln, the man who freed the American slaves and who vies with Nelson Mandela in my mind for the position of dwelling most consistently in the depressive position and thinking under fire in the midst of an impossible set of contending forces. He wrote, 'What next? Free them and make them politically and socially our equals? Our feelings will not admit of this, and if mine would, we know that those of the great mass of whites will not. Whether this feeling accords with justice and sound judgement is not the sole question, if indeed it is any part of it. A universal feeling, whether well or ill founded, cannot be safely disregarded. We cannot then make them equals' (quoted in Sandburg, vol. 2, p. 14). On another occasion, Lincoln said, 'All I ask for the negro is that, if you do not like him, let him alone. If God gave him little, that little let him enjoy' (p. 131). And again, as to all men being born equal: 'Certainly the negro is not our equal in colour perhaps not in many other respects; still, in the right to put in his mouth the bread that his own hands have earned, he is equal to every other man, white or black. In pointing out that more has been given you, you cannot be justified in taking away the little which has been given him' (*Ibid.*).

You may say that it is easy to patronise people who lived before our enlightened times. Let's look, then, at a recent Nobel Prize-winner, that nice man, Konrad Lorenz, who wrote *King Soloman's Ring* (1961) and had the little greylag goslings running after him, believing him to be their mother as a result of biological 'imprinting'. Lorenz was one of the founders of ethology, the scientific study of animal behaviour, the gentlest of the behavioural sciences. He won a Nobel Prize for his pioneering scientific work. I turn to the Austrian scientist's contribution to the Sixteenth Congress of the German Psychological Association in 1938. He is addressing the section on 'Character', subsection 'Heredity': 'This high valuation of our species-specific and innate social behavior patterns is of the greatest biological importance. In it as in nothing else lies directly the backbone of all racial health and power. Nothing is so important for the health of a whole Volk as the elimination of "invirent types": those which, in the most dangerous, virulent increase, like the cells of a malignant tumor, threaten to penetrate the body of a Volk' (quoted in Kalikow, 1978, p. 174).

Two years later, he wrote, 'If there should be mutagenic factors. their recognition and elimination would be *the most important task of those who protect the race,* because the continuing possibility of the novel appearance of people with deficiencies in species-specific social behavior patterns constitutes a danger to Volk and race which is more serious than that of a mixture with foreign races. The latter is at least knowable as such and, after a one-time elimination of breeding, is no longer to be feared. If it should turn out, on the other hand, that under the conditions of domestication no increase in mutations takes place, but the mere removal of natural selection causes the increase in the number of existing mutants and the imbalance of the race, then race-care must consider an even more stringent elimination of the ethically less valuable than is done today, because it would, in this case, literally have to replace all selection factors that operate in the natural environment' (p. 176). Once one penetrates the verbiage, one finds oneself in the midst of fascist ideology, linked to ominous social measures to achieve racial purity by eugenic means.

Where have we got to? First, racism has no natural basis in biological science, except to the extent that racist biologists put it there. It is social, economic, ideological and psychological, with its proximate roots deeply sedimented in the unconscious. Second, psychoanalysis in a racist society will be racist, or at least very selective in the aspects of racism its writers are likely to take up. Third, being enlightened and scientific is no guarantee against racism in the past or present. It is embedded in the culture.

I shall now revert to the literature. Over the years I have developed some skill in finding my way around the literature on topics which interest me. It takes time, but one can get, from footnotes and references and scanning runs of journals, more than one needs to provide a basis for reflecting on a topic in the light of the best writings. Never, never before have I come up with so little, and much of what I've found isn't much use. I am referring to the psychoanalytic literature. As I've said, it's pathetic.

If one turns to novels, oral tradition, cultural studies, films and music, it's another story.

I want to touch now on certain themes – tools my reading has given me for further work. I wont presume to outline Franz Fanon's *Black Skin, White Mask*, John Dollard's *Caste and Class in a Southern Town*, Rae Sherwood's *The Psychodynamics of Race*, Michael Banton's *Racial Theories*, Gunnar Myrdal's *An American Dilemma: the Negro Problem and Modern Democracy* or the useful collections, *Anatomy of Racism*, edited by David Goldberg and *Theories of Race and Ethnic Relations*, edited by John Rex and David Mason. There is a growing literature on the psychology of blacks and various accounts of the holocaust and holocaust victims. There is also a very helpful literature on Native American 'Indians' in which Dee Brown's account from inside the Indian experience, *Bury My Heart at Wounded Knee*, is complemented by a fascinating historical account of white projections – *The White Man's Indian: Images of the American Indian from Columbus to the Present* by Robert F. Berkhofer, Jr. A small number of books – mostly fiction have done as much as my own experience to provide what understanding I do have of these matters: Lillian Smith's *Strange Fruit* and *Killers of the Dream*, Alan Paton's *Too Late the Phalarope*, Alice Walker's *The Color Purple* and Toni Morrison's practically unbearably moving *Beloved*, as well as her more recent novel, *Jazz*.

There are lessons to be learned from the prehistory of racism. Basil Davidson says this: 'What did Europeans think about black people before the rise of racism? How did they estimate the values of black humanity? There are countless indications in the pictorial arts. Think only of the noble portraits of the black monarch among the three kings who journeyed to salute the birth of Christ. Think of the work of the great masters of the Renaissance who painted black persons. Think of Rembrandt, Velasquez, many more. Each of them, without exception, painted black persons from the same standpoint as they painted white persons, whether either of these, white or black, were kings or merchants or ambassadors or servants' (Davidson, 1987, p. 12). Davidson makes these observations in the context of favourably reviewing a remarkable tour de force, *Black Athena: The Afroasiatic Roots of Classical Civilization* by Martin Bernal (1987), in which the author draws on a wide range of classes of evidence to show that the very notion of Aryan purity contained in our idea of the classical Greeks was a social construct, created by late-eighteenth and nineteenth-century scholars to provide a pedigree for their notions of European racial superiority. In fact, he argues, ancient Greek society was contributed to by numerous African and Asiatic strains and was far from 'pure'. Here is a striking instance of the rewriting of history for racist purposes, which is rebutted by a scholar who is dedicated to a different vision of humanity: racist *versus* anti-racist scholarship.

The two writers on racism whom I have found most helpful are Joel Kovel and Eugene Victor Wolfenstein. Both are Marxists, and both say again and again that we must never lose sight of the economic and social interests being served and mediated by racism. They see racism as false consciousness at the social level, scapegoating and rationalisation at the individual level. It is not *sui generis* and is always a mediation of socio-economic issues. What is unique about it is its virulence – the sheer psychotic permissiveness of racist feelings and the actions to which they lead. Kovel uses the same argument about splitting and the scapegoated role of the largely projected Other in his writings on nuclear terror in the service of virulent nationalism (1983). I'll sketch some of the fruits of their analyses.

The key to any attempt to keep economic and social interests in the forefront of our understanding is to try to think dialectically. Things do not only interact: they mutually interpenetrate at many levels; they are mutually constitutive. According to Wolfenstein the key to the dialectic in this matter is a version of Harold Lasswell's formula for understanding the inner and the outer. Lasswell argued that private motives get displaced onto public objects and are then rationalised in terms of the public interest. Wolfenstein is a political scientist and historian as well as a psychoanalyst and wants to start the story at an earlier point. He says that 'Political interests are first reflected into the public sphere, then internalised as character structure and only subsequently displaced into the public realm' (Wolfenstein, 1981, pp. 17–18).

For Wolfenstein, the concept of race manages to obscure both the genuine public issues and the mediation of them through unconscious processes. Hence, racial conflict precludes and obscures class issues and class conflict. Potentially subversive or revolutionary energies get deflected by the lightning rod of the racial object (Wolfenstein, 1977, p. 178). Racism itself is an illusion of a naturally determined social differentiation between racial collectives which serves to justify a particularly violent relationship of domination and subordination. If we adopt his position it becomes clear that slavery was not born of racism but that racism was the consequence of slavery and its sequellae: brown, white, black, yellow, Italian, Chinese, Irish and so on. The economic and social relationship comes first and finds plenty of scope for mediation through human psychic processes. According to Banton (1987), the first evidence of English racism lay in the eighteenth century among Barbados planters who found it convenient to describe their slave workers as beasts without souls. Slavery came first; racism was its rationalisation.

As Kovel tells it, those dark-skinned Africans were treated as descendants of Ham, the son of Noah. According to the *Bible,* Ham looked upon his father naked and had failed to cover the old man, though his brothers had done so. Ham's punishment was that his son Chus (or Canaan) and all his descendants would be black and would be banished from his sight. The crime of Ham – as the Hebraic and early Christian commentators understood perfectly well – was not merely disrespect. It was the castration of the father – the violent rejection of paternal authority and the acquisition of the father's sexual choice. The blackening and banishing of Ham's progeny is the retaliatory castration by the higher Father, God. The transgression which is used to rationalise racism was putatively an Oedipal one.

What is black and banished cannot be seen. The long-term consequence of this was, according to Fanon, that in Europe, that is to say, in every civilised and civilising country, the Negro is the symbol of sin. Whatever is forbidden and horrifying in human nature gets designated as black and projected onto a man whose dark skin and oppressed past fit him to receive the symbols. The id becomes the referent of blackness within the personality, and the various trends within the id make themselves realised in the world as the forms of blackness embodied in the fantasies of race (Kovel, 1970, pp. 63–66).

Once again, Wolfenstein points out that the relationship remains dialectical. It grips the oppressor and the oppressed. In his excellent biography of Malcolm X (the best book on racism I have read), Wolfenstein spells out the relationship as follows: 'Stating the point more generally, we may say the Negro identity (like any other externally imposed and therefore stereotypically limited identity) is a character-form of group-emotion, determined through the mediation of *identification with the oppressor.* Conscience and consciousness are both whitened out, and blackness becomes firmly attached to unacceptable, predominantly aggressive, infantile emotional impulses. Black people and white people alike come to have a character-structure in which the I, including the moral I, is white, and the It is black. Within this relationship, black people can think of themselves as fully human only by denying their true racial identity, while white people secure their humanity only at the price of black dehumanisation. Thus the concept of the emotional-group here emerges in the form of a *dominating-dominated intergroup relationship*. In this relationship the repressed sadistic tendencies of the dominating group become the self-hatred, the masochistic tendency, of the dominated group. Conversely, the alienated self-esteem of the dominated group becomes the narcissism of the dominating one. And through the work of secondary elaboration or rationalisation, the members of both groups are held firmly in the grip of a stereotypical false consciousness' (Wolfenstein, 1981, p. 145). (Please note, once again, that, *mutatis mutandis,* this set of mutual projections exactly parallels those described by Tom Main as characteristic of a bad but stable marriage (above, chapter four).

Wolfenstein reminds us that this emotional process is determined by the political and economic power of the ruling class and that 'Emotional alienation is determined by and is the reproductive mediation of alienated labour'. Thus, by becoming a Negro, 'Malcolm X was learning to play his part in capitalism's dumb show of racial stereotypes, its dialectic of self-preservation' (p. 146).

Kovel says that racism, 'far from being a simple delusion of a bigoted and ignorant minority, is a set of beliefs whose structure arises from the deepest levels of our lives – from the fabric of assumptions we make about the world, ourselves and others and from the patterns of fundamental social activities' (Kovel, 1970, p. 3). The racial Other is the negation of the socially-affirmed self (p. xxix). We reduce the racial object to an alien Other – not me, not human, not clean, not inhibited, not civilised, not whatever I cannot bear or allow in myself.

He breaks racism into a number of subdivisions. *Dominative* racism is the direct oppressive relationship of the southern American states. *Aversive* racism is the exclusion and cold-shouldering of blacks in the northern states. *Metaracism* is the product of an economic and technocratic society. He describes the historical transitions from dominative to aversive to metaracism as parallel to development from slavery to feudalism to industrialisation.

The end of slavery and the arrival of nominal desegregation has not improved certain aspects of the lot of blacks in America. In the decades after the American Civil War, there were 4000 recorded lynchings of black people, who were often hung in groups on festive occasions. Lynchings were ritual occasions, community festivals with magical associations: the fingers, toes and private parts of the victims were highly-prized, as were the links of the chains which bound them and the ropes which strangled them (Buckser, 1992, pp. 18, 22, 23). It was a respectable thing to belong to the Ku Klux Klan. It was celebrated in the first feature film, 'Birth of A

Nation', Woodrow Wilson admired it, and a Chief Justice of the United States Supreme Court was at one time a member.

Moving ahead to recent times, black incomes *fell* relatively between 1970 and 1980, and unemployment rose relatively by five per cent, while that of young people reached fifty per cent. The chances of a black person dying of alcoholism are three times that of white people. The number of homicides is five times that of whites. The number of blacks in prison is a multiple of their percentage of the population. One quarter of young black men is in jail, on probation or otherwise under the control of the law. A black man in Harlem has less chance of living to fifty than the inhabitants of Bangladesh (*Sunday Times* 4 March 1990, p. A18). Similar misfortunes apply to the relationship between black people and the British mental health services. A black person is twice as likely as a white to be diagnosed psychotic, to be locked away against his or her will ('sectioned') and to be given drugs forcibly. The chance of being hospitalised is three times that of a white person ('Hear Say', BBC2, 28 August 1991).

The plight of the Native American 'Indian' is worse and has been dreadful from the moment of 'discovery' of America. (The inverted commas refer to recent recognition that non-European explorers had reached the Western World long before Columbus did in 1492. See Carew, 1988. Moreover, since the country was inhabited, it didn't need to be discovered.). Colonialism and racism were integrally related from the start and decimated red and black and then other peoples: 'Modern colonialism, which began with the European rediscovery of the Americas de-civilised vast areas of the world. It began with a holocaust against Native Americans, twelve million of whom died in the first forty years of the Colombian era, continued against Africans, two hundred million of whom were estimated to have died in the Atlantic slave trade (nine million perished on the ships alone), and then there were countless deaths of Asian peoples as colonialism gained momentum' (Carew, 1988, p. 38). These figures do not include the march West of the American Frontier, which completed the devastation of the Native American way of life. This has been called the longest undeclared war in history. The scale of the carnage was unprecedented in world history and remains unparalleled.

Learned Catholic theologians decreed in 1503 that the permission of Queen Isabella should be given for slavery in the New World, and a degraded view of the natives was a prerequisite to this trade, as was a promise of salvation: 'Being as they are hardened in their hard habits of idolatry and cannibalism, it was agreed that I should issue this decree . . . I hereby give licence and permission . . . to capture them . . . paying us the share that belongs to us, and to sell them and utilise their services, without incurring any penalty thereby, because if the Christians bring them to these lands and make use of their service, they will be more easily converted and attracted to our Holy Faith' (Carew, 1988, p. 48). The European charge of cannibalism was unfounded. Harmless and helpful natives were badmouthed as wild and bestial, thus legitimating the activities of a master race. The savagery of the conquistadors was projected onto their victims, who could then be seen as subhuman and could be treated in subhuman ways – which they extravagantly were.

The ensuing carnage was chronicled by a contemporary observer, Bartolomé de Las Casas, a Catholic cleric who observed that the Indians 'had a greater disposition towards civility than the European people', yet it was 'upon such people that the Spaniards fell as tigers, wolves and lions fall upon lambs and kids. Forty years they ranged those lands, massacring the wretched Indians until in the land of Espanola, which in 1492 had a population estimated at three millions of people, scarcely three hundred Indians remained to be counted. The history of Espanola is the history of Cuba, San Juan [Puerto Rico], and Jamaica. Thirty islands in the neighbourhood of San Juan were entirely depopulated. On the side of the continent, kingdom after kingdom was desolated, tribe after tribe exterminated. Twelve millions of Indians in those continental lands perished under the barbarous handling of the Spaniards. Their property was no more secure than their lives. For greed of gold, ornaments were torn from neck and ear, and as the masked burglar threatens his victim until he reveals the hiding-place of this store, the Indians were subjected to the most cruel tortures to compel the disclosure of mines which never existed and the location of gold in streams and fields in which the Almighty has never planted it. Obedience secured no better treatment than sullenness, faithful service no better reward than that which followed treachery. The meanest Spaniard might violate the family of the most exalted chief, and home had no sanctity in the bestial eyes of the soldier. The courtiers rode proudly through the streets of the New Isabella, their horses terrifying the poor Indians while their riders shook their plumed heads and waved their glistening swords. As they rode along, their lances were passed into women and children, and no greater pastime was practised by them then wagering as to a cavalier's ability to completely cleave a man with one dextrous blow of his sword. A score would fall before one would drop in the divided parts essential to winning the wager. No card or dice afforded equal sport. Another knight from Spain must sever his victim's head from the shoulder at the first sweep of his sword.

Fortunes were lost on the ability of a swordsman to run an Indian through the body at a designated spot. Children were snatched from their mother's arms and dashed against the rocks as they passed. Other children they threw into the water that the mothers might witness their drowning struggles. Babes were snatched from their mothers' breasts, and a brave Spaniard's strength was tested by his ability to tear an infant into two pieces by pulling apart its tiny legs. And the pieces of the babe were then given to the hounds that in their hunting they might be the more eager to catch their prey. The pedigree of a Spanish bloodhound had nothing prouder in its record than the credit of half a thousand dead or mangled Indians. Some natives they hung on gibbets, and it was their reverential custom to gather at a time sufficient victims to hang thirteen in a row, and thus piously to commemorate Christ and the Twelve Apostles. Moloch must have been in the skies . . . I have been an eye-witness of all these cruelties, and an infinite number of others which I pass over in silence' (Las Casas, 1552, quoted in Carew, 1988, pp. 48–9).

Las Casas gives his account island by island, and in practically every case friendly overtures on the part of the natives were repaid with decimation. It was only in the wake of this that the natives became hostile. (It is easy to adopt the other side of the split and ignore the wars between tribes and the human sacrifice involved, for example, in some Central American rituals.) But even then we find a long history of honourable negotiations and treaties, cynically broken and overturned, as Dee Brown's account chronicles. Consequently, the condition of the Indian scarcely improved in the centuries subsequent to the sixteenth, and in the nineteenth century the Americans all but completed their extermination, only to wreak upon them another humiliation in making dime novel and the film western vehicles for symbolising the onward march of the white man's Frontier and the trials of American manhood. Once again, they treated the 'Noble Savage' as wholly ignoble and rapacious, thoroughly deserving diabolisation at the hands of endless paperback cowboys and cinematic John Waynes which echoed, in long marches to alien reservations and at the massacre of Indians at Wounded Knee (which wreaked revenge for the slaughter of US Cavalry at Custer's Last Stand at the Little Big Horn), the behaviour of the Spaniards chronicled by Las Casas three centuries earlier (Slatta, 1990, ch. 12; Buscombe, 1988).

In the wake of physical slaughter, there has been cultural denigration. Offensive terms have found their way into common parlance. For example, the word 'redskin' is derived from bounty hunters who found it burdensome to bring in whole bodies. They were allowed to flay their

victims and deliver their bloody skins in order to receive $60 for a man's
and $40 for a woman's. Similarly, Indian names – including Redskins,
Indians and Braves – are attached to white sports teams, whose cheer-
leaders and fans dress up in ways that offend the Native Americans and
reduce their heritage to foolish garb and frenetic caricatures of war dances.
Contemptuous racist terms were also transferable: Indians were called
'prairie niggers', hipsters who adopted black ways of behaving were 'white
niggers' and civil rights liberals were 'nigger lovers'.

In addition to cultural degradation there is an erosion of the taboos at
the foundation of civilisation. I recently visited Manitoba and met the white
doctor who is responsible for the welfare of Native Canadian children. He
told me that there are whole communities where every member has been
sexually abused by whites or natives or both and that the practice can be
traced through many generations.

The rampant racism of cowboy films is particularly ironic in its portrayal
of blacks and Mexicans as pawns, lazy or bad. Historical research provides
a very different picture of the cowboy: 'In the myth and in the movies he
is always a white Anglo-Saxon. In reality, he was often black or brown.
Texas, the source of so many cowboys, was a slave state, and the coastal
counties where the cattle were raised in Texas before the Civil War had
large slave populations, which in a few of them made up as much as 70
or 80 percent of the total population of the county. Slaves worked cattle,
broke horses, and acquired all the skills exhibited in the movies by white
cowboys. After the war, they were joined by freedmen from all over the
South who went West. Virtually all Texas trail outfits included black
cowboys, and a few, like the one Jim Ellison took to Kansas in the spring
of 1874, were all black. In the 1920s George Saunders estimated that a
third of all hands were either black or Mexican, and numerous cowboy
memoirs and a few surviving photographs of trail outfits bear him out'
(Taylor, 1983, p. 20).

There have been a few films which have sought to redress some of
these historical injustices. For example, 'Broken Arrow' (1950) made a
stand against racism by portraying the hero, James Stewart, as sympathetic
to the Indians. He lived among them and married one. (It is no accident
that the scriptwriter, Albert Maltz, was jailed for refusing to testify to his
political affiliations before the McCarthyite, witch-hunting House Un-
American Activities Committee. Maltz was blacklisted for his communist
beliefs, so a friend put his name to the script, which won many prizes.)
In 'Hombre' (1966), Paul Newman's Indian values, hard as they are, are
seen to show up the hypocrisy of those who were supposed to care for

Indians on reservations but who ruthlessly stole food and supplies from them. In 'Lonesome Dove' (1989), one of the most admirable figures – after the two white Texas Ranger heroes – is black, and his death is one of the most poignant moments. He is felled while rescuing a blind Indian baby. More recently, Kevin Cosner's 'Dances with Wolves' (1991) provides homage to Native American culture, albeit at the expense of making the white soldiers into wooden baddies, even though the reality would have been bad enough. There is an irony in the number of Oscars the picture won, for the film perpetuates the split and presents its mirror image.

The connection between the Indians portrayed in 'Dances with Wolves' and their present-day descendants is spelled out in an article about the film: 'Imagine you were a Native American, living on a reservation in Shannon County, South Dakota where a century ago, your forbears were mown down by the Seventh Cavalry at Wounded Knee. Firstly, you would be poor. Really ground down by poverty. Your place would be on the bottom-most rung of the richest nation in the world. Blacks in Harlem slums and Mississippi shanties would be better off than you. You would have had a substandard education. You would be unlikely to have a job because your race faces a 75 per cent unemployment rate. Much of your meagre welfare benefit probably goes on gambling and drink. Your children are likely to be born crippled because their mother is an alcoholic. Life expectancy would be below 50, the lowest in the United States' (Perry, 1991, p. 19). Indeed, life expectancy of an Indian on a reservation is even lower – 45 years. Alcoholism is the commonest cause of death, and Indians have the highest infant mortality, unemployment and rate of drop-out from education of any group in America. The suicide rate is twice the national average, and one sixth of Indian teenagers have attempted suicide. Jobless and despondent Native Americans in Alaska tend to drink themselves into a numb state and wander out into the sub-zero winter.

These historical data help us to grasp the real human suffering which lies behind Kovel's description of a rationalising process which he calls radical dehumanisation. He describes the 'tracings of a primitive fantasy of dirt upon the more advanced fantasy of Ham and Oedipus' (Kovel, 1970, p. 91). In the history from slavery to the present, the black man moves from being father to child to body to penis to faeces to inanimate thing and finally to nothing – the invisible man of Ralph Ellison's novel. Along with the debasement goes abstraction, until the final point of nothingness is reached. Once again, the black person ceases to be considered as a human being. Kovel reminds us that when Mark Twain's Huckleberry Finn accounted for his lateness to his Aunt Sally he invented an accident aboard a riverboat: 'It wasn't the grounding – that didn't keep us back but a little. We blowed out a cylinder head.' 'Good gracious: anybody hurt?' asked his aunt. 'No'm. Killed a nigger.' 'Well, it's lucky; because sometimes people do get hurt' (quoted p. 92).

The first appearance of the term 'race' in the English language occurred in 1508 and linked it with unconscious forces. It appeared in a poem on the seven deadly sins by a Scot named Dunbar who referred to those who followed envy as including 'bakbyttaris of sindry recis' (backbiters of sundry races; Banton, 1987, p. 1). If we look at treatises on racism, we find them full of very primitive, Kleinian language. Here is a list of terms I have extracted from a book on the psychoanalysis of racism which stresses the projection of intrapsychic phenomena into the political and treats them largely in terms of diseased or malignant internal objects: foreign bodies, germs, pollutants, contaminants, malignancies, poisonous infections, gangrened limbs, dirty, suppurating, verminous (Koenigsberg, 1977). This brings to mind the representation of Jews as gutter rats in Nazi propaganda films and the rhetoric of competing political tendencies discussed by Martin Thom in an article on projection in left sectarian rhetoric, in which opponents were characterised as shitty, nauseating and their ideas as spew, vomit, etc. (Thom, 1978).

At a seminar I gave on racism, I read out the long passage by Las Casas quoted above which described in excruciating detail the genocide of the natives by the conquistadors. A colleague who irritatingly tends to split off compassion from sharp insight said, 'I can see why you are upset, but why are you surprised? That's what happens in the unconscious. The question is what allows it to get acted out'. He was right, of course. That is the whole point of Freud's *Civilization and Its Discontents* and of his theory of civilization. What allows it to get acted out at the supra-familial level is outgrouping, which is most devastating in racism and virulent nationalism. That's not quite adequate, however, since Freud's account makes no distinction between the intrapsychic, the family and groups of different sizes. As I've said, I think he is partly right and partly badly in need of some social thinkers and historians to help him out of his swingeing reductionism. Freud's model begins with the rapaciousness and polymorphous perversity of the of the patriarch. This evokes the creation of civilization by means of the incest taboo, which leads to the Oedipus complex which, in turn, gives us the superego – our only hope when primitive urges are upon us.

What happens in racism and nationalism is that we give our superegos over to the leader, the organisation or group or gang or nation or 'the cause'. The leaders then sanction destructive acting out and selectively remove the veneer of civilisation. As the Indian cultist puts it in 'Gunga Din' (1939), we 'kill for the love of Kali'. We kill in the name of a cause, often a putatively pure cause. This is captured perfectly in that ghastly phase of the moment – 'ethnic cleansing'. It is easy to make a long and distressing list of situations in which some version of that rationalisation was or is operative. My son recently made a television documentary about Yugoslavia during and after the Second World War (D. Young, 1990). The Croatians set up a fascist republic. During its reign soldiers would go up to children and get them to make the sign of the cross. If they made it in the Russian Orthodox way they were shot then and there. At the end of the war the leaders of the fascist group were protected and s muggled abroad by the Vatican. The priest who organised this escape route later became Pope. The documentary has not been shown in any Catholic country and cannot be re-shown here. It says to me that the church and the military are tied for first place in sanctioning genocide in the name of a higher cause.

Sue and Ray Holland (1984) discuss racism inside interracial couples. They draw on Fairbairn's concept of splitting, whereby good or accepted representations remain in the conscious after bad or rejected part-objects and their affiliated bad part-self-representations are relegated to the unconscious. 'The trouble with the rejected part-objects and part self-representations is that, although relegated to the unconscious, they continue to find expression in the behaviour and experience of the adult' (Holland & Holland, 1984, p. 95). These problems can erupt in the couple relationship, as many of us know to our cost. The Hollands adapt this model for describing the depressions of white women in sexual relations with black men from certain colonial cultures. One has here a microcosm of a racist society in the projections, degradations and self-denigrations of these couples, which are inevitably passed on to their children so that attempts at integration at an individual level also perpetuate dimensions of racism in the very process of seeking to overcome it.

Wolfenstein develops his model into the wider group and applies it to situations in which racism involves a leader. Hitler is the obvious example, but Wolfenstein explores the interesting case of the leader of the Black Muslims, the Honorable Elijah Muhammad. Here he adapts Freud's work on group psychology and describes how the member of the sect projects unconscious hostility, felt towards the parents, onto the leader, who authorises its displacement from himself and group members and onto the designated racial enemy. This model is *repression* leading to *projection* leading to *displacement*. He describes racist organisations as dreams, outlets or modes of escape for repressed longings and for specifically irrational unconscious desires (Wolfenstein, 1977, p. 172).

The alien group is perceived as a sexual as well as an aggressive threat. The alien male is a rapacious devil, the female a seductive witch. 'Thus, the image of the racial enemy as a crystallisation of aggressively dominated or limited sexual tendencies. It is formed through the projection and displacement of the group member's infantile self, of the sadistic child who survives within even the most compassionate adult. From which it follows that intra-group life is freed from the pressures of unwelcome infantile sexuality, so that it takes on the character of a relatively aim-inhibited relationship. And if we now translate this conception into the somewhat slippery structural language of psychoanalysis, we may state that the group is to the enemy as ego is to id (as potentially conscious self is to the alienated or unconscious-repressed self), while the group itself is the "number of individuals who have put the same object in the place of their ego ideal and have consequently identified themselves with one another in their ego"' (Wolfenstein, 1977, p. 173, quoting Freud's *Group Psychology*).

In *Killers of the Dream*, Lillian Smith offers a fantasy bargain between the rich owner and the white 'redneck' (the neck gets sunburned from working with heads bowed down in the cotton fields). Let us exploit you, and we will give you the black to dominate, scapegoat, sexually exploit and murder. Mr. Rich White said to Mr. Poor White, 'If you ever get restless when you don't have a job or your roof leaks, or the children look puny and shoulder blades stick out more than natural, all you need to do is remember you're a sight better off than the black man . . . But if you get nervous sometimes anyway, and don't have much to do, and begin to get worried up inside and mad with folks, and you think it'll make you feel a little better to lynch a nigger occasionally, that's OK by me, too; and I'll fix it with the sheriff and the judge and the court and the newspapers so you won't have any trouble afterwards . . . If you once let yourself believe he's human, then you'd have to admit you'd done things to him you can't admit you've done to a human. You'd have to know you'd done things that God would send you to hell for doing . . . And sometimes it was like this: You just hated him. Hated and dreaded and feared him, for you could never forget, there was no way to forget, what you'd done to his women and to those women's children; there was no way of forgetting your dreams of those women . . . No way of forgetting . . . Yes . . . they thought they had a good bargain' (Smith, 1950, pp. 162–65). Once again, we are racist along lines laid down by economic and social stratifications. That's what makes it racism – stereotyping and scapegoating of people as members of groups, rather than treating people as individuals.

I want to turn from those theoretical explorations to current and personal experience. Racism is all around us and in all of us. I once read that spy thrillers chose East Germans as villains, because they were both Krauts and Commies and North Koreans, because they are both slant-eyed and Commies. The final twist to all this, of course, is racist mocking of anti-racism. *Race and Class* has provided analyses of racist writings in the *Sun* newspaper, including stories about London boroughs. Haringey is supposed to have proscribed black dustbin liners and to have spent 50,000 pounds on superloos for gypsy travellers, while Brent and Islington are said to have banned the children's rhyme 'Baa Baa Black Sheep'. Of course, none of these stories was accurate, some were conjured out of thin air, all were misleading and the 'Baa Baa Black Sheep' one began life as a tall tale in a pub. All of this mockingly juxtaposes the ludicrous aliens and their silly do-gooder supporters, on the one hand, with the idealised, homogeneous, organic and otherwise idyllic indigenous white culture, on the other. Alfred Sherman (who was criticised for wanting to bring a French fascist to a Tory conference) feared 'a Procrustean pidgin culture' might 'be imposed on majorities and minorities alike' and deemed this a recipe for 'cultural genocide', which 'in effect outlawed the concept of the English nation'. Mary Kenny thought certain anti-racist proposals would turn 'mild British people into resentful misanthropes . . . as they see everything native to their own traditions scuttled' (Murray, 1986, p.12).

These quotations bring racism out of the realm of high theory and into our own immediate culture. It is also much in the news as a result of the demise of the Soviet empire. Removal of Soviet hegemony has led to a flowering of nationalism, including persecution of local and adjacent minorities, as well as Jews, who are emigrating to Israel in large numbers, only to become part of a Middle East which is itself immersed in the hatreds and degradations of mutual projections and attempted decimation. And then there is former Yugoslavia.

I turn now to my own experience. I cannot say how I learned to persecute Jews and find Catholics oddly different. The first and only person I was caught in bed with (aged five) was a Catholic, and the same was true of my sister (as a teenager). Both of us were criticised in ways that intertwined our sexual misbehaviour with an accusation that, looking back, made us feel as though we'd committed miscegenation. I later had a Catholic girlfriend in my own neighbourhood but was threatened with violence by boys from the local parochial school. The same thing happened when I was a life guard at a working class swimming pool, where I was threatened with maiming by local Catholic boys. In each case the girlfriend broke off the relationship to protect me. I am sure that my sister's eventual conversion to Catholicism was partly a rebellion, as was my marrying a Jew.

I had a close Catholic friend, though, and we were part of the neighbourhood persecution of a boy whose only discernible deviance was going to Hebrew School. He, like others after him, was called 'hebe' and chased home, just as they were called 'kike' and mocked behind their backs and imitated in funny accents. Any sign of meanness led to a nose being stroked and an accusation of being a member of 'the Tribe'. Jewish girls came to our teenage dances; one was elected a Company Queen for an R.O.T.C. (cadet corp) dance, but that led to lots of teasing. Jewish girls, no matter how wealthy or eminent their parents, disappeared from the dances as soon as it was time for debuts to be made into polite society, and no Jews were members of the 'best' country clubs.

There were other retrospectively notable silences and absences. I recall only one working class child in my suburb and school, and he did not stay long. No Mexicans, Chinese, Japanese, Indians, East or Red. And especially no blacks. I never swam in a pool or attended school with a black person until I was eighteen. I never slept under the same roof with one until I was twenty and involved in a Quaker summer project in a mental hospital in another state. I never had a black adult friend until I was in my mid-thirties.

Even so, I think I can date my first awareness of racism. When I was five, my mother simply told me one day that I was no longer to play with my best friend. He was black, lived in the servants' quarters of a neighbour's house, and he and I pranced up and down the local alleyways playing drums (mine was an Indian tom-tom). I asked why and was told that it was because he was a Negro. I protested and cried and felt terrible, but I obeyed – after a relatively small number of spankings – with an astonishing deference that did not apply to other aspects of my parents' authoritarianism.

One particularly cruel irony in all this – and it is true of many a southern American and southern African white – is that I received the only reliable security in my childhood and youth from black women. This extends from my earliest memories until I left home to go to university – deep, abiding, patient, enfolding, caring. Always there and always clear, whereas my parents were either not there or preoccupied with depression, disappointment, bitterness and bigotry. Ask me about childhood care, and you will hear about Odalee, Jessie, Ella May, Sadie (whose surnames I never knew) and Lucy Wilkerson. Stout and loving, neglecting their own children for my sister and me. Lucy worked for my family for nearly forty years and died their servant.

And yet – here is how deep racism cuts – she played practically no part in many years of daily psychoanalysis. Nor have I properly mourned her death. When my mother died, her black nurse, Linda Roberts, was not invited back to the customary family gathering after the funeral. It was she who had been reliably there in Mother's worst period, after my father died.

Where I grew up in Texas in the 1950s, the Ku Klux Klan was still active, as it is again. I unknowingly worked with members – sharecroppers whose farms were uneconomic and who had gone to work in Ford factory in order to hold onto their homes. They seemed decent people, and I had no idea that they were members, until one of them saw me in friendly conversation with a black janitor, a preacher with a Masters degree who was trying to keep his church going, a situation parallel to the sharecroppers. The man who worked most closely with me carefully lowering car bodies onto chassis said, 'Don't never speak to me again. I don't want to have nothing to do with no nigger-lover'. And he never uttered another word to me. A sympathetic co-worker explained that many of the people who worked alongside us were Klansmen.

These people, like racists everywhere, acquired their horrid social attitudes by a process of tacit social learning, whereby their infantile psychotic anxieties, feelings all babies have, got channelled into particular forms of projective identification. I do not think that those rednecks working at the Ford factory were mad or psychopathic, any more than I think my racist father and (rather more genteel) racist mother and sister were evil. As Hannah Arendt has shown us in the case of Adolf Eichmann, it is more banal than that (Arendt, 1963). They were just socialised into the values of that part of the world – just as I was.

I suppose that it is inevitable that this recitation may be found self-indulgent, even offensive. I am raising the question of what enlightenment my own decades of anti-racist work have brought. The answer is practically none at the deeper levels, although I can claim, on the whole, to *behave* well. What I am trying to establish, using the only example I know well, is something about another area of silence – the racism of the inner world of supposedly decent people, even and especially the inner worlds of active anti-racists, whose principled activities are usually, in my experience, born of guilt and an impulse toward reparation. I continue to think that black men are blessed with enviable sexual endowments, have greater potency and make better lovers, that black women are more generous and voluptuous. I have at one time or another – almost always silently in my adult years – despised 'Japs', hated Germans, thought of Latin Americans as unreliable, been embarrassed by Mediterranean wailing, thought of Arabs as fanatics, smiled at Mexicans, regarded Asians as children, and (just as the racist Professor Darlington says) noticed the smells of other cultural groups and found them alien. I have found myself thinking of friends, respected colleagues and lovedones as 'behaving in a Jewish way'. I have reactions to Italians, Pakistanis, Irish people . . . there is no end to it. I could go on and on about all of this – all contrary to my beliefs, efforts and practices. It is still there, layered over by principle and civility but pristine and unreconstructedly primitive. My Jewish mother-in-law once told my wife that 'He will always think of you as a little Jewess'. She was perfectly right. The fact that there were also idealisations mixed in with anti-semitism only makes the problem more complex, as does the fact that two of my children are Jews.

What can we do about all of this? I don't think it would suffice to despise me and notice that by ventilating I am trying to assuage my guilt as well as indulge my racism. I venture to say that, allowing for different cultural experiences, I speak for a great many people, including members of oppressed groups, whose racism I am not competent to explore. My point is that it is *second nature,* and there's the rub. Second nature is history, culture and personal experience disguised as first nature or biology. Indeed, as we have seen, the intellectual racist calls it biology. But it is not first nature or biology. I said above that racism cuts deep. I'd now like to change the image. It is that deeply sedimented by the culture, so deeply embedded that it is not amenable to excision, no matter how enlightened one's subsequent beliefs and practices may be.

My father – with whom I had a terrible relationship – held most of the available forms of bigotry characteristic of the regions he lived in, Alabama, Washington and Texas: toward blacks (though he was called a kind master), toward Jews (some of his best friends were), toward Catholics (ditto, though he never forgave my sister for marrying and becoming one), toward Latin Americans (he was honorary consul for two South American countries). But he was a howling bigot. He once told me that all priests are homosexuals and all nuns are lesbians and that there are tunnels between the monasteries and convents. When I pointed out that he could hold any two of those beliefs but not all three, he said, 'Oh, yeah, you went to college' (so did he and taught in one). When I told the story to my sister, she burst out crying and said that the awful thing is that he really believed what he'd said, no matter how patently absurd it was.

My point in telling this anecdote is that there is only a difference in embedding and surface behaviour between his racism and mine. If this is the case, and if I am not merely an unreconstructed racist who is trying to pass as a decent person and rationalise my bad parts, then what are we to do? The insight that says we accuse others of that which we fear in ourselves, while true, is only a small beginning. It is, I suppose, progress to move from being an active racist to being a less active one and even to work on anti-racist projects. But how can the deep embedding of second nature be scraped away, even if this has to be done millimetre by millimetre?

No amount of 'race awareness training' will cathart away something that is so deeply set in the foundations of cultures. This makes the erection and enforcement of laws and conventions of good behaviour all the more important, because what is bad and underneath will not easily go away. We must be liberal in the public sphere and radical in our knowledge of the deeper issue. This brings us back to the dialectic – the deep, mutually constitutive interrelations between the racist and the oppressed. What binds them together is not only the worst aspects of human nature – aspects that may well be ineradicable.

What makes these destructive aspects take the specific form of racism is historically contingent, and at the root of that contingency is the social and economic organisation of the world that gives order to consent along the lines of economic and nationalistic relationships which are specific to our own age. These are not set in unchippable stone. They are solid but mutable. When we seek to address racism psychoanalytically, we will get nowhere (nor will we with respect to any other matter) unless we grasp and seek to redirect the social, cultural, economic and geopolitical forces which lead our nastiness to take this particularly horrid form. Then, perhaps, we can replace the loud silence with the sounds of scraping and chipping away at our own ways of shaping the destructive side of human nature.

All of this takes me back to the subject of chapter two, in particular, to Freud's pessimism. He pointed out – and Kleinians have been even more sombre about this – that the psychotic and rapacious parts of human nature are kept at bay only by constant effort and that they are omnipresent in phantasy and ever-ready to erupt if sublimation and guilt fail in their work. Racism, then, is not something alien, a throwback. It is the omnipresence of primitive processes, let out of their cage by destructive social, cultural, political, ideological and related forces in nominally civilised communities.

My family lived in a highly-cultured, dropsically wealthy, suburb (the very one where the 'Dallas' television soap opera was set), but it was racist throughout, with a black and Mexican servant class. The emotions and actions we find in racism are part of our own mental worlds, relatively unaltered by the history of the civil rights movement. What has altered, however, is the frequency of violently acting out such feelings, and the means of legal redress have also grown.

Even so, as I write the Sunday paper reports a race riot in Crown Heights, Brooklyn between blacks and orthodox, Lubavitcher Jews (whose world headquarters are in this neighbourhood; see Rayner, 1993). 'The Rev. Al Sharpton, a veteran of these occasions, demanded the arrest of the driver of the car', a Hasidic Jew who had struck and killed a black child, 'and the appointment of a special prosecutor. The rotund preacher denounced the Hasidic Jews as "diamond merchants" and held several of his trademark "Day of Outrage" demonstrations.

'For once, though, Sharpton – who was immortalised as The Rev. Bacon in Tom Wolfe's *The Bonfire of the Vanities* – found himself outflanked by more radical voices. Sonny Carson, a self-styled urban guerrilla, who leads a group called X-clan [after Malcolm X], demanded more action on the streets . . .

'At the funeral of the black child last week, Carson talked of a white plot to destroy black America. "The conspiracy is widespread. I've just come back from Milwaukee. In Milwaukee, they are eating us," he declared in an apparent reference to white serial killer Jeffrey Dahmer, most of whose victims were black' (Sunday Times 1 Sept. 1991).

We have here an accident, involving an innocent child, interpreted by two opposing forms of highly-articulated sectarian, separatist groups, one calling it deliberate, a fat charismatic leader, a self-styled guerrilla, imputed diamond-based wealth, allegations of a genocidal conspiracy and the *cannibalism of blacks* by a self-confessed *white serial killer*. Projective identification of split-off primitive parts are here run riot but based on oppressive inequalities in the heat of summer. As I shall argue in the next chapter, being a Lubavitcher Jew and being a black in that ghetto in this period means that one's identity, one's membership in the group, involves acquiring sets of mutually-stereotyping projective identifications. That is a defining characteristic of belonging, and it is hugely difficult to dismantle, a process which the Israelis and Palestinians and the South African blacks and whites are attempting with great courage to negotiate.

I do not have any wish to claim that life is better for the racially oppressed in economic and social terms. I do say, however, that it is that veneer of civilization we must attend to and not pretend that we can wish or liberalise the feelings away. They are part of what dwells in our inner worlds, inhabitants of our mental space – part of everyday human nature, just below the surface, awaiting the appropriate social and economic conditions to erupt again, with undimmed virulence. That is the lesson of the riot and of recent international relations. Eternal vigilance is the price of civilization. If you take the army away, you'd better have some civil forces at the ready, or humanity will revert to its primitive projective and scapegoating mechanisms. A pity, but I say again that it's best to know what we are up against. Derepression is utterly dangerous unless civil society is strong.

7   AMBIGUOUS SPACE:
PROJECTIVE IDENTIFICATION

In the model for human interrelations I proposed in chapter four, learning was seen to proceed from what we put forth into the world and what comes back. I believe that experience itself is a consequence of projective mechanisms. I now wish to focus on *the basic* projective mechanism and to suggest that it offers the key to understanding how the primitive integrates with the social. I shall argue that it constitutes that which binds us together for good and ill and that it is not at all easy to separate good from evil at the most primitive level of mental functioning.

I begin by suggesting that projective identification is the most fruitful psychoanalytic concept since the discovery of the unconscious. Of course, as soon as something like that is said, competing claims rush forward to be recognised, for example, the significance of the Oedipus complex. Suffice it to say, then, that it is *very* important. Elizabeth Spillius describes it more modestly as Klein's most popular concept (Spillius, 1988, vol. 1, p. 81), and Donald Meltzer calls it the most fruitful Kleinian concept over the past thirty to forty years (Meltzer, 1991). Hinshelwood suggests that as well as being a, if not the, most fruitful Kleinian concept, it is also the most confused and confusing one (Hinshelwood, 1991, pp. 179–208). However, that does not make it mistaken or useless. That's how important ideas develop – by being fruitfully and metaphorically open to different specifications (see Rorty, 1989, Part I). Similar things can be said about the history of the most fundamental concepts in natural science. 'Gravity', 'affinity' and 'natural selection' were, respectively, the most basic ideas in the development of modern physics, chemistry and biology, and the working out of the ambiguities and contradictory claims made on behalf of those essentially metaphorical concepts provided the subject matter of the formative periods in the natural sciences. I have made a special study of the origins and vicissitudes of Darwin's concept of natural selection, which I've called 'Darwin's metaphor', and the parallels are very interesting and reassuring for the prospects of the concept of projective identification (Young, 1985a, ch. 4). Important new ideas are rich in resonances; when they cease to be so, they become literal and mundane, and their fecundity is exhausted (Rorty, 1989, p. 16).

Before plunging into the complexities of projective identification, I want to pause a moment longer at the level of the history of ideas and say that projective identification can be seen as part of a wide network of fundamental developments in the history, philosophy and social studies of science and related subjects. Positivist and empiricist epistemology is in full retreat. In its place is developing a way of thinking about what we know which is not based on the empiricist sequence, whereby we suffer sensations which lead to perceptions and then to ideas. Rather, as I tried to show in my discussion of countertransference, experience is coming to be seen as constructed from the consequences of what we put forth into the world – what we project. Strikingly similar debates are going on in the history, philosophy and social studies of science, in which it is argued that nature and science are socially constructed in ways which depend fundamentally on what questions, hypotheses and frameworks are brought to bear on our experience of the world. (Haraway, 1989, 1991; Young, 1992a, 1994, 1994a–d). Similarly, human relations are the consequences of how we act toward others and what comes back.

In cybernetics this aspect of the process of knowing and adjusting to experience is called 'negative feedback'; one adjusts or fine-tunes ones thoughts and behaviour on receiving back the response to one's overtures, just as a gunnery officer re-sets his angle of fire depending on whether a given shell falls long or short, or a thermo-stat switches the heat on or off, depending on whether the ambient temperature falls below or above the designated one (Wiener, 1950). This is information theory's analogue to the psychoanalytic concept of reality testing. In learning theory, it is called an 'operant'. We modify our behaviour, depending on whether our spontaneous acts are rewarded or not. Not passive conditioning from stimuli but 'operant conditioning' from the feedback from spontaneous acts (Atkinson et al., 1990, pp. 253–62). In the study of human physiology, research on postural control has indicated that we are constantly making subliminal adjustments, depending on the proprioceptive impulses which result from sensing our last movements. We do not manage to stand or sit up or make complex movements solely by means of internal controls but as a result of feedback loops which are constantly leading our musculature to make tiny adjustments. (The tremor of Parkinsonism is one example of what can go wrong with this subtle muscular control system.) I have sketched these developments to indicate analogies which I believe show that Klein's idea of projective identification is in good company. It is part of an epochal change in how we think about knowledge and about nature, human nature and human relations. These approaches are in resonance with phenomenological and hermeneutic thinking in philosophy (and have analogues in the psychoanalytic writings of Lacan and Laplanche).

Returning to the psychoanalytic claims made on behalf of projective identification, Thomas Ogden presents the ideas of Harold Searles, Robert Langs, A. Malin and James Grotstein and describes projective identification as the essence of the therapeutic relationship. Therapy is said to *consist of* dealing with it. It is the basic unit of study of the therapeutic interaction (Ogden, 1979, p. 366). He also tells us that Bion 'views projective identification as the most important form of interaction between the patient and therapist in individual therapy, as well as in groups of all types' (p. 365). In 'Attacks on Linking', Bion says, 'Thus the link between patient and analyst, or infant and breast, is the mechanism of projective identification' (Bion, 1967, p. 106). In the course of a careful review of developments of the concept from its initial formulation in 1946, to the present, Hinshelwood says that for Bion it became 'the basic building block for generating thoughts out of experiences and perceptions' (Hinshelwood, 1991, pp. 189–90). At this same level of generality Segal has described projective identification as 'the earliest form of empathy' and 'the basis of the earliest form of symbol-formation' (Segal, 1973, p. 36). Looking to later developments and more broadly, Hinshelwood describes Bion's notion of 'container-contained' as 'an attempt to raise the concept of projective identification to a general theory of human functioning – of the relations between people, and between groups; of the relationships between internal objects; and of the relationships in the symbolic world between thoughts, ideas, theories, experiences, etc.' (p. 191).

These are large claims – very exciting, uplifting, constructive. Yet this same mechanism is seen to be operative at the heart of autism by Meltzer and his co-workers. He also describes it as '*the* mechanism of narcissistic identification . . . and the basis of hypochondria, confusional states, claustrophobia, paranoia, psychotic depression and perhaps some psychosomatic disorders' (Meltzer *et al.*, 1975, p. 228). It is also the sovereign defence against separation anxiety (Grinberg, 1990, p. 64). Relinquishment of excessive projective identification is described as the precondition of achieving a fully-dimensional inner world. (Meltzer *et al.*, 1975, pp. 226–7). As he says in his essay on 'The Relation of Anal Masturbation to Projective Identification', 'The feeling of fraudulence as an adult person, the sexual impotence or pseudo-potency (excited by secret perverse phantasies), the inner loneliness and the basic confusion between good and bad, all create a life of tension and lack of satisfaction, bolstered, or rather compensated, only by the smugness and snobbery which are an inevitable accompaniment of the massive projective identification' (Meltzer, 1966, p. 104). I have mentioned that in his most recent work, Meltzer describes it as central to the most Social Darwinist forms of ambitious competitive, survivalist conformism, in his concept of 'the claustrum', in which patients use excessive projective identification as a desperate defence against schizophrenic breakdown (Meltzer, 1992). Another Kleinian, Leslie Sohn, recalls that the original thoughts on projective identification in the British Psycho-Analytical Society conceived of it 'as a defence against intolerable envy and as an outcome of hatred of dependence' (Sandler, 1989, p. 190). As I argued in my discussion of racism and shall consider further below, projective identification (of which splitting is an integral part) is also *the* basic mechanism in, sectarianism, virulent nationalism, fanatical religiosity and blind obedience to political and gang leaders.

As if all this wasn't problematic enough, Spillius begins her overview of the concept by telling us that 'the term has gradually become the most popular of Klein's concepts, the only one that has been widely accepted and discussed by non-Kleinians – especially in the United States' (Spillius, 1988, vol. 1, p. 81). The problem is that she goes on to say that 'it is often discussed in terms that are incompatible with Klein's conception' (*Ibid.*). Hinshelwood draws a similarly disconcerting conclusion when he writes, 'There appears to be no consensus on the value of the term "projective identification" outside the Kleinian conceptual framework' (Hinshelwood, 1991, p. 204). It is in danger of degenerating into what he calls 'a catch-phrase for all interpersonal phenomena' (p. 196), a fate similar to that which befell the concept of object relations at the hands of Greenberg and Mitchell, who mistakenly reduced all objects to people so as to bring Klein into closer affinity with American psychoanalytic ideas and those of Harry Stack Sullivan (Greenberg and Mitchell, 1983; *cf.* Kohon, 1985).

American analysts have taken up the concept with enthusiasm and have written extensively about it. Although the best of this work is interesting and rich in clinical examples, these writers have tended to concentrate largely on the interpersonal form of the mechanism at the expense of the purely intrapsychic one. In my opinion this impoverishes the concept and does not allow sufficient scope and space for the inner world and internal objects (Grotstein, 1981; Ogden, 1982; Scharff, 1992).

The key issue here is whether or not a real, external Other, who has been affected by the projection, is essential to the concept. British Kleinians say no; some American interpreters say yes. Spillius' summary is helpful: 'Considerable controversy has developed over the definition and use of the concept. Whether there is a difference between projection and projective identification is perhaps the most frequently raised question, but others have been important too. Should the term be used only to refer to the patient's unconscious phantasy, regardless of the effect on the recipient, or should it be used only in cases in which the recipient of the projection is emotionally affected by what is being projected into him? Should the term only be used for the projection of aspects of the self, or should it also be used for the projection of internal objects? What about the many possible motives for projective identification; should all be included? Should the term be used only in cases where the patient has lost conscious awareness of the quality and part of the self he has projected, or does it also apply to cases in which such awareness is retained? What about the projection of good qualities and good parts of the self; should the concept be used for these as well, as Klein so clearly thought, or should it be reserved for the projection of bad qualities, which has been the dominant tendency? Is a specific bodily phantasy always involved in the projection, as Klein thought, or is it clarifying enough to speak of the phantasy in mental terms?

'Of these many questions, by far the most discussion has been devoted to the question of whether and how projective identification should be distinguished from projection . . . In these discussions the most usual basis for the distinction between projection and projective identification is held to be whether or not the recipient of the projection is or is not affected emotionally by the projector's phantasy . . . But to restrict the term projective identification to such instances greatly diminishes the usefulness of the concept and is in any case totally contrary to what Klein herself meant by it. The English view is that the term is best kept as a general concept broad enough to include both cases in which the recipient is emotionally affected and those in which he is not . . . The many motives for projective identification – to control the object, to acquire its attributes, to evacuate a bad quality, to protect a good quality, to avoid separation – all are most usefully kept under the general umbrella' (Spillius, 1988, vol. 1, pp. 81–3).

Hanna Segal's definition seems to side with those who call for an external object: 'In projective identification parts of the self and internal objects are split off and projected into the external object, which then becomes possessed by, controlled and identified with the projected parts' (Segal, 1973, p. 27). Bion also includes projection 'into an external object' (Bion, 1992, p. 159). Unless we assume that they are written from the point of view of the projector's phantasy, these definitions do not embrace both sides of Spillius' broad approach, which allows for projective identification into an internal object as well as into an external one. It is important to emphasise that projective identification can occur wholly inside the unconscious of the projecting person and need not be involved at all with behaviour which is unconsciously designed to elicit a response from another person. The Other can dwell exclusively in the inner world of the person who creates the projective identification and supplies the response from his or her phantasy of the *dramatis personae* in the mind. In this case it is a relationship between one part of the inner world and another. Where behaviour is involved, the process of eliciting the unconsciously desired resonance from the Other can be very subtle, indeed. Betty Joseph has made the detailed understanding of these interactions an area of special study. In particular, she draws attention to the patient's uncanny ability to 'nudge' the therapist to act out in accordance with the patient's projection – to evoke the disowned feelings from the therapist's repertoire and induce the therapist to experience and perhaps reproject them (Joseph, 1989, esp. chs. 7, 9–12).

There are further elaborations: 'Projective identification has manifold aims: it may be directed towards the ideal object to avoid separation, or it may be directed towards the bad object to gain control of the source of the danger. Various parts of the self may be projected, with various aims: bad parts of the self may be projected in order to get rid of them as well as to attack and destroy the object, good parts may be projected to avoid separation or keep them safe from bad things inside or to improve the external object through a kind of primitive projective reparation. Projective identification starts when the paranoid-schizoid position is first established in relation to the breast, but it persists and very often becomes intensified when the mother is perceived as a whole object and the whole of her body is entered by projective identification' (Segal, 1973, pp. 27–8).

Mutual projective processes are powerfully described in the essay by Tom Main which I quoted at length above (pp. 62–3). He provides excellent analyses of projective mechanisms in individuals, couples and large and small groups. I repeat his conclusion: 'Certain pairs come to live in such locked systems, dominated by mutual projective phantasies with each not truly married to a person, but rather to unwanted, split off and projected parts of themselves. But the husband, dominant and cruel, and the wife, stupidly timid and respectful, may be miserably unhappy with themselves and with each other, yet such marriages, although turbulent, are stable, because each partner needs the other for narcissistic pathological purposes. Forcible projective processes, and especially projective identification, are thus more than an individual matter; they are object-related, and the other will always be affected more or less. The results are a variety of joint personality deplenishments and invasions and interpersonal disturbances' (Main, 1975, pp. 100–01).

None of the above descriptions sufficiently emphasises *projective identification into parts of one's own mind,* a topic well-expressed (in the context of envy) by Joseph Berke, whose book, *The Tyranny of Malice* (1989), can be seen as a compendium on splitting and projective identification: 'Projection and projective identification are activities that influence different parts of the self. These, of course, include phantasized or internal representations of actual relationships. Thus a person can indeed feel under attack because he is attacking mental images of his own father or teacher or therapist.

'However, a more ominous reaction occurs when, beset by envy, the envier tries to preserve himself from himself by splitting up and protectively identifying his spite and malice with and into parts of his own mind. Consequently the envier contains a multitude of envious others all threatening to attack him from within. These exist as split off and extremely hostile representations of his own envious self or of envious parents and parental substitutes.' This process leads to an over-severe and envious superego and saps the individual's progressive and creative capacities.

'In order to avoid such a psychic catastrophe, whereby a host of inner enviers assault each other, the afflicted person may utilise projective processes to deflect these enmities outward. The net effect is like picking out a pack of piranhas and throwing them into the air. Because of the action of projective identification, when these vicious little enviers land on something, and they always do, the envious person (fleeing from his own envious selves) inevitably converts elements of external reality (benign people, places, or things) into malevolent entities (witches, evil influences, bad omens). But instead of solving the problem, this manoeuvre compounds it, for the individual feels threatened by malignity emanating from within himself and from without. Thus the envier becomes the envied, and the hunter becomes the hunted' (Berke, 1989, p. 67).

Donald Meltzer's book, *The Claustrum*, is entirely devoted to projective identification into internal objects. He is at pains to reveal the evolution of his thinking. He had for some years been uncomfortable with a bias in Klein's paper 'On Identification' (1955a) and came to 'discover the real reason for my dissatisfaction: the tendency of Mrs. Klein's paper to continue treating projective identification as a psychotic mechanism and one which operated with external objects, primarily or exclusively' (Meltzer, 1992, p. 13). He emphasises that an important part of mental space is inside internal objects (p. 118) and that entry into projective identification is a 'ubiquitous phenomenon in early childhood' (p. 118). More generally, he concludes that 'the existence of one or another infantile part either living in projective identification or easily provoked to enter the claustrum of internal objects is fairly ubiquitous' (p.134; *cf.* p. 153).

There is one more aspect of projective identification to which I want to refer before moving onto a broader canvas. I have already stressed the intrapsychic form, where both parts are played inside the inner world. I now want to draw attention to a feature of the process when it occurs between people. In much of the literature on this topic, reference is made to 'projecting *into* the Other, whether externally or internally. I believe that there is an important distinction which is, as yet, not fully worked out. It concerns putting something into another person as distinct from *eliciting something from the repertoire of their responses, exaggerating it and evoking a reprojection of that aspect of their personality.* The process its one of the projection *finding a home* and of unconscious collusion on the part of the person receiving the projection. In my opinion this is by far the most common manifestation of the interpersonal form of the process, as distinct from being invaded by something entirely alien, a strange feeling in oneself. What is strange in the case of evoked and exaggerated feelings is the intensity. The recipient reprojects a degree or strength of feeling that is surprising, but, though an exaggeration or enhancement, it is still his or hers.

The person who has made most of this point is Harold Searles, who is not a Kleinian and does not stress the term. His writings have centred on the honesty required to acknowledge the patient's prescience. In describing his findings in his first paper on the subject, he says of himself that he 'has very regularly been able to find some real basis in himself for those qualities which his patients – *all* his patients, whether the individual patient be more prominently paranoid, or obsessive-compulsive, or hysterical, and so on – project upon him. It appears that all patients, not merely those with chiefly paranoid adjustments, have the ability to "read the unconscious" of the therapist. This process of reading the unconscious of another person is based, after all, upon nothing more occult that an alertness to minor variations in the other person's posture, facial expression, vocal tone, and so on, of which the other person himself is unaware. All neurotic and psychotic patients, because of their need to adapt themselves to the feelings of the other person, have had to learn as children – usually in association with painfully unpredictable parents – to be alert to such nuances of behavior on the part of the other person' (Searles, 1978–9, pp. 177–78; 1979; Young, 1992).

The patient's hook catches its fish in the analyst's unconscious and reels it in. In my view, much of the striking originality of Searles' work stems from this important insight, one which has been grasped by some Kleinians, for example, Irma Brenman Pick (1985, esp. p. 41; above, p. 69), Betty Joseph (1989) and Michael Feldman (1992, pp. 77, 87), but its implications are far from being taken in by most writers on the subject. There is too little awareness of how nearly fully interactive the processes is, and I believe this is a remnant of objectivist attitudes on the part of therapists, who do not grant the fundamental role of the countertransference in therapy, as in the rest of life (see chapter four).

I have, in an attempt to lay the groundwork for my argument, raised rather a lot of possibilities. As I near the end of my review of the concept, I have to add that Segal reports that Klein seems to have defined it almost casually and doubted its value because of the ease with which it could be misused (Spillius, 1988, vol. 1, p. 81). That need not worry us: the same could be said of Freud's introduction of countertransference, and look where that has led. Where are we, then? Projective identification is the basis of all relationships, yet the basic mechanism in some of our most alarming mental disorders and some of our worst inhumanities, as well as for the therapeutic process. At the same time, the tacit injunction to our patients – 'Take back the projections' – is a useful way of characterising the goal of helping her or him to dwell as much as possible in the depressive position, and, as we have seen, the effort to shift from the paranoid-schizoid to the depressive position is, according to Brenman Pick, the aim of every interpretation (Brenman Pick, 1985, p. 37). So – in one Kleinian formulation it is the model for the process, while in another its diminution is the goal of that process.

What sense can we make of all this? First, I have to say that it's *all* true. There are a number of forms of the process of projective identification, and it would not be fruitful to legislate away any of them. We have to try to live with the mixture in the depressive position and bear the consequences and the anxieties. That sends us back to basics. That's always best, and directs us to what many believe to be Klein's most important single text, 'Notes on Some Schizoid Mechanisms', delivered on 4 December in 1946 – a good point in history for taking back projections, you might say, in the wake of the Second World War and at the genocidal dawn of the Atomic Age.

Klein concludes seven pages on the fine texture of early paranoid and schizoid mechanisms as follows: 'So far, in dealing with persecutory fear, I have singled out the oral element. However, while the oral libido still has the lead, libidinal and aggressive impulses and phantasies from other sources come to the fore and lead to a confluence or oral, urethral and anal desires, both libidinal and aggressive. Also the attacks on the mother's breast develop into attacks of a similar nature on her body, which comes to be felt as it were as an extension of the breast, even before the mother is conceived of as a complete person. The phantasied onslaughts on the mother follow two main lines: one is the predominantly oral impulse to suck dry, bite up, scoop out and rob the mother's body of its good contents . . . The other line of attack derives from the anal and urethral impulses and implies expelling dangerous substances (excrements) out of the self and into the mother. Together with these harmful excrements, expelled in hatred, split-off parts of the ego are also projected onto the mother or, as I would rather call it, *into* the mother. [Klein adds a footnote at this crucial point, to the effect that she is describing primitive, pre-verbal processes and that projecting '*into* another person' seems to her 'the only way of conveying the unconscious process I am trying to describe'. Much misunderstanding and lampooning of Kleinianism could have been avoided if this point was more widely understood.] These excrements and bad parts of the self are meant not only to injure but also to control and to take possession of the object. In so far as the mother comes to contain the bad parts of the self, she is not felt to be a separate individual but is felt to be *the* bad self.

'Much of the hatred against parts of the self is now directed towards the mother. This leads to a particular form of identification which establishes the prototype of an aggressive object-relation' (Klein, 1946, pp. 7–8). Note carefully that *we have here the model* – the template, the fundamental experience – *of all of the aggressive features of human relations.* Six years later Klein adds the following sentence: 'I suggest for these processes the term "projective identification"' (*Ibid.*).

She goes on to say that if the infant's impulse is to harm, the mother is experienced as persecuting, and that in psychotic disorders the identification of the object with hated parts of the self 'contributes to the intensity of the hatred directed against other people', that this process weakens the ego, that good parts are also projected and that 'The processes of splitting off parts of the self and projecting them into objects are thus of vital importance for normal development as well as for normal object-relations' (pp. 8–9). In the course of all this, Klein makes it quite clear that the very same processes involve 'anxieties characteristic of psychosis' (p. 2). I am relating these matters in the way that I am in order to make it apparent that the very same mechanisms are at work in a wide range of internal processes.

This leaves me with a painful, rather Aristotelian, point to make here – at the centre or pivotal passage in my argument. What is crazy and murderous and what is essential to all experience and human relations are the same. *The same*. It is all a matter of degree, and all we can hope to do is attempt to find and hold onto something akin to Aristotle's ethical principle, 'The Golden Mean'. This is contrary to what we are taught in the nosologies of the psychopathologists, where normal and pathological are sharply distinguished and lie on either side of diagnostic dichotomies. As I understand the Kleinian notion of projective identification (as with much else in Kleinian metapsychology), *there is no sharp line to be drawn between normal and pathological, between benign as compared to virulent or malignant projective identification.* The relevant division concerns points on a continuum representing *the force* with which the projection is phantasied, along with other criteria which do not arise inside this primitive mechanism. I am not suggesting that good is the same as bad. There are all-important distinctions to be drawn between benign and virulent manifestations of projective identification. They are based on content, motive, situation and moral criteria, but the psychological mechanism involved in all of these is the same.

Tom Main makes the distinction clearly: 'It must be emphasised that externalising defences and fantasies can involve positive as well as negative aspects of the self; and that projection of impulses and projective identification of parts of the self into others are elements in "normal" mental activity. When followed by reality testing, trial externalisation of aspects of the self help an individual to understand himself and others . . . It is when projective processes are massive and forceful that they are difficult to test or reverse. In malignant projective identification this difficulty arises not only because of the forcefulness of the projection but also because, with the ego impoverished by loss of a major part of the self, reality testing becomes defective. Thus unchecked and uncheckable pathological judgements may now arise about oneself and the other, quasi-irreversible because of the pains of integration. Malignant projective processes are to be found in both neurotic and psychotic patients, and may be temporarily observable also in "normal" people suffering major frustrations.' In the temporary and benign cases, reality testing helps one to get over it. 'By contrast, in malignant projective systems the self is impoverished, reality testing fails, the other is not recognized for what he is but rather as a container of disowned aspects of the self, to be hated, feared, idealized, etc., and relations are unreal and narcissistically intense up to the point of insanity' (Main, 1975, p. 105).

As we have seen, Klein began in earlier papers by attempting to specify fixation points for paranoia and depression (Klein, 1935). She went on to specify developmental points. Bion and others completed the universali-zation of the paranoid-schizoid (ps) and depressive (d) positions by putting a double-headed arrow between them and emphasising that we move back and forth in the mundane processes of daily and moment-to-moment experience: ps$\leftrightarrow$d.

Lest you think my position utterly eccentric in lumping all things together and then domesticating them, I can claim that I am not alone in discerning this broad view of projective identification in the literature. After reviewing the development of the concept, Torras de Beà writes, 'These authors consider that projective identification is the basic mechan-ism of empathy and primitive communication and also of the defence mechanism which consists of dissociating and projecting anxiety in order to be rid of it. I agree with this and think also that what we call projective identification is the active element in every communication from empathy to the most pathological and defensive' (Torras de Beà, 1989, p. 266). He concludes that it is 'the mechanism basic to all human interaction' (p. 272).

Faced with all this conceptual muddle and the close proximity between constructive and destructive aspects of our most basic ways of feeling and relating, what hope is there for sorting out our personal and collective feelings and forms of co-operation and conflict? Not a lot, I have to say, but we are at least in a position to see where the problems lie for individuals and beyond. An important place where they lie for all of us is in the mapping of these mechanisms onto groups, institutions, organisations, customs and nations which legitimate these processes and allow us to experience the virulent as though it is benign and part of the definition of a good social order. Recall that in his reflections on *Civilization and Its Discontents,* Freud taught us that repression, guilt and sublimation are absolutely essential for the existence of civilization (Freud,

1930; see above, chapter two). Klein, Bion, Elliott Jaques, Isabel Menzies Lyth, Hinshelwood, Berke and others are supplementing this sombre truth with an equally sombre one: the institutionalisation of destructive forces is a result of the need to erect defences against psychotic anxieties (above, chapter five). What we need to be civilised and the ways we organise our incivilities are desperately and distressingly close. Differentiating between them is a matter of degree and of moral criteria which are not intrinsic to this mechanism.

Moving now to groups and institutions, I want to share an initial bewilderment. If you look in the index to a number of important texts in this sphere, you will find no entry for projective identification in, for example, Jaques' classic, *The Changing Culture of a Factory* (1951), Malcolm Pines' edited collection on *Bion and Group Psychotherapy* (1985; no mention of 'container-contained', either), Gareth Morgan's highly-regarded *Images of Organization* (1986), Hinshelwood's excellent *What Happens in Groups* (1987), Windy Dryden and Mark Aveline's collection on *Group Therapy in Britain* (1988), Didier Anzieu's *The Group and the Unconscious* (1984). As recently as the mid-1980s, Leonard Horowitz claimed that the concept of projective identification 'has failed to gain wide currency in either the psychoanalysis or the group psychotherapy literature' and set out to explain this failure, which he largely attributes to conceptual muddle (Horowitz, 1983, pp. 21, 22). As with all separations in the real world, however, the cleavage is not complete. I did find some fleeting references in a couple of S. H. Foulkes' books and many more in the two volumes of the A. K. Rice Series – *Group Relations Readers.* – including Horowitz's musings (references in the 1985 volume are a multiple of those in the 1975 one – Colman and Bexton, 1975; Colman and Geller, 1985).

I am not embarking on a pedant's tour of indexes but emphasising the contrast between very recent literature and the immediate present, where it can rightly be said, as, indeed, it was said by Lise Rafaelsen in the journal, *Group Analysis,* 'Projective Identification is a fashionable concept. "We see it here, we see it there, we see it everywhere", just like the Scarlet Pimpernel during the French Revolution. However, in spite of its elusiveness, it is one of the few concepts that describes and catches the process in and the relationship between the intrapsychic and the interpersonal' (Rafaelsen, 1992, p. 55).

It could be argued that by seeing projective identification here, there and everywhere, we are spreading the concept so thin that it cannot properly cover anything. I believe that this is potentially a real danger, but

I do not think we are yet at the danger point. At a time like the present in the history of a concept, it is often worth while to be permissive and to ask what we can learn from viewing familiar ideas from the point of view of the apparently ubiquitous, promiscuous and all-powerful concept. A number of familial and group phenomena are obvious candidates for consideration in terms of projective identification: the 'designated patient' in a family; the use of a group member as a spokesperson; scapegoating of all kinds; the phenomenon of 'role suction' (see Horowitz, 1983, pp. 29–30).

My purpose, however, is a fundamentally political one. I do not mean 'political' in the party-political sense (partly, in my case, because I have never found a real world party which elicited my enthusiasm). I mean politics in the sense of ways of embodying values in groups, structures, institutions and the distribution of power and resources. Now most people who have turned to psychology with public questions in mind have done so warily, because they have rightly feared that they might fall prey to reductionism. I believe that this wariness is wholly justified. As we have seen, Freud was quite explicitly and unequivocally reductionist in avowing his belief that all social, cultural and political phenomena were only the familiar phenomena of id, ego and superego, along with the Oedipal triangle, operating in a new sphere (Gay, 1988, p. 547). He even avowed that 'Strictly speaking, there are only two sciences: psychology, pure and applied, and natural science' (Freud, 1933, p. 179). There is, according to Freud, no place for truly social explanations; sociology 'cannot be anything but applied psychology' (*Ibid.*).

Social scientists are prone to tear their hair out at this point, and sociologists of knowledge indulge in a knowing smile. All knowledge is relative to its time, to contending interests, to particular cultures. Freud was, in my view, pretty naive about this, as I have argued elsewhere (Young, 1973; 1988a; above, chapter two). But I do not think that this leaves us marooned or prone to the well-known pitfalls of psychohistory, in which cultures and nations get mapped onto a developmental scheme which would embarrass any half-informed social anthropologist (Lowenberg, 1985; Cocks and Crosby, 1987).

I suggest that two or three things can rescue us. However, before specifying them I need to add an important cautionary note: what we need rescuing *from* is the erroneous belief that psychoanalysis can or should be sufficient to understand groups, culture, society, nations and other supra-individual phenomena, any more than it is sufficient to understand the individual. The rescue operation is designed to make connections –

articulations – between the intrapsychic and the historical, socio-economic
and ideological factors that largely constitute our characters, personalities
and behaviour in groups. The connections I shall specify are not merely
links; they are *embeddings*.

Now, to revert to the rescue operation. The first helpful notion is one
we have encountered before: Victor Wolfenstein's marxist critique of a
well-known maxim in political science known as 'Lasswell's Formula'
(Lasswell, 1930; Wolfenstein, 1981, pp. 17–18), which states that private
interests get projected onto the public realm and then represented as the
common good. This is a particularly socially harmful form of rationalisation. The ruthless economic self-interest of a Rockefeller is defended
as generating good for all. He used the analogy of competition among
roses leading to the American Beauty Rose, his pretty analogy for the
competitive success of his firm, Standard Oil, a company which has
recently been cosmetically renamed EXXON, presumably in an attempt to
refurbish its corporate image, since Standard Oil was associated with
ruthless monopolistic practices. (This soon backfired when the Exxon
Valdeez oil spill occurred off the coast of Alaska. Another instance of this
kind was the renaming of Windscale as Sellafield in a vain attempt to
escape some of the opprobrium connected with nuclear pollution.)
Versions of this rationalising maxim have been offered throughout history,
for example, in the self-assigned civilising missions of colonialists or
imperialists. It forms the basis of the self-justifications of factory owners
throughout the history of the labour process in industrial capitalism,
including, in our own era, Taylorist 'scientific management' and softer
versions of it in the 'human relations movement' associated with the work
of Elton Mayo. Indeed, as Peter Barham and I have attempted to point
out, it provides one way of mounting a critique of some aspects of the
group relations movement and the forms of consultancy which grew out
of the work of the Tavistock Institute of Human Relations after it ceased
to be funded by granting bodies (including, especially, the Rockefeller
Foundation), and its consultants became 'guns for hire' in industry
(Barham, 1984; Young, 1990b). At the individual level, politicians from
time immemorial have rationalised their private interests and represented
them as the common good.

What provides us with the perspective of critique with respect to
Lasswell's formula is Wolfenstein's important move in starting the story a
stage further back. Where did the particular conception of private interests
come from *before* they got rationalised as the public good? This is both a
familial and an ideological question. It invites us to look at both the

psychoanalytic and the socialising process of development. Freud famously pointed out that the child does not acquire the parent's values but the parents' superego. This has an inherently conservative influence on the personality and provides a significant brake on social change (Freud, 1933, p. 67). Our task is to investigate the microprocesses of how we acquire values in the family. We are greatly aided in doing so by recent research on the transmission of superego in particularly distressing family histories – those of holocaust survivors. Both Haydée Faimberg (1988) and Ilony Kogan (1989) have shown us how direct and coercive these forms of inherited distress are and how they come to be acted out 'unto the seventh generation' – or at least in the generations to which we have so far had analytic access.

The transmission of trauma in Holocaust survivor provides a model for how values get implanted in the process of socialisation and passed down through the generations. Psychoanalytic writers of varying degrees of radicalism have essayed about this, basing their own work on attempts to make sense of the rise of Nazism and its aftermath. I am thinking of the classical writings of the liberal Eric Fromm, the anarchic libertarian Wilhelm Reich, and the libertarian marxist Herbert Marcuse. Whatever one may feel about their respective politics and views on specific theoretical issues in psychoanalysis, these men wrote powerfully about how an epoch's values get into the unconscious value systems of people. I am thinking of Fromm's essays (1971) from the 1930s, when he was in liaison with the Frankfurt School and his book, *Fear of Freedom* (called *Escape from Freedom* in America, 1941); of Reich's essays (1929–34) collected as *Sex-Pol* (1972) and his masterpiece, *The Mass Psychology of Fascism* (1933). With respect to Marcuse, I have in mind his remarkable philosophical investigation into Freud, *Eros and Civilization* (1955, discussed above (pp. 25–8), the companion volume in which he mounts a critique of the ideology of industrial capitalism, *One Dimensional Man* (1964) and his essays on how conformist pressures are eroding the role of the father, the superego and the family, collected in *Five Lectures* (1970). Making due allowance for the consequences of their differing views on how change comes about and how refractory human nature is, they share a psychoanalytic perspective on how we come to conform – how consent is organised, how hegemony is instanced in the hearts and minds (especially the unconscious minds) – of human beings. I admire this body of work and have found it consistently illuminating.

But – as many radical critics of the Freudo-Marxist literature have reluctantly concluded – they did not delve deeply enough. This fact brings us back to projective identification by way of Bion and those whose work was inspired by his. I said above that I could think of two or three things which might rescue us from experiencing Freud's reductionism as hopelessly ignorant of the importance of social causation. The first was to look deeper than Lasswell's Formula and investigative how certain public values and structures got into the unconscious before they got projected and rationalised as the public interest. The second reason for hope was adumbrated in a motto of Freud's: 'If I cannot bend the higher powers, I will stir up the lower depths' (Freud, 1900, p. ix) . As we saw in chapter five, Bion takes us further into the lowest depths – the most primitive and most refractory defences of all: defences against psychotic anxieties which arise in the paranoid-schizoid and depressive positions. He considers these to be the 'source of the main emotional drives of the group' (Bion, 1961, p. 188) and 'the ultimate sources of all group behaviour' (p. 189). As well as working through the problems posed by family patterns, groups must cope with splitting and projection and the part-object relationships to which they give rise. The move from the individual to the group does not raise new issues about explanation. He says a little further on, 'The apparent difference between group psychology and individual psychology is an illusion produced by the fact that the group brings into prominence phenomena which appear alien to an observer unaccustomed to using the group' (p. 169).

I want to look again at the work following on from Bion's experiences in groups. Elliott Jaques (1955) and Isabel Menzies Lyth conducted research in various organisations and found the same mechanisms at work, with the defences embodied in the mores and structures of the institutions. I believe that this model is at work in innumerable situations – neighbourhood gang, school, workplace, country club, religion, racial, political and international conflict. When one comes into contact with the group, subculture or institution, the psychic price of admission is to enter into that group's splits and projective identifications.

In her classical paper on 'The Function of Social Systems as a Defence Against Anxiety', Menzies Lyth describes the link as it applies to student nurses: 'Although, following Jaques, I have used the term "social defence system" as a construct to describe certain features of the nursing service as a continuing social institution, I wish to make it clear that I do not imply that the nursing service *as an institution* operates the defences. Defences are, and can be, operated only by individuals. Their behaviour is the link between their psychic defences and the institution' (Menzies Lyth, 1959, p. 73). There is a complex and subtle interaction, resulting in a matching between the individual's defences and the institution's. The processes 'depend heavily on repeated projection of the psychic defence system into the social defence system and repeated introjection of the social defence system into the psychic defence system. This allows continuous testing of the match and fit as the individual experiences his own and other people's reactions.

'The social defence system of the nursing service has been described as a historical development through collusive interaction between individuals to project and reify relevant elements of their psychic defence systems. However, from the viewpoint of the new entrant to the nursing service, the social defence system at the time of entry is a datum, an aspect of external reality to which she must react and adapt. Fenichel makes a similar point (1945). He states that social institutions arise through the efforts of human beings to satisfy their needs, but that social institutions then become external realities comparatively independent of individuals which affect the structure of the individual' (pp. 73–4). The student nurse has to adapt her defences to those of the institution. The latter are relatively immutable, so she shapes hers until they are congruent with the institution's. The primitive psychic defences from infancy are brought by the individual to the fraught and literally life-threatening setting of the hospital. 'These defences are oriented to the violent, terrifying situations of infancy, and rely heavily on violent splitting [and, I would add, projective identification – R. M. Y.] which dissipates the anxiety. They avoid the experience of anxiety and effectively prevent the individual from confronting it. Thus, the individual cannot bring the content of the phantasy anxiety situations into effective contact with reality. Unrealistic or pathological anxiety cannot be differentiated from realistic anxiety arising from real dangers. Therefore, anxiety tends to remain permanently at a level determined more by the phantasies than by the reality. The forced introjection of the hospital defence system, therefore, perpetuates in the individual a considerable degree of pathological anxiety.

'The enforced introjection and use of such defences also interferes with the capacity for symbol formation . . . The defences inhibit the capacity for creative, symbolic thought, for abstract thought, and for conceptualization. They inhibit the full development of the individual's understanding, knowledge and skills that enable reality to be handled effectively and pathological anxiety mastered' (pp. 74–5).

I have quoted this passage – one which will be familiar to many – to invite you to reflect on the appropriateness of this description for understanding how a person comes to think and feel not only like a nurse but also like a racist or a virulent nationalist or a member of a street gang or a religious or psychoanalytic sect. I believe that the mechanisms are the same and that the process of taking in the values as 'a given', adapting one's own primitive anxieties to that group's particular version of splitting, projection, stereotyping and scapegoating, leads to the same kind of impoverishment that nurses experience – of the ability to think and feel with moderation and to deal with reality and anxiety. It is projected into the structure or the Other and given back – not detoxified, but – as an injunction to behave inhumanely toward patients, Lacanians, Jews, Armenians, 'the Evil Empire', Bosnians or whomsoever. It is by this means that I became certain, without thinking about it or meeting many, if any, of the people involved, that Germans are sadistic, Japanese cunning, Italians sexist, Mexicans lazy, French romantic, English decent, Scots dour, Canadians boring, Swiss efficient, Dutch tidy, Scandinavians cold, Spaniards romantic, Russians passionate, Turks depraved, Arabs fanatical, Jews avaricious, Hawaiians friendly, Australians gauche, Chinese inscrutable, Africans rhythmic, White South Africans racist and authoritarian. I have been sure of all these things all my conscious life, but, as I indicated at the end of chapter five, I do not recall learning any of them

How, if at all, does this differ from any other theory of socialisation into a belief system? The answer is two-fold. Most conceptions of socialisation in social psychology, sociology and social anthropology have a civility and blandness, reminiscent of learning theory in psychology, as if to say, 'This is how Dick and Jane learn to be good citizens, members of the tribe, team-players, or whatever'. I believe that it is an implication of fundamental importance that the level of explanation following on from Bion's insistence that Freud missed out 'the ultimate sources of all group behaviour' is that we are dealing with a whole new level of *grip*. In terms of a domestic analogy the comparison is between the bonding power of a glue stick, on the one hand, and superglue, on the other. The projective identifications of membership are bonded with the unconscious equivalent of superglue – cemented at the most primitive level of feeling that we have. I recall a series of sexual jokes that were popular some years ago. 'Plumbers do it with pipe.' 'Surfers do it with wet suits.' 'Radio hams do it with short waves.' 'Teachers do it with discipline.' 'Psychotherapists do it with insight.' 'Marxists do it with class.' The analogous slogan would be: 'Members do it with projective identification.' I mean members of families, couples, groups, institutions, tribes, cultures, sects, armies and so on.

I have another set of images in mind, which I offer in an attempt to emphasise the grip or adhesiveness or deep registration of these phenomena. Recent work with survivors of catastrophes shows that the trauma acts like a homing device and ransacks or searches out the history of the victim until it finds a congruent, early experience. It latches onto that – tightly – and can only be dislodged with the greatest difficulty (Caroline Garland, personal communication). Another image is of hungry birds in a nest – heads vertical, beaks open, cheeping. You may think that they are only craving, but they are also projecting like mad, and what mother thrusts down their throats on her return goes deep. What is true of worms served up as food for birds is also true of people with respect to prejudices and other deeply held beliefs. They become so deeply implanted or sedimented that they are 'second nature'.

In the context of what I have been saying, I want to ponder a passage from Hanna Segal about the political implications of Klein's views on how hunger gnaws: 'From the beginning the infant forms some object relationships, predominantly in phantasy. In her view, the outward deflection of the death instinct postulated by Freud creates the fantasy of a deathly bad object . . . First we project our destructiveness into others; then we wish to annihilate them without guilt because *they* contain all the evil and destructiveness' (Segal, 1988, pp. 50–51). When we read accounts of the genocide of the Conquistadors, the Stalinists, the Germans, the Kampucheans, the Americans or the Iraqis, we must ask what has been projected into these people from the most primitive parts of their tormentors. Similarly, when we see the behaviour of drunken Indians or Esquimos or the fawning of black film actors such as Step'n Fetchit or the behaviour of Mafiosi as represented by Brando, Jews like Dickens' Fagin as played by Alec Guiness or Americans as played by John Wayne – then we must note how such projections take root and evoke stereotypes which people, in society as in fiction, perform so convincingly that they reinforce the projective process and confirm the original degrading depiction.

Once we have adopted this way of thinking about the relationship between the individual and the group process, familiar matters begin to appear in a new light. What are Bion's three basic assumptions which sunder sensible work group functioning – dependence, pairing, fight-flight (see below, p. 157) – but projective identifications? What is the mechanism of becoming a follower, as described in Freud's *Group Psychology and the Analysis of the Ego* (1921), except projective identification of desired parts into the leader, who gives back an identity and frees one from the obligation of being responsible for one's own superego? Wolfenstein gives a moving account of this in his writings about the black American revolutionary, Malcolm X, and his relationship – of protégé, heir

apparent and then apostate – with respect to the leader of the Black
Muslims, The Honorable Elijah Muhammad (Wolfenstein, 1981;.1991, esp.
pp 527–41). What is being a fan of a movie star or a groupie of a rock
star other than romantic, idealising projective identification? Main makes
just this point: 'Where positive aspects of the self are forcefully projected
similar degrees of depersonalization occur, with feelings of personal
worthlessness and with dependent worship of the other's contrasting
strengths, powers, uncanny sensitivity, marvellous gifts, thoughts, knowledge, undying goodness etc. This is the world of the devotee, cults and
hero-promotion' (Main 1975, p. 106). It is also a world in which people
will do anything a Bhagwan (Milne, 1986) or a Charles Manson (Sanders,
1972) or a Rev. James Jones or a David Koresh tells them to do – from
sexual licence to senseless murder to mass suicide. The same suspension
of one's own sense of right and wrong is at work in the followers L. Ron
Hubbard in the Church of Scientology as in the helter-skelter minds of
the devotees of Charles Manson, killing rich Californians, and in the
convictions of bombers and perpetrators of sectarian murders in Northern
Ireland or terrorists from Lybia, though the ideologies of the respective
group leaders may have utterly different apparent or real justifications.

The example of my experience at a group relations conference which
I gave at the end of chapter five is of an idealised internal group, with
which I was in projective identification of a kind. I now want to speak
about another kind of group. You will recall that I have offered two sorts
of hope for rescuing us from the charge that psychoanalysis is reductionist
with respect to groups and institutions. The first was to look behind
Lasswell's Formula about rationalising private interests and claiming that
they represent the public good. Following Wolfenstein, we discovered
how social forces shaped conceptions of private interests and should be
considered as an earlier stage in the process. The second basis for hope
lay in looking deeper, with Bion and his successors, into how institutional
and group values get imbedded, as if superglued, in the unconscious via
projective identification as a way of dealing with psychotic anxieties. I
now offer a third way in which groups and group dynamics are at work
in the unconscious. I am thinking of recent ideas about the *'institution in
the mind'*. David Armstrong has developed other notions of Isabel
Menzies Lyth's *to locate institutional dynamics, whether benign or malign,
in the unconscious of the individual* (Armstrong, 1991, 1992).

A further group presence in the unconscious is in the notion of
'pathological organisations' in borderline psychotic states, the subject of
a burgeoning literature (Spillius, 1988, vol. 1, Part 4; Steiner, 1987, 1993;

cf. Searles, 1986, who considers these phenomena in different terms). In discussing this, Herbert Rosenfeld explicitly describes the individual as in projective identification with a *'gang in the mind'*: 'The destructive narcissism of these patients appears often highly organised, as if one were dealing with a powerful gang dominated by a leader, who control all the members of the gang to see that they support one another in making the criminal destructive work more efficient and powerful. However, the narcissistic organisation not only increases the strength of the destructive narcissism, but it has a defensive purpose to keep itself in power and so maintain the *status quo*. The main aim seems to be to prevent the weakening of the organisation and to control the members of the gang so that they will not desert the destructive organisation and join the positive parts of the self or betray the secrets of the gang to the police, the protecting superego, standing for the helpful analyst, who might be able to save the patient' (Rosenfeld, 1971, p. 174).

My aim in this chapter has been to look at a variety of conceptions of projective identification, to explore the fecundity of the concept and its operation at a number of levels of individual, group, institutional, cultural, political and international relationships. The examples I have given have, for the most part, been negative ones, and I have underemphasized the positive function of the mechanism. That aspect was emphasised in chapter four, on the special sort of projective identification called countertransference. Rosenfeld remarked that 'It is important to realise that in so far as projective identification is communicative it is a benign process, which means that the object into which projection has taken place is not changed by the projective process' (Rosenfeld, 1987, p. 160). In the container-contained relationship between mother and baby or patient and therapist, the person into whom the projection is put *is* changed, as is the projection itself, in the process of detoxification. One way of distinguishing benign from virulent projective identification is whether or not it allows experience to be thought about – for its complexity to be borne, for it to feed depressive functioning. Feldman also points out that 'projective identification may also involve good parts of the self. – projected in love, or in an attempt to protect something valuable from internal attack' (Feldman, 1992, p. 76). He goes on to make a point similar to mine on the question of degree: 'Up to a point, this process is a normal one, necessary for the satisfactory growth of our relationships, and is the basis, for example, for what we term "empathy". If it is excessive, on the other hand, there is an impoverishment of the ego, and an excessive dependence on the other person who contains all the good parts of the self' (*Ibid.*)

One of the guiding principles in my choice of examples has been to draw attention to crossover points between individual and group processes. Another has been to indicate places where it is perhaps surprising to find the group and social forces: deep in the unconscious of the individual. Finally, I have been concerned to emphasise the primitiveness and the adhesive, binding power of projective identification. Connections, once made, are not easily dislodged. That makes it a profoundly conservative mechanism, hard at work at the heart of human nature – in infants, nominal grown-ups, groups, societies, cultures, nations. It is deeply problematic for any hopes former Soviets may have for a Confederation of Independent States, much less for all our hopes that humankind may entertain for truly United Nations. No wonder it is so hard to change and no wonder that decades of willed, imposed change, for example, in Eastern Europe, can melt away as soon as military repression is removed. This is a startling example of the return of the suppressed. To revert to a mythological figure I have already mentioned, if we are to make more of benign projective identification, we must set about our task as tirelessly as Sisyphus and perhaps be prepared to accept the satisfactions of what we can accomplish along the way, rather than keeping our eyes fixed on an ultimate goal. 'There is no sun without shadow, and it is essential to know the night' (Camus, 1955, p. 91).

8 POTENTIAL SPACE: TRANSITIONAL PHENOMENA

I wish to insert here an exposition of Winnicott's ideas about culture. It could be argued that discussion of his ideas about transitional space and transitional phenomena belong in chapter two, where I examined psychoanalytic ideas about culture. Indeed, I did include a brief discussion of his ideas there. But I want to linger longer over them in this chapter, partly because I think they are lovely and partly because I want to dwell more on the topic of chapter three – the notion of mental space itself. I find Winnicott's way of writing about these matters quite congenial for rumination: good food for thought. They are an example of what they advocate: they offer space for pondering.

I'm not sure why this is so. My Kleinian friends are scathing about them. I recall an eminent Kleinian training analyst saying, rather grumpily, 'There *are* no transitional phenomena, only failed primary object relationships'. I take it that he meant that the use of objects like blankets, teddy bears, a thumb or a rag are not, after all, a constructive path from near-total dependence on maternal presence, toward relative independence on the part of the infant, but that they are a sign of a developmental failure, leading to a – hopefully temporary – fetishism. There is also a philosophical issue: for Kleinians psychoanalysis is solely about internal objects. The very idea of something that is partly internal, partly external, or of a zone or third world between the internal and the external, is to them a sloppy thinking. Yet that sense of intermediateness is exactly what I feel sitting in a theatre, listening to music, reading, watching a sunset. I cannot say where my hopes, dreams and longings end and what I am taking in from the experience begins. There is a merging, a congruence, a suspension of boundaries. I am in the theatre, *in* my mind and *in* the cultural experience – all at once as in Nanci Griffith's song, 'Dollar Matinee' (1982).

There is also a significant difference in tone and atmosphere between Winnicottian and Kleinian ideas about creativity and culture. Put simply, Winnicott treats cultural phenomena as something positive and constructive, occurring in a reparative space, mending or filling an absence or lack. Kleinians treat culture and creativity as a form of atonement, a reparation on the part of the infantile self. This reparation is an attempt to make up for the devastation caused by the phantasy attack on the mother, which is in retaliation for the sense that the mother's absence was itself an abandonment, experienced as persecution. The absence is a form of starvation, and the hunger gnaws.

One way of making the contrast stark is to say that Winnicottians learn to look after themselves, filling the space created by the mother's deliberate, loving and controlled abandonment, while reparation in the Kleinian sense is rather more like war reparations, where the infantile forces have been wilfully destructive, as we have seen in previous chapters, in particular, in the phenomena of racism and in the case of Helen Keller's satisfaction after smashing her doll, followed by an attempt to put it back together again once she had entered the realm of symbolism and culture (pp. 17–19). For a Winnicottian, cultural space is warm and loving, a fulfilment. For a Kleinian it is a move from the fragmented, persecuted, part-object world of the paranoid-schizoid position, through reparation, to the whole-object, depressive position, where responsibility and concern for others are characteristic feelings. The mood is less wholesome than relieved. For the time being, I want to place these issues in the background and explore Winnicott's ideas on their own terms. Although I am, in general, inclined toward Kleinian ideas, I find Winnicott's notions about the transitional so appealing that I want to keep them before our eyes in the hope that some sort of alliance between them will turn out to be possible.

I dare say that this brief chapter will be experienced as breaking both the flow and the mood of my argument. So be it. I know it is important, while I cannot integrate it with what I have been saying about the negative aspects of our basic natures. In the course of writing this book I have had a growing sense of having located in the psychoanalytic literature three fundamental features of human nature – psychotic anxieties, projective identification, and transitional objects and phenomena. It is tempting to call them three fundamental particles of human nature, but I wish to eschew scientistic authority, except in the loosest, metaphorical sense. If we pursue that rhetoric for a moment, I feel like the sort of scientist who has located the elements but doesn't yet know much about how the chemistry works – how they combine and interact. If we put the point more humanistically, I'm not sure how they fit into people's stories, but I am satisfied that they are basic. Moreover, I feel strongly that the way Kleinians turn their noses up at Winnicott's ideas is a mistake. Their psychology was a strong reaction to the neo-Freudian tendency to give too little weight to human destructiveness, but they left themselves with too little understanding of how and why people are constructive, loving and creative. While I was revising this book, I had an exploratory conversation with a particularly thoughtful Kleinian analyst about this, who said that reparation is simply not enough to account for all of culture. Something more – something playful and celebratory – is needed, as well. He lamented the doctrinaire unwillingness of the Kleinian establishment to make room for this idea.

I think it is fair to say that Winnicott is, at present, the most popular psychoanalyst in the world. His popular books and essays remain in print in relatively inexpensive paperbacks, while his writings for fellow-professionals are steady sellers. His broadcasts for mothers, parents, teachers are utterly accessible. The book he wrote in which he developed his original (1951) paper on transitional objects and phenomena, *Playing and Reality,* went through five printings between 1971 and 1985.

The idea put forward in that book is the most well-known of his ideas and is extraordinarily and intuitively appealing. It is that most infants have an object that they insist on having with them for a period of months or years. It is typically a rag, a pacifier, a small blanket, favourite doll or teddy bear. In Schultz' 'Peanuts' It is called Linus' 'security blanket', and he is always trailing it behind him, just as Christopher Robin trails Winnie the Pooh bump, bump down the stairs. If this object cannot be found when the family is going out for the day, there is an instant crisis. The child can't live without it. It mustn't be washed or altered, even if it becomes threadbare. The child must be allowed to abandon it in its own time and its own way. It is not mourned; it is left behind, 'relegated to the limbo of half-forgotten things at the bottom of a chest of drawers, or at the back of the toy cupboard' (Winnicott, 1989, p. 56). I should add that the 'object' need not be a thing. It can be a song, the edge of a curtain, the mother herself, an image in the mind. However, having made this point, I shall develop the idea in terms of material objects.

My experience is that everyone, on first hearing about the concept of transitional objects, immediately recognises the phenomenon in their own and their children's experience. Winnicott moves on from this anecdotal description to make large claims. He sees it as the fundamental element of culture, the way into the worlds of play, creativity, including the arts, religion and science. The ability of a child to inhabit this realm is the *sine qua non* for being a member of the civilized human race. It is the rite of passage for entering the realms of symbolism and culture.

The transitional object is not the first object, but it is the first possession. This means that it is not a Kleinian internal object, which is a concept (Winnicott, 1951, pp. 231, 237) and purely a matter of the inner world (Winnicott, 1989, p. 58). It is the first 'not-me' (Davis and Wallbridge, 1981, p. 69). It stands for the breast and is a symbolic part-object (Winnicott, 1951, pp. 231, 233). The mental space it occupies is neither subjective nor objective but partakes of both (p. 231). It develops into a space 'that is intermediate between the dream and the reality, that which is called cultural life' (Winnicott, 1965, p. 150). Cultural life is the adult equivalent of transitional phenomena of infancy, wherein communication is not referred to as subjective or objective (Winnicott, 1965, p. 184).

It is this quality of cultural life as occupying a *space* between subjective and objective that I find particularly appealing in Winnicott's thinking. Kleinians give one a very rich inner world at the expense of the outer world and allow little or nothing in between. Similarly, in traditional epistemology one is taught to think of a line between subject and object, but – as we saw in chapter four in the case of interpersonal perception and communication – this is too simple a model. What exists between subject and object is in some sense a zone and in some sense a permeable boundary with constant traffic both ways and with objects often multiply represented.

Winnicott says that in addition to the inner world and external reality 'there is the third part of the life of a human being, a part that we cannot ignore, an intermediate area of *experiencing,* to which inner reality and external life both contribute. It is an area which is not challenged, because no claim is made on its behalf except that it shall exist as a resting-place for the individual engaged in the perpetual human task of keeping inner and outer reality separate yet inter-related' (1951, p. 230). 'This third area might turn out to be the cultural life of the individual' (1989, p. 57).

It is important that it is an *area* or space. It is not the sharp boundary-maintenance referred to as reality-testing. It is intermediate: '*illusion,* that which is allowed to the infant, and which in adult life is inherent in art and religion' (*Ibid.*). He acknowledges that 'infants and children and adults take external reality in, as clothing for their dreams, and they project themselves into external objects and people and enrich external reality by their imaginative perceptions' (1989, p. 57). But he means something more than the inner world, external reality and the commerce between them: 'But I think we really do find a third area, an area of living which corresponds to the infant's transitional phenomena and which actually derives from them. In so far as the infant has not achieved transitional phenomena I think the acceptance of symbols is deficient, and the cultural life is poverty-stricken' (*Ibid.*).

What begins as a child's first possession widens out not only into 'that of play and of artistic creativity and appreciation, and of religious feeling 'and of dreaming', but also of 'fetishism, lying and stealing, the origin of loss and affectionate feeling, drug addiction, the talisman of obsessional rituals, etc.' (Davis and Wallbridge, 1981, p. 72). There is a direct development from the earliest transitional phenomena to playing, to shared playing and from this to cultural experience (p. 73). For Winnicott, this process is central to the mother's role in fostering the child's development. She must at first allow the infant the '*illusion* that her breast is part of the infant. It is, as it were, under magical control. The mother's eventual task is gradually to disillusion the infant, but she has no hope of success unless at first she has been able to give sufficient opportunity for illusion' (Winnicott, 1951, p. 238). (A Kleinian would object to the notion that the breast is ever seen as other than fully an object or part-object.)

I shall now quote at length from his original, highly evocative statement: 'It is well known that infants as soon as they are born tend to use fist, fingers, thumbs in stimulation of the oral erotogenic zone, in satisfaction of the instincts at that zone, and also in quiet union. It is also well known that after a few months infants of either sex become fond of playing with dolls, and that most mothers allow their infants some special object and expect them to become, as it were, addicted to such objects' (1951, p. 229).

'There is a wide variation to be found in sequence of events which starts within the new-born infant's fist-in-mouth activities, and that leads eventually on to an attachment to a teddy, a doll or soft toy, or to a hard toy . . . I have introduced the terms "transitional object" and "transitional phenomena" for designation of the intermediate area of experience, between the thumb and teddy bear, between the oral erotism and true object relationship, between primary creative activity and projection of what has already been introjected, between primary unawareness of indebtedness and the acknowledgement of indebtedness ("Say: ta!")' (pp. 229–30).

He then speaks about the development from playing with one's hands and lips to relating to part of a sheet, blanket or bit of cloth which is sucked or caressed. He continues, 'One may suppose that thinking, or fantasising, gets linked up with these functional experiences.

'All these things I am calling *transitional phenomena*. Also, out of all this (if we study any one infant) there may emerge some thing or some phenomenon – perhaps a bundle of wool or the corner of a blanket or eiderdown, or a word or tune, or a mannerism, which becomes vitally important to the infant for use at the time of going to sleep, and is a defence against anxiety, especially anxiety of the depressive type. Perhaps some soft object or cot cover has been found and used by the infant, and this then becomes what I am calling a *transitional object*. This object goes on being important. The parents get to know its value and carry it round when travelling. The mother lets it get dirty and even smelly, knowing that by washing it she introduces a break in continuity in the infant's experience, a break that may destroy the meaning and value of the object to the infant' (p. 232).

He suggests that the use of such objects can begin anytime between four and twelve months, purposely leaving room for variations.

'Patterns set in infancy may persist into childhood, so that the original soft object continues to be absolutely necessary at bed-time or at time of loneliness or when a depressed mood threatens. In health, however, there is a gradual extension of range of interest, and eventually the extended range is maintained, even when depressive anxiety is near. A need for a specific object or a behaviour pattern that started at a very early date may reappear at a later age when deprivation threatens' (p. 232).

The outcome of the child's relationship to this object is that 'Its fate is to be gradually allowed to be decathected, so that in the course of years it becomes not so much forgotten as relegated to limbo. By this I mean that in health the transitional object does not "go inside" nor does the feeling about it necessarily undergo repression. It is not forgotten and it is not mourned. It loses meaning, and this is because the transitional phenomena have become diffused, have become spread out over the whole intermediate territory between "inner psychic reality" and "the external world as perceived by two persons in common", that is to say, over the whole cultural field' (p. 233).

Winnicott adds, 'the term transitional object, according to my suggest-ion, gives room for the process of becoming able to accept difference and similarity. I think there is use for a term for the root of symbolism in time, a term that describes the infant's journey from the purely subjective to objectivity; and it seems to me that the transitional object (piece of blanket,

etc.) is what we see of this journey of progress towards experiencing'
(pp. 233–4).

In conclusion, he says, 'The transitional objects and transitional
phenomena belong to the realm of illusion which is at the basis of the
initiation of experience . . . This intermediate area of experience, unchal-
lenged in respect of its belonging to inner or external (shared) reality,
constitutes the greater part of the infant's experience and throughout life
is retained in the intense experiencing that belongs to the arts and to
religion and to imaginative living, and to creative scientific work' (p.242)

In this and a related paper on 'Psychoses and Child Care' (1952)
Winnicott presents diagrams which illustrate the move from illusion to the
transitional object and the epistemological space occupied by transitional
objects and phenomena (Winnicott, 1975, pp. 225, 240).

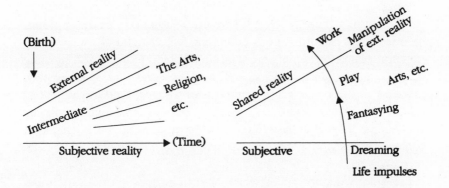

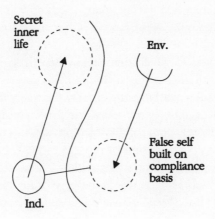

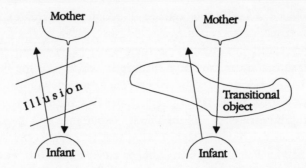

In my opinion, the lines he draws between the subjective, the transitional and the objective should be dotted, so as to indicate their permeability, rather like a cell membrane, across which all sorts of metabolites selectively move back and forth.

In reflecting on Winnicott's notions, it is important to distinguish them from fetishism, where an object is perversely substituted for the appropriate one. Critics claim that he is describing fetishism, but the answer lies in the process of consigning the transitional object to limbo and opening out the ongoing transitional space of the third world – the space of play, creative symbolism and culture. True fetishism is more rigid and is unlikely to fade without treatment or substitution of another symptom. I think that no other psychoanalyst has offered anything approaching the richness of Winnicott's description of cultural space and its ongoing links with infantile processes.

I also think that the space which opens out does not preclude other transitional objects in latency, adolescence and adulthood (see Kahne, 1967). By this I mean that having abandoned the blanket, doll or teddy, one can still attach similar significance to other objects with a less addictive intensity. The sensuous, comforting quality and the sense of something that is favourite and to which one turns when in danger of depressive anxiety applies to all sorts of special things. Everyone's list will be different, but these days walkmans have this quality for many adolescents, as do portable computer games for pre-teens and computers for adult devotees, whether they be merely enthusiastic word processors or totally committed 'hackers'. The same can be said of mountain bikes, fancy roller skates, expensive trainers, certain fashions in clothes – Champion sweatshirts and sweatpants and Timberland shoes in the case of my children.

The advertising industry is predicated on getting in touch with this area of need and comfort and can succeed brilliantly with jeans, body oils, perfumes, bath oils and cremes, shampoos and conditioners. I think the burgeoning of The Body Shop phenomenon and the need for chemists such as Boots to emulate them (all their shops revamped under the banner 'Health Care and Beauty') only makes sense if seen in the light of providing transitional satisfactions. Advertising for cars and motorcycles evokes the same quality of luxuriousness and comfort. This is particularly true of sports cars and powerbikes. The sensuous quality of Braun products (black brushed metal) and certain beers, rums and bourbons evoke the satisfactions of the transitional realm, as does Cadbury's Milk Tray (or so the advertisers would have it). For me, much the most satisfying experiences of this sort come from favourite music played on a home or in-car stereo, where one is bathed in totally enfolding sound. The experience is somehow both soothing and ecstatic, like a return to the womb, and certain pieces of music make the experience almost overwhelmingly comforting, as can certain films on video.

Apparently mundane objects can occupy the transitional realm if they are experiences by the consumer in that way. A leather personal organiser – an original Filofax or a comparable notebook – gives the illusion that one has one's life under some sort of control. In my case it literally acts as a container, a portable file for all sorts of bits of paper, reminders, addresses, phone numbers, tickets – all of which would be routinely mislaid if it were not for this lovely leather portmanteau. How otherwise can we explain the proliferation of such products and the ludicrous prices people are willing to pay for what is fundamentally a utilitarian object and some bits of paper with holes punched in them? It is useful, stylish and a metaphor for the attempt to contain in one's mind all the obligations and opportunities of a busy life.

I think all of these things can function as adult security blankets and teddy bears. I also think that the more we are deprived of deep satisfactions in an alienated society, the more we comfort ourselves with such things. I am not suggesting that favourite clothes, adornments, accessories or listening to Mahler's Eighth or Emmylou Harris and Willie Nelson singing 'Gulf Coast Highway' are not truly soul-satisfying experiences. I am suggesting, however, that we may well turn more and more to such experiences as luxurious foaming bath cremes or Jacuzzis, to Gucci shoes and gold chains, as rather sad compensations for the lack of a better quality of society and social relations. Otherwise why smile sheepishly at the slogan: 'I consume therefore I am'? (I have given further consideration to these issues in Young, 1989c.)

Think back to Meltzer's lovely description in which dimensions of mind are added, moving on from the house with no insides – a paper thin world of surfaces – to three dimensions and to the fourth one of development and the ability to learn from experience. We are now in a position to fill that space and that lifetime with – with what? With work which has moral purpose and relationships of love and concern? With lots of expensive commodities and plenty of chemical substances for highs and lows? With ambition and status? With envy and spite? Mental space and the transitional realm come with no guarantees of the quality of life. They provide only the potentiality. Winnicott's third world is a 'potential space'; what one makes of it is exquisitely contingent. What use one makes of objects depends on moral qualities that are not explicitly under consideration here.

Much has been made of Winnicott's ideas. Indeed, there is a large collection of essays covering a wide range of topics, *Between Reality and Fantasy* (Grolnick *et al.,* 1978), as well as an ongoing debate in the literature, including at least one swingeing (but, to me, unconvincing) critique: 'Transitional Objects: Idealization of a Phenomenon' (Brody, 1980).

One of the more interesting applications of the concept is a paper by André Green, 'Potential Space in Psychoanalysis: The Object in the Setting', which, among other interesting ideas, treats the psychoanalytic relationship as transitional. He says, 'Analytic technique is directed towards bringing about the capacity for play with transitional objects. The essential feature is no longer interpreting, but enabling the subject to live out creative *experiences* of a new category of objects' (Green, 1978, p. 176). 'The analytic object is neither internal (to the analysand or to the analyst), nor external (to either the one or the other), but is situated *between* the two. So it corresponds exactly to Winnicott's definition of the transitional object and to its location in the intermediate area of *potential space,* the space of "overlap" demarcated by the analytic setting. When a patient terminates his analysis, it is not only that he has *internalised* the analytic interplay, but also that he can take away with him the potential space in order to reconstitute it in the outside world, through cultural experience, through sublimation and, more generally, through the possibility of pairing or (let us rather say) of coupling' (p. 180). In the same vein, Adam Phillips suggests that a good interpretation, like a transitional object, cannot be given to a patient; it can only be offered and found meaningful (Phillips, 1988, p. 115).

Klein's biographer reports that until he wrote 'Transitional Objects and

Transitional Phenomena' in 1951, Winnicott considered himself a Kleinian. He wrote it for inclusion in the classical collection of Kleinianism, *New Directions in Psycho-Analysis* (1955). She wanted him to revise it so as to incorporate her ideas more clearly, and he refused. As far as Klein was concerned, that was the end of their relationship, although he remained committed to certain of her ideas, particularly the depressive position, while disagreeing about the death instinct, the paranoid-schizoid position and innate envy (Grosskurth, 1985, pp. 397–8; *cf.* pp. 399–400).

Klein's was a sharper, sterner view, in which we reach the stars through the bars – *ad astra per aspera* – while he, according to his wife, Claire, suffered from 'benignity' (Grosskurth, 1985, p. 399). His work is optimistic and not immersed in the ongoing, unresolvable struggle between good and evil in the human spirit. He was inclined to refer to 'capacities', with rather unclear boundaries, while she specified clear, distinct 'positions' with oscillations from moment to moment. His notion of 'good enough mothering' was anathema to her. Indeed, a latter-day Kleinian said to me contemptuously, 'What's all this about real mothers? That's not psychoanalysis, which is exclusively concerned with internal objects.' Winnicott put much more onto the environment and saw the baby-and-mother as a unity.

I cannot, at present, offer a mediation or adjudication between Kleinian object relations and Winnicottian ones. (Indeed, this is only a tiny part of a problem which seems to me not to have been seriously addressed: how *very different* the theories of the three founders of object relations were. For example, Klein saw internal objects as the *sine qua non* of having a mind, while Fairbairn saw all internal objects as pathological.) I do, however, want to hold on to the idea of a space between the inner world and the outer one. I inhabit it much of the time, I'm glad to say, and I'm not inclined to let my appreciation of Kleinian psychoanalysis lead me to abandon it, just because it's not kosher Klein. Kleinian writings on culture and aesthetics strike me as having a precious quality and indulge in an esotericism to which I find it hard to relate. They fail to do something that I think any account of human nature (or of anything, come to that) ought to do: give one back one's familiar experiences with additional illumination. I get illumination of unconscious phantasy aplenty and am glad to have it. But what about my experiences of music, film, exhibitions? I shall keep trying, but in the meantime I find this idea of transitional space good enough to be getting on with. I am glad to say that broader and deeper use of Winnicott's ideas on culture are becoming more widespread. For example, they are evident in a special issue of *The Psychoanalytic Review*, entitled *Illusion and Culture: A Tribute to Winnicott* , which contains a number of essays which are close to my own reading of the fruitfulness of his ideas on culture and epistemology (Lerner, 1992). Winnicott's ideas have been applied to literature in a collection edited by Peter Rudnytsky (1993) and to film in the work of Phyllis Creme (1991). I look forward to further developments of his ideas and to an eventual rapprochement between them and Kleinian thought. Nicola Worledge (1993) has made a promising beginning on this project.

9 MISPLACED CONCRETENESS AND HUMAN STORIES

Our humanity and civility are being squeezed from a number of directions. One is philosophical in a formal sense. That is, the legacy of the combined revolutions in science, capitalism and religion has left precious little space for thinking about our humanity which is not impoverished, reified, alienated and wretched. It would be silly and inconsistent with my own critique to think of psychoanalysis as lying completely outside these traditions, since Freud saw himself as a scientist, was philosophically sophisticated, focused on the individual in the family and was heir to the Judeo-Christian tradition. Indeed, two of the most interesting interpretative works about him (both regularly reprinted) are Philip Rieff *Freud: The Mind of the Moralist* (1960) and David Bakan's *Freud and the Jewish Mystical Tradition* (1958). I mention these studies, concerned, respectively, with the central roles of morality and Judaism in his work, lest it be thought that the strand of scientism is dominant in Freud. I see his work as profoundly *of* its culture and involving scientific, philosophical, humanistic, moral and religious strands.

My aim in the foregoing chapters has been to explore the ways we think about the inner world in the hope of helping to make our ways of doing so more congenial, more capacious, more constructive and more hopeful. But even when we try to free our notions from a reifying scientism we come up against what Freud would call realism but feels, to me at least, like extreme pessimism, though, if it is realistic, it behoves us to know what we are up against. This is the second direction whence comes constriction of our humanity and civility. In the concluding section of chapter two I said that worse to come from Bion and other Kleinians, and I have sought to add that perspective in chapters five, six and seven, in which I have characterised the forces which constrain and constrict mental space and thereby eliminate or pollute our capacity to live constructively, generously, hopefully.

Put simply, Bion and other followers of Melanie Klein have argued that primitive, psychotic processes play a much larger role in our lives – especially in groups, institutions and culture – than was evident in classical Freudianism. This is another way of saying that the primitive is never transcended. One could say that the essence of the Freudian position is that the bulwarks of civilization are designed to keep at bay something which is crazy enough, thank you: polymorphously perverse sexuality, in particular, incest. But the Kleinian position emphasises something even more primitive and claims that much, if not most, of our group behaviour and institutional arrangements are quite specifically and exquisitely designed to avoid consciously experiencing psychotic anxiety. Moreover, psychotic processes are in danger of breaking through from moment to moment. Since the structure of groups and institutions makes up a large portion of the extended sense of culture I outlined in chapter two, these findings should be integrated with psychoanalytic ideas about 'high' and popular culture.

As we have seen, the psychoanalytic writers who have had most to say about these matters are Bion, Elliott Jaques, and Isabel Menzies Lyth. Much of their work had been admirably summarized and illustrated in R. D. Hinshelwood's *What Happens in Groups,* while his *A Dictionary of Kleinian Thought* provides the best single source of understanding of Kleinian concepts. A useful summary of this way of thinking, which shows clearly how it connects to Freud's writings on groups and culture, is the conclusion to Bion's contribution to the book from which Winnicott's paper on transitional phenomena was excluded, *New Directions in Psychoanalysis: The Significance of Infant Conflict in the Pattern of Adult Behaviour* (Klein *et al.,* 1955). Bion's essay, 'Group Dynamics: A Review' summarises pioneering work he did with soldiers during World War Two and which he carried on at the Tavistock Institute of Human Relations. It is no exaggeration to say that it laid the foundations for the tradition of 'group relations' work which has inspired (with other contributions) over twenty institutions around the world, for example, The Grubb Institute, The A. K. Rice Institute, The Australian Institute of Social Administration.

The ideas in this essay were distilled from a series of papers which he collected in his classic, *Experiences in Groups* (1961) and which have been described and quoted above (pp. 86–7, 136). He concludes the essay by saying, 'To recapitulate: any group of individuals met for work shows group activity, that is mental activity designed to further the task in hand'

(Bion, 1955, p. 476; 1961, p. 188). I think of such people operating within the boundaries of civilized behaviour, sublimating, suffering guilt, getting on with it. But the veneer of civilization is thinner and more vulnerable than we may have thought. Group processes evoke psychotic anxieties appertaining to primitive part-object relations and are 'the source of emotional drives to aims far different either from the overt task of the group or even from the tasks that would appear to be appropriate to Freud's view of the group as based on the family group' (Bion, 1955, p. 474).

I shall now sketch Bion's three basic assumptions, but it is not part of my purpose to explore them. I am at present concentrating on the *kind* and *level* of feelings and their relations with classical Freudian ideas of the inner world. The first basic assumption is *dependency*: 'that the group is met in order to be sustained by a leader on whom it depends for nourishment, material and spiritual, and protection' (p. 444). The basic assumption of *pairing* involves a Messianic hope that something or someone as-yet unborn, not-yet present or not yet in role will save the group 'from feelings of hatred, destructiveness and despair, of its own or of another group, but in order to do this, obviously the Messianic hope must never be fulfilled' (pp. 446–8). The third basic assumption is *fight or flight*: 'that the group has met to fight something or run away from it' (p. 448), the emotions appropriate to the physiological emergency response of the sympathetic nervous system, energised by adrenaline. He contends that 'panic flight and uncontrolled attack are really the same' (p. 469). Menzies Lyth comments that 'They have in common massive splitting and projective identification, loss of individual distinctiveness or depersonalization, diminution of effective contact with reality, lack of belief in progress and development through work and suffering' (Menzies Lyth, 1959, p. 21).

Bion stresses that these are in no way voluntary, conscious reactions: 'Participation in basic assumption activity requires no training, experience or mental development. It is instantaneous, inevitable and instinctive . . . ' (Bion, 1955, p. 449; cf. p. 458). All of the basic assumptions involve a leader, but this need not be a person; it could be an idea or inanimate object (p. 450). When the 'leader' *is* a person, he or she 'is as much the creature of the basic assumption as any other member of the group . . . The "loss of individual distinctiveness" applies to the leader of the group as much as to anyone else – a fact which probably accounts for some of the posturing to which leading figures are prone' (p. 467).

These defensive actions derive from group processes which lead individuals to regress. Once again, he places the main emphasis on the primitiveness of the reactions: 'It will be seen from this description that the basic assumptions now emerge as formations secondary to an extremely early primal scene worked out on a level of part objects, and associated with psychotic anxiety and mechanisms of splitting and projective identification . . . characteristic of the paranoid-schizoid and depressive positions. Introjection and projection of the group, which is now the feared investigator, now the feared object of investigation, form an essential part of the picture and help to add confusion to the scene unless recognised as being very active' (p. 457).

In my critique of Freud's reductionism I lamented his swingeing reductionism of group, social and cultural phenomena to the familial and to the interplay of id, ego and superego. Bion shares Freud's view but insists that the true sources lie even deeper in the individual, as indicated above. He adds here, in a footnote which partly anticipates his conclusions, that 'there are aspects of group behaviour which appear strange unless there is some understanding of M. Klein's work on the psychoses' (p. 461n).

In the very next chapter in *New Directions*, 'Social Systems as Defence Against Persecutory and Depressive Anxiety', Elliott Jaques draws on Kleinian ideas in the context of his research in industry. He begins by commenting that 'many social phenomena show a striking correspond-ence with psychotic processes in individuals'; that 'institutions are used by their individual members to reinforce individual mechanisms of defence against anxiety, and in particular against recurrence of the early paranoid and depressive anxieties'; that mechanisms of projective and introjective identification operate in linking individual and social behav-iour; and he puts forward the hypothesis that '*one* of the primary cohesive elements binding individuals into institutionalised human association is that of defence against psychotic anxiety' (Jaques, 1955, pp. 478–9).

Jaques starts out from Freud's ideas in *Group Psychology and the Analysis of the Ego* (1921), in particular, the phenomenon of identification with the leader and other members of the group. He quotes Freud on how primitive this mechanism is: 'identification is known to psycho-analysis as the earliest expression of an emotional tie with another person' (Jaques, 1955, p. 480). He also refers to Paula Heimann's claim 'that introjection and projection may lie at the bottom of even the most complex social processes' (p. 481). We are immersed here in the alimentary view of experience, knowledge and culture discussed in chapter three. Once again, all knowledge is mediated by the mother's body; the primitive is never transcended and continues to operate. Heimann says, 'Such taking in and expelling consists of an active interplay between the organism and the outer world; on this primordial pattern rests all intercourse between subject and object, no matter how complex and sophisticated such intercourse appears. (I believe that in the last analysis we may find it at the bottom of all our complicated dealings with one another)' (quoted by Jaques, 1955, p. 481n).

Jaques' model emphasises the role of unconscious defences: 'I shall try to show how individuals make unconscious use of institutions by associating in these institutions and unconsciously co-operating to reinforce internal defences against anxiety and guilt. These social defences bear a reciprocal relationship with the internal defence mechanisms. For instance, the schizoid and manic defences against anxiety and guilt both involve splitting and projection mechanisms, and, through projection, a link with the outside world. When external objects are shared with others and used in common for purposes of projection, phantasy social relationships may be established through projective identification with the common object. These phantasy relationships are further elaborated by introjection; and the two-way character of social relationships is mediated by virtue of the two-way play of projective and introjective identification' (pp. 481–2).

You will recall that Meltzer made relinquishing excessive projective identification the prerequisite for attaining mental four-dimensionality, i. e., a mind with the capacity to contain experience and to develop. He also argued that since Klein first described the mechanism, her followers had come to see it as '*the* mechanism of narcissistic identification and could be confidently looked to as the basis of hypochondria, confusional states, claustrophobia, paranoia, psychotic depression and perhaps some psycho-somatic disorders' (Meltzer *et al.*, 1975, p. 228). He sees it as 'the mechanism par excellence of narcissistic identification in a three-dimensional world' (*Ibid*). In a lecture given in 1990, he added that it is used as *the* defence against schizophrenic breakdown by excessively conformist, ambitious and competitive adherents to institutions – people who inhabit a world of projective identification which he calls 'the claustrum', inside the anus. Introjective identification, by contrast, is described as 'coming into play to raise the mental life out of the sphere of narcissism in specific connection with four-dimensionality' (Meltzer *et al.*, 1975, p. 228).

I can think of no more convincing and sobering example of Bion's (and Jaques' – see above pp. 87–8) conclusions than Isabel Menzies Lyth's classic study of group dynamics in nursing, aspects of which were considered in chapter seven. After Bion's *Experiences in Groups,* this is probably, and rightly, the best-known piece of research to emerge from the work of the Tavistock Institute of Human Relations. Combined with her other Kleinian investigations of social and institutional settings, her collected papers constitute, in my opinion, the most important body of psychoanalytic work on the social bearings of the psyche. She has turned her approach to such diverse topics as the wearing of crash helmets on motorcycles, the dynamics of the Fire Brigade, family patterns of consumption and the fantasies surrounding ice cream, conflicts between psychiatric hospitals and the communities they serve (Menzies Lyth, 1988, 1989).

The intimate and confidential nature of much of the research she has undertaken means that it is often difficult and sometimes impossible to publish her findings. For example, she was asked by the British Psycho-Analytic Society to look into the structure and consequences of its fifty-year-long compromise, whereby the training and committee structure of the Institute should be balanced so as to protect the interests of all three of the prevailing tendencies: Contemporary (or Anna) Freudian, Kleinian and Independent Groups. Her brief, presumably, was to look into the consequences of this long-standing 'gentlemen's (actually ladies') agreement' to see if it may be appropriate to make other arrangements, perhaps even to dissolve the groups and attempt to function as a single group with a mixture of tendencies and beliefs. The prevailing structure was created in order to avoid a split in the Society in the wake of the acrimonious Controversial Discussions between the followers of Melanie Klein and Anna Freud and those who had no wish to be followers of either woman There is no doubt that the present arrangements – whereby there is representation of each group on all main committees and training involves a commitment to one group with exposure to the ideas of the others – has kept a species of peace. There is also no doubt that the British Psycho-Analytic Society has been remarkably prolific of ideas and has had (perhaps unique) world-wide influence throughout the period of this pact. It could be argued, however, that there are sclerotic aspects of the structure and that it institutionalises conflicts, projections and reprojections which might otherwise wane.

We may never know what she has discovered and recommended. I am told that it is unlikely that her findings will ever be published. On the other hand, there is a precedent in the publication of the original Controversial Discussions half a century after they began (King and Steiner, 1991). There is more in this example than gossip. First, this investigation is an excellent example of the work at which she excels, and the whole psychoanalytic culture stands to benefit from her counsel, even if her report remains confidential. Second, it illustrates – with wonderful irony – that psychoanalysts (and psychotherapists, for that matter) are not immune to the processes that they investigate. As Bion pointed out, the therapist or leader in group processes is not immune to such processes. He said elsewhere that the problem in analysis is like that in war: somehow to manage to think under fire.

It is a feature of analytic institutions that they exhibit the same factionalism, splits and other forms of primitive processes that other institutions do. A prominent non-Kleinian member of the British Psychoanalytical society is fond of saying that there was something 'really crazy' about the Controversial Discussions. It has always struck me that this is the simple truth, and it would be unsurprising to him if he was a Kleinian. This problem of 'physicians' who cannot heal themselves is particularly ironic in the case of the group relations movement. It turns out that the world centre of such researches – The Tavistock Institute of Human Relations – underwent a series of the very kind of splits that its members were renowned for illuminating in their research and consultancy work. My response to this is ambivalent. Part of me is sad and sardonic and asks how one could have thought it would be otherwise. Doctors are notoriously bad patients, and people who have insight about others when in role cannot be expected to be so good at it when outside the consulting room or consultancy role. But another voice says that it reflects on psychoanalysis and the group relations movement – consummately reflexive disciplines – if their practitioners behave in their institutions as badly as lay people and if group relations consultants cannot conduct civil group relations in *their* own institutions. The truth is that they have had acrimonious splits, with lamentable departures of key personnel, some of whom have remained embittered. The analogy which occurs to me is those evangelical preachers who keep getting caught at the very forms of sinnin' that they so vehemently denounce from their pulpits. This is not, of course, only ironic, since we set out to help others in the spheres where we are – or have been – troubled and hopefully have made some progress, however fragile.

One might think that institutions explicitly designed for the enhancement of human welfare and the alleviation of suffering would be altruistic through and through. Put another way, one might hope that the 'helping professions' would be helpful in their institutional arrangements. Yet another formulation, which would seem only common sense, is that 'the first duty of a hospital is not to spread disease'. Yet that is exactly what Menzies Lyth's most celebrated study shows that they do – not bacteria and viruses, mind you, but something as distressing: defences against potentially overwhelming feelings which lead to inhumanity.

I worked for a number of years as a psychiatric aide, nurse and medical student, before I began teaching in a university and medical school. I was appalled by the rigidity, thoughtlessness, even callousness and cruelty I saw and – to some extent – got caught up in. I did not stay in any role or institution long enough to become fully socialised into a professional identity, but my distress about these matters has remained fresh in my mind. I am sorry to say that when I was subsequently in institutions long enough to gain some insight into their dynamics, they have always had a large component of the features described by the writers on group relations. I have found this in medical and academic institutions, cultural politics, television, publishing and the subculture of psychoanalysis and psychotherapy, especially their training institutions (Young, 1981, 1986, 1990a, 1993a, 1993b). Lest it be thought that I am taking swipes, I remind the reader that distressing factional and personal relations were characteristic of Freud's inner circle, as Phyllis Grosskurth has shown (1991). But the same can be said of the building of the great civil engineering projects in and around New York City (Caro, 1974) and of the political process in the United States (Caro, 1983, 1990) and of espionage (Wright, 1987) and of making movies (McClintick, 1982; Bach, 1985; Boorman, 1985).

It was always thus. What has changed is people's willingness to write about such matters in a way which is not idealised and not merely prurient. I have had occasion to work closely with many Victorian lives and letters, where a veil was drawn over the intimate relationships and unadmirable aspects of great men (Young, 1987). It was a breath of fresh air when Lytton Strachey began writing biography which gave due weight to people's less admirable qualities (1918). I believe that writings about people and their milieus has benefited greatly by a more balanced rendition of the mixture of Eros and Thanatos in their characters and careers, even though opinions will differ about the authors' motives – to tell as much of the full truth as they can (Lash, 1971, 1980; Hodges, 1983; Grosskurth 1985; Branden, 1986; Gay, 1988; Sutherland, 1989; Brady, 1990; Monk, 1990; Richardson, 1991; McBride, 1992) to be iconoclastic (Goldman, 1981, 1988), to criticise (Bower, 1991; Cannon, 1991; von Hoffman, 1988) to make lots of money (Kelly, 1986, 1991). I believe that reading biographies which let it all hang out helps my clinical work as well as being illuminating and entertaining. They also make the point that lives are stories, narratives lived inside history and subject to a whole variety of determinations which are not reducible to a single, scientistic account of basic mental mechanisms. For reasons which this whole book has sought to make attractive and persuasive, I believe that the training and the reading habits of psychoanalysts and psychotherapists would do well to include a significant component of biographical reading. Biographies and accounts of activities like making movies or surviving as a hostage certainly make it abundantly clear that containment and the lack of it are not the exclusive prerogatives of the analytic consulting room. Human nature should be told about in human stories, told as fully as one can manage. One of the conclusions toward which my entire account in these pages has been meandering is the advocacy of narrative and story telling as more illuminating than formalistic and scientistic accounts. Narrative, sensitively crafted, is the epitome of evocative knowledge.

A flood of light was cast on the complex and distressing relations between individuals and institutions which I had experiences in various contexts when I read Menzies Lyth's study of the institutional arrangements in the nursing service of a general teaching hospital in London. Among the problems that led to commissioning the study was the high dropout rate among trainees and those who completed the training. This amounted to a wastage rate of 30–50% in various hospitals (Menzies Lyth, 1959, p. 61), and those who left were among the most sympathetic nurses. There were also problems in the internal arrangements which threatened a complete breakdown in the system of allocation of practical work (p. 45).

What she discovered is what we would expect from the work of Bion (her analyst) and Jaques (on whose work hers was modelled): nursing is highly stressful work which evokes primitive anxieties, so that the institution will go to absurd lengths to avoid its staff having to experience them. The trainees are socialised into these arrangements, however bizarre and inhuman they seem, because they unconsciously want a place to hide from psychic pain.

'The objective situation confronting the nurse bears a striking resemblance to the phantasy situations that exist in every individual in the deepest and most primitive levels of the mind. The intensity and complexity of the nurse's anxieties are to be attributed primarily to the peculiar capacity of the objective features of her work to stimulate afresh these early situations and their accompanying emotions' (pp. 46–7). She provides a lucid exposition of the parallel between the infant's developmental experiences and their revival in the stressful, existentially life-threatening hospital setting. I shall not attempt to summarise her account but heartily commend it to the reader.

The accumulated, relentless evocations of infantile anxieties lead members of the organisation to develop 'socially-structured defence mechanisms, which appear as elements in the organisation's structure, culture and mode of functioning' (p. 30). Menzies Lyth spells out the relationship between the individual and the institution. Individual defences come to match those of the social defence system. If the discrepancy is too great, some breakdown between individual and institution 'is inevitable' (p. 73), whether it be illness, acting out, becoming a rebel, getting expelled/sacked, leaving. The chances of an individual bringing about reform are slight, and those of a group doing so are remote.

I shall list the defensive techniques she discovered and then add a few examples: splitting up the nurse-patient relationship; depersonalization, categorisation, and denial of the significance of the individual; detachment and denial of feelings; the attempt to eliminate decisions by ritual task-performance; reducing the weight of responsibility in decision-making by checks and counter-checks; collusive social redistribution of responsibility and irresponsibility; purposeful obscurity in the formal distribution of responsibility; the reduction of the impact of responsibility by delegation to superiors; idealisation and underestimation of personal development possibilities; avoidance of change (pp. 51–63).

Two examples rang painfully true to my own experience. The first falls under the category of 'depersonalization, categorisation, and denial of the significance of the individual'. 'The protection afforded by the task-list system is reinforced by a number of other devices that inhibit the development of a full person-to-person relationship between nurse and patient, with its consequent anxiety. The implicit aim of such devices, which operate both structurally and culturally, may be described as a kind of depersonalisation or elimination of individual distinctiveness in both nurse and patient. For, example, nurses often talk about patients not by name, but by bed numbers or by their disease or a diseased organ: "the liver in bed 10" or "the pneumonia in bed 15". Nurses themselves deprecate this practice, but it persists. Nor should one underestimate the difficulties of remembering the names of, say, thirty patients on a ward, especially the high-turnover wards' (p. 52). The patient is not seen as whole person needing care but a number, an illness, or a damaged part of the body, that is, 'a part-object only, the retreat into part-objects being another feature Bion attributes to basic assumption group phenomena' (Menzies Lyth, 1969, p. 16).

A similar depersonalization occurs for the hospital staff through the use of identical uniforms with a rigid hierarchy of roles and tasks appropriate to various levels of seniority. The nurses *become* their roles and skills, and are thereby experienced and experience themselves less as individuals: charge nurse, staff, student, aide. Like a soldier or policeman, they are cloaked in their uniforms and positions in society and are thereby more respectable (one of Florence Nightingale's intentions), while both less vulnerable and less accessible. The starch is a powerful barrier; so are the colours of the uniforms and their quasi-military markings. The bizarre hats are part of a code whereby those in the know can locate a nurse's training hospital in the complex culture of the hierarchy of trainings, like a college or club tie or the insignia of a nun's order.

The problem of depersonalization is made even more acute by the fact that shortages – due to the factors here described – lead to increased use of agency nurses who are quite often present on a given ward for a single shift and in an entirely different hospital the next working day. Callousness can also be born of boredom and doing routine tasks with only prostrate bodies for company. If one is sitting alone in a recovery room waiting for a patient to come round from an anaesthetic, conversation from a passing colleague is very welcome and unlikely to take account of the fact that the patient may be taking in what is said as he or she regains consciousness. When I was thirteen, I was wheeled in my bed from my hospital room for a test. On the way back, when the nurses pushing the bed thought I was asleep or unconscious, they were discussing my alarmingly low pulse and respiration rates and speculating that I would not survive another night. Once I realised what was being said, I kept quiet for fear of being caught eavesdropping.

My second example is of underemployment of nurses and getting them to do stupid things. This is the example always cited from the paper, because it is so familiar to people who have spent time in hospitals. Hospital routines are 'routinely' followed slavishly to the point that common sense utterly disappears: 'Underemployment of this kind stimulates anxiety and guilt, which are particularly acute when under-employment implies failing to use one's own capacities fully in the service of other people in need. Nurses find the limitations of their performance very frustrating. They often experience a painful sense of failure when they have faithfully performed their prescribed tasks, and express guilt and concern about incidents in which they have carried out instructions to the letter but, in so doing, have practised what they consider to be bad nursing. For example, a nurse had been told to give a patient who had been sleeping badly a sleeping draught at a certain time. In the interval he had fallen into a deep natural sleep. Obeying her orders, she woke him up to give him the medicine. Her common sense and judgement told her to leave him asleep and she felt very guilty that she had disturbed him' (p. 69).

In industry this is called 'working to rule' and is considered to border on industrial sabotage. Doing *exactly* what one is told is a characteristic of the roles of prisoners, people in the military and children under the yoke of particularly authoritarian parents. And to follow orders to the letter, without using one's discretion and common sense, very frequently leads to disaster, which is why so much slapstick comedy illustrates this form of revenge against silly rules and rulers. The outstretched hands, accompanied with a shrug and a look of pseudo-innocence, completes the moment of Oedipal triumph, just before the chase by the would-be punisher begins. Having been addressed like an idiot and told to do 'exactly as I say', one then behaves like a fool, thereby protecting the vulnerable, sensible self from further humiliation. Charlie Chaplin, Harold Lloyd, Stan Laurel and Lou Costello got some of their most reliable laughs this way.

The defences described here and in the essays by Bion and Jaques do not, to say the least, bring out or reflect the best in people. 'These defences are oriented to the terrifying situations of infancy, and rely heavily on violent splitting which dissipates the anxiety. They avoid the experience of anxiety and effectively prevent the individual from confronting it. Thus the individual cannot bring the content of the phantasy anxiety situations into effective contact with reality. Unrealistic or pathological anxiety cannot be differentiated from realistic anxiety arising from real dangers. Therefore, anxiety tends to remain permanently at a level determined more by the phantasies than by the reality. The forced introjection of the hospital defence system therefore perpetuates in the individual a considerable degree of pathological anxiety' (pp. 74–5).

My reaction to this outcome is to feel that we have been here before – in Whitehead and Burtt's descriptions, discussed in chapter one, of the impoverishing effect on our humanity of the reifications of the scientific world view: the Cartesian ontological dualism of mind and body and the associated epistemological dualism of subject and object. The problems I have been discussing here take us full circle and back to the question of finding a place for our humanity in a world of material, extended substances and descriptions of mind as analogous to the conceptual languages of the natural sciences. Indeed, the effect on our humanity is surprisingly parallel to the effects of scientific reductionism. In the passage immediately following the one quoted above, Menzies Lyth points out that the effect of these defences is, in effect, *to push the nurse out of the symbolic and cultural realm:* 'The enforced introjection and use of such defences also interferes with the capacity for symbol-formation' (p. 75). She refers us to a previous passage about pathological *symbolic equation.* Through the projection of infantile phantasy situations into current work situations, 'the individual sees elements of the phantasy situations in the objective situations that come to symbolise the phantasy situations. Successful mastery of the objective situations gives reassurance about the mastery of the phantasy situations. To be effective, such symbolisation requires that the symbol *represents* the phantasy object, but *is not equated* with it. Its own distinctive, objective characteristics must also be recognized and used. If, for any reason, the symbol and the phantasy object become almost completely equated, the anxieties aroused by the phantasy object are aroused in full intensity by the symbolic object. The symbol then ceases to perform its function in containing and modifying anxiety' (p. 49) 'The defences inhibit the capacity for creative, symbolic thought, for abstract thought, and for conceptualisation. They inhibit the full development of the individual's understanding, knowledge and skills that enable reality to be handled effectively and pathological anxiety mastered. Thus the individual feels helpless in the face of new or strange tasks or problems. The development of such capacities presupposes considerable psychic integration, which the social defence system inhibits. It also inhibits self-knowledge and understanding, and with them realistic assessment of performance' (p. 75).

Once again, I have the strong feeling that we have been here before. She has given, quite independently as far as I know, a description of the institutional equivalent of Whitehead's fallacy of misplaced concreteness (above, ch. 1), whereby *abstractions are created for a quite distinct purpose, but that purpose is forgotten and one becomes stuck with them and equates them with reality, substituting them for direct experience, which comes to be experienced in terms of the equation between that set of abstractions and reality itself.*

At the heart of both Whitehead's and Menzies Lyth's critiques lies a single humanistic impulse. In her case, the infantile phantasy situations are symbolically equated with the realistic situations (pp. 49–50), while in his 'we have mistaken our abstractions for concrete realities' (Whitehead, 1925, p. 69). Life and mind thereby become impoverished to the point that our humanity is squeezed out of the conceptual scheme of modern thought, leading to a scientized form of psychoanalysis in which structures, forces, energies, economics, biological development and adaptation come to replace resonant accounts of people's lives. The parallel in institution-alised defence systems has been movingly described in her account of the world of nursing (and in others; see especially 'Action Research in a Long-Stay Hospital', 1987). In my view, this form of impoverishment is the consequence of the same set of impulses which framed the conceptual scheme of the modern era, whereby our humanity was brought to conform to a set of arrangements which subordinated individual consciousness and welfare to the requirements of a mode of production that placed order, quantification and profit before human welfare. The Scientific Revolution, Capitalism and Protestantism brought us to this pass, so it should not be surprising to find astonishingly congruent critiques by profound analysts of different aspects of the overall system – Whitehead and Burtt on the philosophical basis of the external world and Bion, Jaques and Menzies Lyth on the social bearings of the most primitive aspects of the inner world.

In a passage immediately preceding the ones quoted above, Menzies Lyth recalls a thought of Fenichel (1945) which perfectly echoes, with respect to institutional arrangements, the notion of misplaced concreteness as applied to the scientific world view: 'He states that social institutions arise through the efforts of human beings to satisfy their needs, but that social institutions then become external realities comparatively inde-pendent of individuals which affect the structure of the individual' (Menzies Lyth, 1959, p. 74).

Are they *so* independent that the despair one might derive from Freud's pessimism, driven deeper by the role of psychotic anxieties in the erection of our group relations and institutions, should lead to a truculent stoicism? I hope not.

It is time to take stock and conclude. I began in chapter one by pointing out the baleful consequences of Cartesian dualism in modern thought and drew particular attention to the fact that mind, feelings and the personal realm were left with no language of their own within the scientific world view. I drew on the writings of Burtt and Whitehead to show just how fundamental this problem is in the metaphysical foundations of our ontology and epistemology. Both were quite explicit about the disastrous effects of success in physics for being able to think about beauty and human nature. The history of attempts to represent mental phenomena is one of analogies drawn from physics, chemistry, biology and other formalistic disciplines which are scientistic, for example, linguistics and systems theory. Orthodox psychoanalysis has been no exception to this rule, and the use of concepts of force, energy, cathexis, etc. became fashionable in orthodox Freudian and neo-Freudian accounts of the inner world. The other domain in which people have thought about themselves is the humanities, and this made up some of the most profound dimensions of Freud's thought and has been reasserting itself in recent claims that narratives and stories can and should lie at the heart of the psychoanalytic project, just as it does the best of other branches of the humanities and what is often, contradictorily and confusingly called 'the human sciences'.

I next offered accounts of culture drawn from psychoanalysis and drew attention to the regrettable reductionism in Freud's own analysis of civilisation and its discontents. The argument could have stopped there and turned away from psychoanalysis for illumination of group, social and cultural phenomena. I want to repeat here that I in no sense wish to claim that psychoanalysis can do the work of historical, ideological, social, cultural, economic and political analysis. On the other hand, I do think that by going deeper than the Freudian level we can gain much more insight into these matters than might be thought. By that I mean that when we recombine psychoanalytic and other modes of discourse, psycho-analysis will make a more subtle and profound contribution to a full account. In the succeeding chapters I attempted to do just that by analysing concepts which I believe to be foundational for a non-scientistic account of psychoanalysis: countertransference, psychotic anxieties, projective identification, transitional objects and phenomena and the exploration of these concepts a work in group and social settings, in particular, institutions, racism and virulent nationalism.

There is a congruence between what the reductionist side of Cartesian dualism and the reductionist tradition in psychoanalysis do to our humanity, on the one hand, and what psychotic anxieties and the defences we mount against them do to individuals and groups, on the other. That is the beauty of the example from Menzies-Lyth given above, When I said at two points, 'We have been here before', I was drawing attention to that congruence between three forms of alienation, reification and misplaced concreteness: in the modern world view, in psychoanalytic theory and in the effects of primitive defences on people in stressful institutional settings.

It should be obvious from the examples I have used and the texts I have drawn upon that I believe that Kleinian ideas are relatively free from scientistic and mechanistic reductionism which characterises much of orthodox and neo-Freudian theory. This strong bias on my part will put some people off, even though one of my motives in writing about them was to make them more accessible and attractive. Regardless of whether I have succeeded or failed in that aim, my general point about mental space does not depend on my Kleinian perspective. I think it does depend on turning away from physicalist analogies, and I have found Kleinian ideas very resonant with my own personal and therapeutic experience. I also think that any body of ideas which promises to help us must be one which looks deeper into human desperation in an attempt to account for our destructive and desperate feelings and activities.

I want to turn, in closing, to the work of Richard Rorty (who was my first philosophy tutor), which I make no pretence of summarising, since, like that of so many writers I have mentioned in the foregoing chapters, I'd much prefer to entice you into reading. My reason for doing so is that I want to end on a note of pointing to broader horizons for the ideas I have been advocating, and I believe that his perspective is very hopeful and enabling. His writings bear on the philosophical status of the system of ideas I was outlining and criticising in chapter one. He has set out to persuade his growing audience that there is a perfectly credible alternative to systematic and scientistic philosophy. He urges us to see such ideas as just another way of framing reality and sets alongside it *edifying* writers who place narrative prose, stories, and just plain yarns on a par with the intimidating systematics and abstruse philosophising of the world view of modern science and the framers of scientistic analogies in the human sciences and humanities. As I have said, he argues that truth is made, not found, that poetry and metaphor are as valid as any other path to the illumination and edification of human nature.

In a powerful and brilliant essay on 'The Contingency of Selfhood' (Rorty, 1989, ch. 2), he attributes to Freud profound support for the humanistic, as opposed to the scientistic, way of thinking. His text is an extended reflection on the last part of a poem by Philip Larkin (p. 23):

> And once you have walked the length of your mind, what
> you command is as clear as a lading-list.
> Anything else must not, for you, be thought
>   To exist.
>
> And what's the profit? Only that, in time
> We half-identify the blind impress
> All our behavings bear, may trace it home.
>   But to confess,

> On that green evening when our death begins,
> Just what it was, is hardly satisfying,
> Since it applied only to one man once,
>   And that one dying.

Having explored the competing claims of different ways of framing the individual and having concluded that none should be seen as truer or more basic than the others, he comments: 'Strong poetry, common-sense morality, revolutionary morality, normal science, revolutionary science, and the sort of idiosyncratic fantasy which is intelligible to only one person, are all, from a Freudian point of view, different ways of dealing with blind impresses: or, more precisely ways of dealing with different blind impresses – impresses which may be unique to an individual or common to the members of some historically-conditioned community. None of these strategies is privileged over others in the sense of expressing human nature better' (pp. 37–8).

Rorty wants to undermine the privileged standing of systematic, formal and scientistic thought and give at least equal warrant to poetry and fiction: 'The final victory of poetry in its ancient quarrel with philosophy – the final victory of metaphors of self-creation over metaphors of discovery – would consist in our becoming reconciled to the thought that this is the only sort of power over the world that we can hope to have. For that would be the final abjuration of the notion that truth, and not just power and pain, is to be found "out there"' (p. 40).

I find this inspiring, and it confers on mental space a liberation from Cartesian dualism and scientism which is profoundly human, but the price of this abjuration is that the depressive position requires that pain of contingency be borne in the mixture of experiences and concern for others. It cannot be avoided by system, formalism, groups or institutions, unless one is prepared to pay the price of impoverishment of experience, diminished imagination and debased culture. To my own decades-long period of rumination of Willie Nelson's lines (1981):

> You'd think me loco
> To rub for a geenie
> While burning my hand on the lamp

I now have to say yes to all three: yes, loco; yes, rubbing; yes, burned. The geenie may not have appeared, but the lamp is burnished.

BIBLIOGRAPHY

Place of publication is London unless otherwise specified.
(* indicates edition quoted in text)

Abercrombie, M. L. J. (1960) *The Anatomy of Judgement: an Investigation into the Processes of Perception and Reasoning.* Hutchinson; reprinted Free Association Books, 1989.

Alexandris, Athina and Vaslamatzis, Grigoris, eds. (1993) *Countertransference: Theory, Technique, Teaching.* Karnac.

Amacher, Peter (1965) *Freud's Neurological Education and Its Influence on Psychoanalytic Theory. Psychological Issues* Vol. 4 no. 4, Monograph 16. International Universities Press.

Anderson, Benedict (1983) *Imagined Communities: Reflections on the Origin and Spread of Nationalism.* Verso.

Anderson, Robin, ed. (1992), *Clinical Lectures on Klein and Bion.* Routledge.

Anon. (1902) 'Phrenology', in *The New Volumes of the Encyclopedia Britannica, constituting . . . the Tenth Edition.* Edinburgh: Black, 1902, vol. 31, pp. 709–10.

Anthias, Floya (1990 'Race and Class Revisited – Conceptualising Race and Racisms', *Sociol. Rev.* 38: 19–43.

Anzieu, Didier (1984) *The Group and the Unconscious.* Routledge & Kegan Paul.

Appignanesi, Lisa, ed. (1989) *Postmodernism: ICA Documents.* Free Association Books.

Arendt, Hannah (1963) *Eichmann in Jerusalem: A Report on the Banality of Evil.* N. Y.: Viking Penguin; revised and enlarged, 1965; reprinted Harmondsworth: Penguin, 1977.

Armstrong, David (1991) 'The "Institution in the Mind": Reflections on the Relation of Psycho-analysis to Work with Institutions', paper read to the conference on Psychoanalysis and the Public Sphere, Polytechnic of East London, 1–2 November.

—— (1992) 'Names, Thoughts and Lies: the Relevance of Bion's Later Writings for Understanding Experiences in Groups', *Free Assns.* (no. 26) 3: 261–82.

Atkinson, R. L. *et al.* (1990) *Introduction to Psychology,* 10th ed. Harcourt Brace Janovich.

Bach, Steven (1985) *Final Cut: Dreams and Disaster in the Making of Heaven's Gate.* Cape.

Bakan, David (1958) *Sigmund Freud and the Jewish Mystical Tradition.* N. Y.: Schocken; reprinted Free Association Books, 1990.

Banton, Michael (1987) *Racial Theories.* Cambridge.

Barham, Peter (1984) 'Cultural Forms and Psychoanalysis: Some Problems', in B. Richards, ed. (1984), pp. 38–55.

Barnard, F. M. (1973) 'Culture and Civilization in Modern Times', in P. P. Wiener, ed. (1968–74) vol. 1, pp. 613–21.

Bell, David. (1992) 'Hysteria – A Contemporary Kleinian Perspective', *Brit. J. Psychother.* 9: 169–80.

Berke, Joseph (1989) *The Tyranny of Malice: Exploring the Dark Side of Character and Culture.* Simon and Schuster.

Berkhofer, Robert. F. Jr. (1978) *The White Man's Indian: Images of the American Indian from Columbus to the Present.* N. Y.: Knopf; reprinted N. Y.: Vintage Books, 1979.

Bernal, Martin (1987) *Black Athena: The Afroasiatic Roots of Classical Civilisation. Vol. 1: The Fabrication of Ancient Greece 1785–1985.* Free Association Books.

Bernfeld, Siegfried (1944) 'Freud's Earliest Theories and the School of Helmholtz', *Psychonal. Quart.* 13: 341–62.

—— (1949) 'Freud's Scientific Beginnings', *Amer. Imago* 6: 3–36.

—— (1951) 'Sigmund Freud, M. D., 1882–1885', *Int J. Psycho-Anal.* 32: 204–17.

Berry, David (1983) 'Science in Society', *New Statesman* 28 Oct., pp. 10–12.

Bettleheim, Bruno (1983) *Freud and Man's Soul.* Chatto and Windus/Hogarth.

Bion, Wilfred R. (1955) 'Group Dynamics – a Re-view', in Klein *et al.*, eds. (1955), pp. 440–77; reprinted in Bion (1961), pp. 141–91

—— (1961) *Experiences in Groups and Other Papers.* Tavistock.

—— (1967) *Second Thoughts: Selected Papers on Psycho-Analysis.* Heinemann Medical; reprinted Maresfield, 1984.

—— (1970) *Attention and Interpretation.* Tavistock.

—— (1992) *Cogitations.* Karnac.

'Birth of a Nation' (1915) B & w, silent. D. W. Griffith, Harry E. Aitken.

Blejer, J. (1966) 'Psychoanalysis of the Psycho-analytic Frame', *Int. J. Psycho-Anal.* 48: 511–19.

Bloor, David (1976) *Knowledge and Social Imagery.* Routledge & Kegan Paul.

Bollas, Christopher (1987) 'Expressive Uses of the Counter-transference', in *The Shadow of the Object: Psychoanalysis of the Unthought Known.* Free Association Books, pp. 200–35.

—— (1989) *Forces of Destiny: Psychoanalysis and Human Idiom.* Free Association Books.

Boorman, John (1985) *Money into Light: The Emerald Forest. A Diary.* Faber and Faber.

Bower, Tom (1991) *Maxwell: The Outsider.* William Heinemann.

Brady, Frank (1990) *Citizen Welles: A Biography of Orson Welles.* Hodder and Stoughton.

Branden, Barbara (1986) *The Passion of Ayn Rand: A Biography.* N. Y.: Doubleday.

Brenman Pick, I. (1985) 'Working Through in the Counter-transference', *Int. J. Psycho-Anal.* 66: 157–66; reprinted in Spillius, ed. (1988), vol. 2, pp. 34–47.

Breuer, Josef and Freud, Sigmund (1895) *Studies on Hysteria.*, in Freud (1953–73), vol. 2.

Britton, Ronald (1989) 'The Missing Link: Parental Sexuality in the Oedipus Complex', in Britton *et al.* (1989), pp. 83–102.

—— (1992) 'The Oedipus Situation and the Depressive Position', in R. Anderson, ed. (1992), pp. 34–45.

—— *et al.* (1989) *The Oedipus Complex Today: Clinical Implications.* Karnac.

Brody, S. (1980) 'Transitional Objects: Idealisation of a Phenomenon', *Psychoanal. Quart.* 49: 561–605

'Broken Arrow' (1950) Technicolor TCF. Produced by Julian Blaustein, directed by Delmer Daves, written by 'Michael Blankfort' (pseud. for Albert Maltz).

Brown, Dee (1978) *Bury My Heart at Wounded Knee: An Indian History of the American West.* Chatto.

Bruner, Jerome (1951) 'Personality Dynamics and the Process of Perceiving', in R. V. Blake and G. V. Ramsey, eds. *Perception: an Approach to Personality.* New York: Ronald Press.

Buckser, Andrew S. (1992) 'Lynching as Ritual in the American South', *Berkeley J. Sociol.* 37:11–28.

Burtt, Edwin. A. (1932) *The Metaphysical Foundations of Modern Physical Science,* 2nd ed., Routledge.

Buscombe, Ed (1988) *The BFI Companion to the Western.* Deutsch.

Cannon, Lou (1991) *President Reagan: The Role of a Lifetime.* Simon and Schuster.

Camus, Albert (1955) 'The Myth of Sisyphus' in *The Myth of Sisyphus and Other Essays.* N. Y.: Knopf; reprinted N. Y.: *Vintage, pp. 88–91

Carew, Jan (1988) 'Columbus and the Origins of Racism in the Americas', *Race and Class* 29: 1–19; 30: 33–57.

Caro, Robert S. (1974) *The Power Broker: Robert Moses and the Fall of New York.* N. Y.: Knopf; reprinted N. Y.: Vintage, 1975.

—— (1983) *The Years of Lyndon Johnson: The Path to Power.* Knopf.

—— (1990) *The Years of Lyndon Johnson: Means of Ascent.* Knopf.

Cassirer, Ernst (1953–57) *The Philosophy of Symbolic Forms,* 3 vols. Yale University Press.

Caughey, John and LaRee (1977) *Los Angeles: Biography of a City.* University of California Press.

'Chinatown' (1974) Technicolor. Panavision. Paramount/Long Road. Produced and written by Robert Towne; directed by Roman Polanski

Cocks, G. and Crosby, T. L. (1987) *Psychohistory: Readings in the Method of Psychology, Psychoanalysis, and History.* Yale.

Colman, A, D. and Bexton, W. H. (1975) *Group Relations Reader 1.* Washington, D. C.: A. K. Rice Institute.

—— and Geller, M. H. (1985) *Group Relations Reader 2.* Washington, D. C.: A. K. Rice Institute.

Coltart, Nina (1986a) '"Slouching towards Bethlehem" . . . or Thinking the Unthinkable in Psychoanalysis', in Kohon, ed. (1986), pp. 185–99.; reprinted in *Slouching towards Bethlehem . . . and Further Psychoanalytic Explorations.* Free Association Books, 1992, pp. 1–14.

Cooper, David (1972) *The Death of the Family*. Harmondsworth: Penguin.

Creme, Phyllis (1991) 'Winnicott and the Cinema', paper read to annual conference of THERIP (The Higher Education Network for Research and Teaching in Psychoanalysis).

'Dances with Wolves' (1990) Directed by Kevin Costner.

Darlington, C. D. (1969) *The Evolution of Man and Society*. Allen & Unwin.

Darwin, Charles R. (1874) *The Descent of Man, and Selection in Relation to Sex*, 2nd ed., revised and augmented. Murray, 1889.

Davidson, Basil (1987) 'The Ancient World and Africa: Whose Roots? *Race & Class* 29: 1–15.

Davis, Madeleine and Wallbridge, David (1981) *Boundary and Space: An Introduction the Work of D. W. Winnicott*. Karnac; reprinted Harmondsworth: Penguin, 1983

Descartes, René (1637) *Discourse on the Method of Properly Conducting One's Reason and of Seeking the Truth in the Sciences*, in *Discourse on Method and The Meditations*. Harmondsworth: Penguin, 1968, pp. 25–91

Deutsch, Felix, ed. (1959) *On the Mysterious Leap from the Mind to the Body: A Workshop Study of the Theory of Conversion*. N. Y.: International Universities Press.

Deutsch, H. (1926) 'Occult Processes Occurring during Psychoanalysis', in G. Devereux, ed. (1953) *Psychoanalysis and the Occult*. New York: International Universities Press.

Dollard, John (1937) *Caste and Class in a Southern Town*; reprinted Garden City, N. Y.: Doubleday Anchor, 1957.

Douglas, Mary (1966) *Purity and Danger: An Analysis of the Concepts of Pollution and Taboo*; reprinted *Penguin, 1970.

—— (1975) *Implicit Meanings: Essays in Anthropology*. Routledge.

Dryden, Windy and Aveline, Mark, eds. (1988) *Group Therapy in Britain*. Open University Press.

Dunne, J. G. (1982) 'Chinatowns', *New York Review of Books*. 21 October, pp. 6–10.

During, Simon, ed. (1993) *The Cultural Studies Reader*. Routledge.

Dworkin, Dennis L. and Roman, Leslie G. (1993) *Views Beyond the Border Country: Raymond Williams and Cultural Politics*. Routledge.

Eigner, J. B. (1986) 'Squid and Projective Identification', *Free Assns*. 7: 75–8.

Ellison, Ralph (1953) *Invisible Man*. Gollancz; reprinted Harmondsworth: Penguin, 1965.

Epstein, L. and Feiner, A. H. (1983) *Countertransference: The Therapist's Contribution to the Therapeutic Situation*. Aronson.

Faimberg, Haydée (1988) 'The Telescoping of Generations: Genealogy of Certain Identifications', *Contemp. Psychoanal*. 24: 99–118.

Fairbairn, W. Ronald D. (1952) *Psychoanalytic Studies of the Personality*. Routledge & Kegan Paul.

Fanon, Franz (1967) *Black Skin, White Masks*. N. Y.: Grove.

Feldman, Michael (1992) 'Splitting and Projective identification', in Anderson, R., ed. (1992), pp. 74–88.

Fenichel, Otto (1941) *Problems in Psychoanalytic Technique*, New York: Psychoanalytic Quarterly.

—— (1945) *The Psychoanalytic Theory of Neurosis* New York: Norton.

Figlio, Karl (1978) 'Chlorosis and Chronic Disease in Nineteenth-century Britain: the Social Constitution of Somatic Illness in a Capitalist Society', *Internat. J. Health Services* 8: 589–617.

—— (1979) 'Sinister Medicine: A Critique of Left Approaches to Medicine', *Radical Sc. J.* 9: 14–68.

—— (1984) 'Freud's Exegesis of the Soul', *Free Assns.* Pilot Issue: 113–21.

—— (1985) 'Medical Diagnosis, Class Dynamics, Social Stability, in L. Levidow and R. M. Young, eds., *Science, Technology and the Labour Process: Marxist Studies,* Free Association Books, Vol. 2, pp. 129–65.

—— (1990) 'The Environment: Topographies of the Internal and External Worlds', talk delivered to the Centre for Psycho-analytic Studies, University of Kent.

Finlay, Marike (1989) 'Post-Modernizing Psychoanalysis / Psychoanalysing Post-Modernity', *Free Assns.* 16: 43–80.

Foucault, Michel (1967) *Madness and Civilisation: A History of Insanity in the Age of Reason.* Tavistock.

Foulkes, S. H. (1948) *Introduction to Group-Analytic Psychotherapy.* Heinemann Medical; reprinted Maresfield, 1983.

—— (1964) *Therapeutic Group Analysis.* Allen and Unwin; reprinted Maresfield, 1984.

Freeman, Jo (1970) 'The Tyranny of Structurelessness', pamphlet reprinted in *Berkeley J. Sociol.*; reprinted Leeds Women, n.d.

Freud, Sigmund (1891) *On Aphasia: A Critical Study.* N. Y.: International Universities Press, 1953.

—— (1891a) 'Psycho-physical Parallelism'. *S. E.* 14, pp. 206–8.

—— (1895) 'Project for a Scientific Psychology'. *S. E.* 1, pp. 283–397.

—— (1900) *The Interpretation of Dreams. S. E.* 4 and 5.

—— (1905) 'Fragment of an Analysis of a Case of Hysteria'. *S. E.* 7, pp. 1–122.

—— (1910) 'The Future Prospects for Psycho-analytic Therapy'. *S. E.* 11, pp. 139–51.

—— (1912) 'The Dynamics of Transference'. *S. E.* 12, pp 97–108.

—— (1912a) 'Recommendations to Physicians Practising Psycho-analysis'. *S. E.* 12, pp. 109–20.

—— (1912–13) *Totem and Taboo. S. E.* 13, pp. 1–161.

—— (1921) *Group Psychology and the Analysis of the Ego. S. E.* 18, pp. 67–143.

—— (1922) 'Some Neurotic Mechanisms in Jealousy, Paranoia and Homosexuality'. *S. E.* 18, pp. 221–232.

—— (1923) *The Ego and the Id. S. E.* 19, pp. 1–66.

—— (1926) 'The Question of Lay Analysis: Conversations with an Impartial Person'. *S. E.* 20, pp. 177–258.

—— (1927) *The Future of an Illusion. S. E.* 21, pp. 3–56.

—— (1930) *Civilization and Its Discontents. S. E.* 21, pp. 59–145.

—— (1930) *Moses and Monotheism. S. E.* 22, pp. 3–127.

—— (1932) 'The Acquisition and Control of Fire'. *S. E. 22*, pp. 185–93.

—— (1933)*New Introductory Lectures on Psycho-analysis. S. E.* 22, pp. 1–182.

—— (1953–73) *The Standard Edition of the Complete Psychological Works of Sigmund Freud*, 24 vols. Hogarth (*S. E.*).

Fromm, Erich (1941) *Fear of Freedom;* U. S. title – *Escape from Freedom.* N. Y.: Rinehart & Co.

—— (1971) *The Crisis of Psychoanalysis: Essays on Freud, Marx and Social Psychology.* Cape.

Frosh, Stephen (1991) *Identity Crisis: Modernity, Psychoanalysis and the Self.* Macmillan

Gay, Peter (1988) *Freud: A Life for Our Time.* Dent.

Gedo, John. E. (1986) *Conceptual Issues in Psychoanalysis: Essays in History and Method.* New York: Analytic Press.

Giovacchini, P. L. (1989) *Countertransference: Triumphs and Catastrophes.* Aronson.

Glover, Edward (1927) 'Lectures on Technique in Psychoanalysis', *Int. J. Psycho-Anal.* 8: 311–38.

Goffman, Erving (1961) *Asylums.* N. Y.: Anchor Books

Goldberg, D. T., ed. (1990) *Anatomy of Racism.* Minneapolis: Minnesota.

Goldman, Albert (1981) *Elvis.* Allen Lane.

—— (1988) *The Lives of John Lennon.* Bantam Press.

Gordon, Paul (1990) 'Souls in Armour: Thoughts on Psychoanalysis and Racism' (typescript).

Green, André (1978) 'Potential Space in Psychoanalysis: The Object in the Setting', in Grolnick *et al.,* eds. (1978), pp. 167–90.

Greenberg, Jay R. and Mitchell, Stephen A. (1983) *Object Relations in Psychoanalytic Theory.* Harvard.

Griffith, Nanci (1982) 'Dollar Matinee', *There's a Light Beyond these Woods.* Philo 1097.

Grinberg, L. (1990) *The Goals of Psychoanalysis: Identification, Identity and Supervision.* Karnac.

Grolnick, S. *et al.,* eds. (1978) *Between Reality and Fantasy Transitional Objects and Phenomena.* Aronson.

Grossberg, Larry *et al.,* eds. (1992) *Cultural Studies.* Routledge.

Grosskurth, Phyllis (1985) *Melanie Klein: Her World and Her Work.* Hodder and Staughton.

—— (1991) *The Secret Ring: Freud's Inner Circle and the Politics of Psychoanalysis.* Yale.

Grotstein, James (1981) *Splitting and Projective Identification* Aronson.

'Gunga Din' (1939) B & w. RKO. Directed and produced by George Stevens, written by Joel Sayre *et al.*

Hann-Kende, F. (1933) 'On the Role of Transference and Countertransference in Psychoanalysis', in Devereux, ed. (1953).

Haraway, Donna (1989) *Primate Visions: Gender, Race, and Nature in the World of Modern Science.* Routledge.

—— (1990) *Simians, Cyborgs and Women: The Reinvention of Nature.* Free Association Books.

—— (1992) 'The Promises of Monsters: A Regenerative Politics for Inappropriate/d Others', in Grossberg *et al.*, eds. (1992), pp. 295–337.

Harris, Emmylou and Nelson, Willie (1990) 'Gulf Coast Highway', Emmylou Harris, *Duets.* Reprise 7599–25791–2.

Hartmann, Heinz (1958) *Ego Psychology and the Problem of Adaptation.* N. Y.: International Universities Press.

—— (1964) *Essays on Ego Psychology: Selected Problems in Psychoanalytic Theory.* N. Y.: International Universities Press.

——, Kris, Ernst and Lowenstein, R. M. (1946) 'Comments on the Formation of Psychic Structure', *The Psychoanalytic Study of the Child* 2: 11–38.

Harvey, David. (1980) *The Condition of Postmodernity.* Basil Blackwell.

Hatch, Elvin. (1985) 'Culture', in A. and J. Kuper, eds., *The Social Science Encyclopedia.* Routledge & Kegan Paul, pp. 178–81.

Heimann, Paula. (1949–50) 'On Counter-transference', in Heimann (1990), pp. 73–9.

—— (1959–60) 'Counter-transference', in Heimann (1990), pp. 151–60.

—— (1990) *About Children and Children No Longer: The Work of Paula Heimann.* Routledge.

Hesse, Mary. B. (1980) *Revolutions and Reconstructions in the Philosophy of Science.* Brighton: Harvester Press.

Hinshelwood, Robert D. (1987) *What Happens in Groups.* Free Association Books.

—— (1991) *A Dictionary of Kleinian Thought*, 2nd ed. Free Association Books.

Hodges, Andrew (1983) *Alan Turing: The Enigma of Intelligence.* Burnett Books/Hutchinson; reprinted Unwin Counterpoint, 1985.

Hoggart, Richard (1957) *The Uses of Literacy.* Chatto & Windus; reprinted Pelican, 1958.

Holland, Sue and Holland, Ray (1984) 'Depressed Women: Outposts of Empire and Castles of Skin', in B. Richards, ed. (1984), pp. 92–101.

'Hombre' (1967) DeLuxe Panavision TCF/Hombre Productions. Produced by Martin Ritt and Irving Ravetch, directed by Martin Ritt, written by Irving Ravetch and Harriet Frank.

Horowitz, L. (1983) 'Projective Identification in Dyads and Groups', *Int. J. Group. Psychother.* 33: 259–79. reprinted in *Colman and Geller, eds. (1985), pp. 21–35.

Horton, Robin (1967) 'African Traditional Thought and Western Science' *Africa* 37: 50–71, 155–87.

Huxley, Thomas H. (1865) 'Emancipation – Black and White', in *Lay Sermons, Addresses and Reviews*. Macmillan, 1903, pp. 17–23.

Ilahi, Nasir (1988) 'Psychotherapy Services to the Ethnic Communities' (typescript).

Ingleby, David (1972) 'Ideology and the Human Sciences: Some Comments on the Role of Reification in Psychology and Psychiatry', in T. Pateman, ed., *Counter Course: A Handbook for Course Criticism*. Harmondsworth: Penguin, pp. 51–81.

Isaacs, Susan (1952) 'The Nature and Function of Phantasy', in Klein *et al.* (1952), pp. 67–121.

Jacoby, Russell (1981) *Dialectic of Defeat: Contours of Western Marxism*. Cambridge.

Jameson, Frederic (1991) *Postmodernism or, The Cultural Logic of Late Capitalism*. Verso.

Jaques, Elliott (1951) *The Changing Culture of a Factory: A Study of Authority and Participation in an Industrial Setting*. Routledge & Kegan Paul.

—— (1955) 'Social Systems as a Defence against Persecutory and Depressive Anxiety', in Klein *et al.*, eds. (1955), pp. 478–98.

Jay, Martin (1973) *The Dialectical Imagination: A History of the Frankfurt School and the Institute of Social Research, 1923–1950*. Little, Brown & Co.

—— (1984) *Marxism and Totality: The Adventures of a Concept from Lukács to Habermas*. Polity.

Jones, Ernest (1949) *Hamlet and Oedipus*. N. Y.: Doubleday Anchor.

Jordanova, Ludmilla, ed. (1986) *Languages of Nature: Critical Issues on Science and Literature*. Free Association Books.

—— (1989) *Sexual Visions: Images of Gender in Science and Medicine between the Eighteenth and Twentieth Centuries*. Harvester Wheatsheaf.

Joseph, Betty (1983) 'Transference: The Total Situation', in Joseph (1989), pp. 156–67.

—— (1989) *Psychic Equilibrium and Psychic Change: Selected Papers*. Routledge.

Kahne, M. J. (1967) 'On the Persistence of Transitional Phenomena into Adult Life', *Int. J. Psycho-Anal,* 48: 247–58.

Kahrl, W. L. (1982) *Water and Power: The Conflict over Los Angeles' Water Supply in the Owens Valley*. University of California Press.

Kalikow, T. J. (1978) 'Konrad Lorenz's "Brown Past": a Reply to Alec Nisbett', *J. Hist. Behav. Sci.* 14: 173–80.

Kaufman, M. Ralph and Heiman, Marcel, eds. (1964) *Evolution of Psychosomatic Concepts. Anorexia Nervosa: A Paradigm*. N. Y.: International Universities Press.

Keller, Helen (1903) *The Story of My Life*.; reprinted N. Y.: Scholastic Book Services, 1967.

Kelly, Kitty (1986) *His Way: The Unauthorised Biography of Frank Sinatra*. N. Y.: Bantam.

—— (1991) *Nancy Reagan: The Unauthorised Biography*. Simon and Schuster.

King, Pearl & Steiner, Ricardo, eds. (1991) *The Freud-Klein Controversies 1941–45*. Tavistock/Routledge.

Klein, Melanie (1928) 'Early Stages of the Oedipus Conflict'; reprinted in *W. M. K.* I, pp. 186–98.

—— (1935) 'A Contribution to the Psychogenesis of Manic-Depressive States'; reprinted in *W. M. K.* II, pp, 262–89.

—— (1945) 'The Oedipus Complex in the Light of Early Anxieties'; reprinted in *W. M. K.* I, pp. 370–419 and in Britton *et al.* (1989), pp. 63–82.

—— (1946) 'Notes on Some Schizoid Mechanisms'; reprinted in *W. M. K.* III, pp. 1–24.

—— (1952) 'The Origins of Transference'; reprinted in *W. M. K.* III, pp. 48–56.

—— (1955) 'The Psycho-Analytic Play Technique: Its History and Significance'; reprinted in *W. M. K.* III, pp. 122–40.

—— (1955a) 'On Identification; *W. M. K.* III, pp. 141–75.

—— (1958) 'On the Development of Mental Functioning'; reprinted in *W. M. K.* III, pp. 236–46.

—— (1959) 'Our Adult World and Its Roots in Infancy'; reprinted in *W. M. K.* III, pp. 247–63.

—— (1975) *The Writings of Melanie Klein*, 4 vols. Hogarth. Vol. I: *Love, Guilt and Reparation and Other Works., 1921–1945*. Vol. II: The Psycho-Analysis of Children. Vol. III: *Envy and Gratitude and Other Works; 1946–1963*; Vol. IV: *Narrative of a Child Analysis*. all reprinted Virago, 1988. (*W. M. K.*)

—— *et al.* (1952) *Developments in Psycho-Analysis*. Hogarth.

—— *et al.*, eds. (1955) *New Directions in Psycho-Analysis: The Significance of Infant Conflicts in the Patterns of Adult Behaviour*. Tavistock; reprinted Maresfield,

Klein, Sydney (1980) 'Autistic Phenomena in Neurotic Patients', *Int. J. Psycho-Anal.* 61:395–402.

Koenigsberg, R. A. (1977) *The Psychoanalysis of Racism, Revolution and Nationalism*. N. Y.: Library of Social Science.

Kogan, Ilony (1989) 'The Search for the Self', *Int. J. Psycho-Anal.* 70: 661–71.

Kohon, Gregorio (1985) 'Objects are Not People', *Free Assns.* 2: 19–30.

—— (1986) 'Countertransference: an Independent View', in Kohon, ed. (1986a), pp. 51–73.

—— (1986a) *The British School of Psychoanalysis: The Independent Tradition*. Free Association Books.

Kovel, Joel (1970) *White Racism: A Psychohistory*. N. Y. Pantheon; reprinted Free Association Books, 1988.

—— (1983) *Against the State of Nuclear Terror*. Free Association Books.

Kreeger, Lionel, ed. (1975) *The Large Group: Dynamics and Therapy*. Constable; reprinted Maresfield.

Kren, George (1987) 'The Holocaust and the Foundations of Moral Judgement', *J. Value Inquiry* 21: 55–64.

Kris, Ernst (1950) 'The Significance of Freud's Earliest Discoveries', *Int. J. Psycho-Anal.* 31: 108–16.

—— (1950a) 'On Preconscious Mental Processes', *Psychoanal. Quart.* 19: 540–60.

Kuhlenbeck, Hertwig (1957) *Brain and Consciousness: Some Prolegomena to an Approach of the Problem.* Basel/N. Y.: Karger.

—— (1958) 'The Meaning of "Postulational Psychophysical Parallelism"', *Brain* 81:588–603

Laing, Ronald D. (1960) *The Divided Self: An Existential Study in Sanity and Madness.* Tavistock; reprinted Penguin, 1965.

—— and Esterson, A. (1970) *Sanity, Madness and the Family: Families of Schizophrenics.* Harmondsworth: Penguin.

Langer, Suzanne K. (1942) *Philosophy in a New Key: A Study in the Symbolism of Reason, Rite and Art.* Cambridge, MA: Harvard University Press.

Langs, Robert and Searles, Harold F. (1980) *Intrapsychic and Interpersonal Dimensions of Treatment: A Clinical Dialogue.* Aronson.

Laplanche, Jean and Pontalis, J.-B. (1983) *The Language of Psycho-Analysis.* Hogarth; reprinted Maresfield.

Las Casas, Bartolomé de (1552) *The Devastation of the Indes: A Brief Account.* Johns Hopkins, 1992.

Lash, Joseph P. (1971) *Eleanor and Franklin: The Story of Their Relationship, based on Eleanor Roosevelt's Papers.* N. Y.: Norton.

—— (1980) *Helen and Teacher: The Story of Helen Keller and Anne Sullivan Macy.* Delacorte Press/Seymour Lawrence; reprinted *Penguin, 1981.

Lasswell, Harold. D. (1930) *Psychopathology and Politics.* N. Y.: Viking.

Lawrence, W. G. (1991) 'Won from the Void of the Infinite: Experiences of Social Dreaming', *Free Assns.* (no. 22) 2: 259–94.

Lerner, Leila, ed. (1992) *Illusion and Culture: A Tribute to Winnicott,* special issue of *Psychoanal. Rev.* 79 (no. 2).

Levidow, Les (1978) 'A Marxist critique of the IQ debate', *Radical Sci. J.* 6/7: 13–72.

Little, Margaret (1950) 'Countertransference and the Patient's Response to It', in Little (1986), pp. 33–50.

—— (1957) '"R" – The Analyst's Total Response to His Patient's Needs', in Little (1986), pp. 51–80.

—— (1985) 'Winnicott Working in Areas where Psychotic Anxieties Predominate', *Free Assns.* 3: 9–42.

—— (1986) *Transference Neurosis and Transference Psychosis: Toward Basic Unity.* Aronson; reprinted Free Association Books/ Maresfield Library.

—— (1987) 'On the Value of Regression to Dependence', *Free Assns.* 10: 7–22.

—— (1989) Review of *Selected Letters of D. W. Winnicott, Free Assns.* 18: 133–8.

—— (1990) *Psychotic Anxieties and Containment: A Personal Record of an Analysis with Winnicott.* Aronson.

'Lonesome Dove' (1989) US Television, based on the novel by Larry McMurtry.

Lorenz, Konrad (1961) *King Solomon's Ring.* Methuen.

Low, Barbara (1935) 'The Psychological Compensation of the Analyst'. *Int. J. Psycho-Anal.* 16: 1–8.

Lowenberg, Peter (1985) *Decoding the Past: The Psychohistorical Approach.* University of California Press.

Lowenstein, R. M. (1963) 'Some Considerations on Free Association', J. *Amer. Psychoanal. Assn.* 11:451–73.

Lynn, Kenneth S. (1987) *Hemmingway.* Simon and Schuster.

Main, Tom (1975) 'Some Psychodynamics of Large Groups', in L. Kreeger, ed. (1975), pp. 57–86; reprinted in **The Ailment and Other Psychoanalytic Essays.* Free Association Books, 1989, pp. 100–22.

Marcuse, Herbert (1955) *Eros and Civilization: A Philosophical Inquiry into Freud.* Boston: Beacon; 2nd ed., with a new preface by the author, Allen Lane: The Penguin Press, 1969.

—— (1958) *Soviet Marxism: A Critical Analysis.* Routledge & Kegan Paul; reprinted Pelican, 1971.

—— (1964) *One Dimensional Man: Studies in the Ideology of Advanced Industrial Societies.* Routledge & Kegan Paul; reprinted Ark, 1986.

—— (1969) 'Repressive Tolerance', in R. P. Wolff, *et al.*, *A Critique of Pure Tolerance.* Cape, pp. 95–142.

—— (1969a) *An Essay on Liberation.* Boston: Beacon Press

—— (1970) *Five Lectures: Psychoanalysis, Politics, and Utopia.* Allen Lane: The Penguin Press.

McBride, Joseph (1992) *Frank Capra: The Catastrophe of Success.* Faber and Faber.

McDougall, Joyce (1980) 'Countertransference and Primitive Communication', in *Plea for a Measure of Abnormality.* Madison, CT: International Universities Press; reprinted Free Association Books, 1990, pp. 247–98.

McClintick, David (1982) *Indecent Exposure: A True Story of Hollywood and Wall Street.* N. Y: Morrow; reprinted N. Y.: Dell.

Meltzer, Donald (1966) 'The Relation of Anal Masturbation to Projective Identification', *Int. J. Psycho-Anal,.* 47: 335–42; reprinted in Spillius (1988), vol. 1, pp 102–16.

—— (1978) *The Kleinian Development Part I: Freud's Clinical Development; Part II: Richard Week-by-Week; Part III: The Clinical Significance of the Work of Bion.* Strath Tay: Clunie.

—— (1991) Lecture on Projective Identification and the Claustrum (tape).

—— (1992) *The Claustrum: An Investigation of Claustrophobic Phenomena.* Strath Tay: Clunie.

—— *et al.* (1975) *Explorations in Autism: A Psycho-Analytical Study.* Strath Tay: Clunie.

Meltzer, Donald and Harris Williams, M. (1988) *The Apprehension of Beauty: The Role of Aesthetic Conflict in Development, Art and Violence.* Strath Tay: Clunie Press.

Menninger, Karl (1938) *Man Against Himself.* Rupert Hart Davis; reprinted Harvest/HBJ.

Menzies Lyth, Isabel (1959) 'The Functions of Social Systems as a Defence Against Anxiety: A Report on a Study of the Nursing Service of a General Hospital', *Human Relations* 13: 95–121; reprinted in *Lyth (1988), pp. 43–88

—— (1969) 'A Personal Review of Group Experiences', in Lyth (1989), pp. 1–18.

—— (1987) 'Action Research in a Long-Stay Hospital', in Lyth (1988), pp. 130–207.

—— (1988) *Containing Anxiety in Institutions: Selected Essays, vol. 1.* Free Association Books.

—— (1989) *The Dynamics of the Social: Selected Essays, vol. II.* Free Association Books.

Miller, Eric (1990) 'Experiential Learning Groups I: The Development of the Leicester Model', in E. Trist and H, Murray, eds., *The Social Engagement of Social Science: A Tavistock Anthology, Vol. 1: The Socio-Psychological Perspective.* Free Association Books, pp. 165–85.

—— (1990a) Experiential Learning Groups II: Recent Developments in Dissemination and Application', in *Ibid.*, pp. 186–98

Milne, A. A. (1926) *Winnie the Pooh.* Methuen.

Milne, Hugh (1986) *Bhagwan: The God That Failed.* Caliban.

'The Miracle Worker' (1962) Black & white. UA/Playfilms. Produced by Fred Coe; directed by Arthur Penn; written by William Gibson.

Money-Kyrle, Roger (1956) 'Normal Counter-transference and Some of its Deviations, *Int. J. Psycho-Anal.* 37: 360–66.; reprinted in *The Collected Papers of Roger Money-Kyrle.* Strath Tay: Clunie, 1978, pp. 330–42 and Spillius, ed. (1988), vol. 2, pp. 22–33.

Monk, Ray (1990) *Ludwig Wittgenstein: The Duty of Genius.* Cape.

Morgan, G. (1986) *Images of Organization.* Sage.

Morrison, Toni (1987) *Beloved.* Chatto and Windus

—— (1992) *Jazz.* Chatto and Windus

Murray, N. (1986) 'Anti-racists and Other Demons: the Press and Ideology in Thatcher's Britain', *Race & Class* 27(3): 1–20.

Myrdal, Gunnar *et al.* (1944) *An American Dilemma: The Negro Problem and Modern Democracy.* N. Y.: Harper. N. Y.: Holt, Rinehart & Winston.

Natterson, J. (1991) *Beyond Countertransference: The Therapist's Subjectivity in the Therapeutic Process.* Aronson.

Nelson, Willie (1981) 'I'd Have to be Crazy', *Willie Nelson's Greatest Hits (and Some that Will Be).* Columbia CGK 37542.

Ogden, Thomas K. (1979) 'On Projective Identification', *Int. J. Psycho-Anal.* 60: 357–73.

—— (1982) *Projective Identification and Psychotherapeutic Technique.* Aronson.

Orr, D. W. (1988) 'Transference and Countertransference: a Historical Survey', in Wolstein, ed. (1988), pp. 91–110.

O'Shea, James (1991) *The Daisy Chain: How Borrowed Billions Sank a Texas S&L.* Simon and Schuster.

Pagel, Walter (1958) 'Medieval and Renaissance Contributions to Knowledge of the Brain and its Functions', in F. N. L. Poynter, ed., *The History and Philosophy of Knowledge of the Brain and its Functions*. Oxford: Blackwell, pp. 95–114.

Paton, Alan (1971) *Too Late the Phalarope*. Harmondsworth: Penguin.

Perry, G. (1991) 'The First Face of America', *Sunday Times Magazine Section, 3* Feb., pp. 19–24.

Phillips, Adam (1988) *Winnicott*. Fontana.

Pines, Malcolm, ed. (1985) *Bion and Group Psychotherapy*. Routledge.

'Prime Cut' (1972) Technicolor. Panavision. Cinema Center. Produced by Joe Wizan; directed by Michael Ritchie; written by Robert Dillon.

Racker, Heinrich (1968) *Transference and Countertransference.* Hogarth; reprinted Maresfield Reprints, 1982.

Rafaelsen, Lise (1992) 'Glimpses of Projective Identification in Inpatient Groups and in Life', *Group Anal.* 25: 55–59.

Rank, Otto (1912) *The Incest Theme in Literature and Legend: Fundamentals of a Psychology of Literary Creation*. Johns Hopkins University Press, 1992.

Rapaport, David (1959) 'The Structure of Psychoanalytic Theory: a Systematizing Attempt', in S. Koch, ed., *Psychology: A Study of a Science. Study I: Conceptual and Systematic*. Vol. 3: *Formulations of the Person in the Social Context*. N. Y.: McGraw-Hill, pp. 55–183; reprinted *Psychological Issues,* Vol. 2 no. 2, Monograph 6, 1960.

—— (1967) *The Collected Papers of David Rapaport.* N. Y.: Basic Books.

—— (1974) *The History of the Concept of Association of Ideas*. N. Y.: International Universities Press.

—— and Gill, Merton M. (1959) 'The Points of View and Assumptions of Metapsychology', *Int. J. Psycho-Anal.* 40: 1–10.

Rayner, Eric (1991) *The Independent Mind in British Psychoanalysis.* Free Association Books.

Rayner, Jay (1993) 'Ghetto v. Ghetto', *The Guardian Weekend, 17* April 1993, pp. 22–34.

Reich, Annie (1951) 'On Countertransference'. *Int. J. Psycho-Anal.* 32: 25–31.

Reich, Wilhelm (1933) *Character Analysis: Principles and Techniques for Psychoanalysts in Practice and Training,* 2nd ed., New York: Orgone Institute.

—— (1933) *The Mass Psychology of Fascism*; reprinted Penguin, 1975.

—— (1972) *Sex-Pol: Essays, 1929–1934.* N. Y.: Vintage

Rex, John and Mason, David, eds. (1986) *Theories of Race and Ethnic Relations.* Cambridge. University Press.

Ribot, Th. (1873) *English Psychology*. King.

Richards, Barry, ed. (1984)*Capitalism and Infancy: Essays on Psychoanalysis and Politics*. Free Association Books

Richardson, John (1991) *A Life of Picasso. Vol. I: 1881–1906*. Cape.

Rieff, Philip (1960) *Freud: The Mind of the Moralist*. Gollancz, 3rd ed., Chicago, 1979.

Riese, Walther (1958) 'Freudian Concepts of Brain Function and Brain Disease', *J. Nerv. & Ment. Dis.* 127: 287–307.

Riviere, Joan (1952) 'General Introduction', in Klein *et al.* (1952), pp. 1–36.

—— (1952a) 'On the Genesis of Psychical Conflict in Early Infancy', in Klein *et al.* (1952), pp. 37–66.

Rorty, Richard (1980) *Philosophy and the Mirror of Nature*. Oxford: Blackwell.

—— (1982) *Consequences of Pragmatism (Essays: 1972–80)*. Minneapolis: University of Minnesota Press.

—— (1989) *Contingency, Irony, and Solidarity*. Cambridge University Press.

Rosenfeld, Herbert (1971) 'A Clinical Approach to the Psychoanalytic Theory of the Life and Death Instincts: An Investigation into the Aggressive Aspects of Narcissism', *Int. J. Psycho-Anal.* 52: 169–78; reprinted in Spillius (1988), vol. 1, pp. 239–55.

—— (1987) 'Projective Identification in Clinical Practice', in *Impasse and Interpretation: Therapeutic and Anti-Therapeutic Factors in Psychoanalytic Treatment of Psychotic, Borderline, and Neurotic Patients*. Routledge, pp. 157–90.

Rudnytsky, Peter L. (1987) *Freud and Oedipus*. N. Y.: Columbia.

——, ed. (1993) *Transitional Objects and Potential Spaces: Literary Uses of D. W. Winnicott*. Columbia.

Rustin, Margaret (1989) 'Identity: Fragmentation and Recovery in Psychoanalytic Psychotherapy'. *Discourse Social/Social Discourse* 2: 311–19.

Sandburg, Carl (1925) *Abraham Lincoln: The Prairie Years – II*. N. Y.: Scribner's, The Sagamon Edition, 1926.

Sanders, Ed (1972) *The Family: The Story of Charles Manson's Dune Buggy Attack Battalion*. Rupert Hart-Davis; reprinted Panther.

Sandler, Joseph (1987) *From Safety to Superego: Selected Papers*. Karnac Books.

——, ed. (1989) *Projection, Identification, Projective Identification*. Karnac Books.

Sandler, Joseph and Sandler, Anne-Marie (1978) 'On the Development of Object Relations and Affects', *Int. J. Psycho-Anal. 59: 285–96*.

Scharff, Jill S. (1992) *Projective Identification and the Use of the Therapist's Self*. Aronson.

Schulz, C. M. (1976) *Peanuts Jubilee: My Life and Art with Charlie Brown and Others*. Allen Lane.

Searles, Harold F. (1960) *The Nonhuman Environment: In Normal Development and in Schizophrenia*. Madison, CT: International Universities Press.

—— (1975) 'The Patient as Therapist to His Analyst', in Searles (1979), pp. 380–459.

—— (1976) 'Transitional Phenomena and Therapeutic Symbiosis', in Searles (1979), pp. 503–76.

—— (1978–9) 'Concerning Transference and Countertransference', *J. Psychoanal. Psychother.* 7: 165–88 (written in 1949).

—— (1979) *Countertransference and Related Subjects*. Madison, CT: International Universities Press.

—— (1986) *My Work with Borderline Patients*. Aronson

Segal, Hanna (1957) 'Notes on Symbol Formation', *Int. J. Psycho-Anal.* 38: 391–7; reprinted in *Segal (1981), pp. 49–65.

—— (1973) *Introduction to the Work of Melanie Klein*. Hogarth; reprinted Karnac, 1988.

—— (1981) *The Work of Hanna Segal: A Kleinian Approach to Clinical Practice*. Aronson; reprinted Free Association Books/ Maresfield Library, 1986.

—— (1988) 'Silence is the Real Crime', in J. B. Levine *et al.*, eds., *Psychoanalysis and the Nuclear Threat: Clinical and Theoretical Studies*. Hillside, NJ: Analytic Press, pp. 35–58

Sharpe, Ella (1930) 'The Technique of Psychoanalysis'. *Int. J. Psycho-Anal.* 2: 361–86.

Sherwood, Rae (1980) *The Psychodynamics of Race: Vicious and Benign Spirals*. Brighton: Harvester.

Slakter, E., ed. (1987) *Countertransference*. Aronson.

Slatta, R. W. (1990) *Cowboys of the Americas*. Yale.

Smith, Lillian (1944) *Strange Fruit*. Ace Books, 1959.

—— (1950) *Killers of the Dream*. Cresset.

Spillius, Elizabeth B. (1992) 'Clinical Experiences of Projective Identification', in Anderson, ed. (1992), pp. 59–73.

—— , ed. (1988) *Melanie Klein Today*, 2 vols. Routledge

Spoerl, Howard D. (1935–6) 'Faculties versus Traits: Gall's Solution', *Character and Personality* 4: 216–31.

Steiner, John (1987) 'The Interplay between Pathological Organizations and the Paranoid-Schizoid and Depressive Positions', *Int. J. Psycho-Anal.* 68: 69–80; reprinted in Spillius, ed. (1988), vol. 1, pp. 324–42.

—— (1994) *Psychic Retreats: Pathological Organizations in Psychotic, Neurotic and Borderline Patients*. Routledge.

Stern, A. (1924) 'On the Countertransference in Psychoanalysis'. *Psychoanal. Rev.* 2: 166–74.

Strachey, James (1934) 'The Nature of the Therapeutic Action of Psychoanalysis', *Int. J. Psycho-Anal.* 15: 127–59.

Strachey, Lytton (1918) *Eminent Victorians*; reprinted Collins, 1959.

Sulloway, Frank J. (1979) *Freud, Biologist of the Mind: Beyond the Psychoanalytic Legend*. Burnett Books/André Deutsch

Sutherland, John D. (1989) *Fairbairn's Journey into the Interior*. Free Association Books.

Symington, Neville (1986) 'The Analyst's Act of Freedom as Agent of Therapeutic Change', in Kohon, ed. (1986a), pp. 253–72.

Taylor, Charles (1964) *The Explanation of Behaviour*. Routledge & Kegan Paul.

Taylor, Lonn (1983) 'The Open-Range Cowboy of the Nineteenth Century', in Lonn Taylor and Ingrid Marr, *The American Cowboy*. Harper and Row, pp., 16–27.

Theory, Culture and Society (1988) *Postmodernism*. Special Issue, vol. 5, numbers 2–3.

Thom, Martin (1978) 'Anti-racism – Infections of Language', *Wedge* no. 3 (winter), 14–22.

Torras de Beà, E. (1989) 'Projective Identification and Differentiation', *Int. J. Psycho-Anal.* 70: 265–74.

Turquet, Pierre (1975) 'Threats to Identity in the Large Group', in L. Kreeger, ed. (1974), pp. 87–144.

Tustin, Frances (1986) *Autistic Barriers in Neurotic Patients.* Karnac.

Tyson, Phyllis and Tyson, Robert L. (1990) *Psychoanalytic Theories of Development: An Integration.* Yale.

von Hoffman, Nicholas (1988) *Citizen Cohn.* Harrap.

Walker, Alice (1983) *The Color Purple.* Women's Press.

Warren, Howard C. (1921) *A History of the Association Psychology.* Constable.

Whitehead, Alfred N. (1925) *Science and the Modern World* N. Y.: Macmillan; reprinted *Free Association Books, 1985.

Wiener, Norbert (1950) *The Human Use of Human Beings: Cybernetics and Society.* N. Y.: Houghton Mifflin; reprinted Free Association Books, 1989.

Wiener, Philip P., ed. (1968–74) *Dictionary of the History of Ideas.* N. Y.: Scribner's, 8 vols.

Williams, Raymond (1958) *Culture and Society 1780–1950.* Chatto and Windus; reprinted Penguin, 1961.

—— (1961) *The Long Revolution.* Chatto and Windus; reprinted Pelican, 1965.

—— (1974) *Television: Technology and Cultural Form.* Fontana.

—— (1976) *Keywords: A Vocabulary of Culture and Society.* Fontana.

—— (1979) *Politics and Letters: Interviews with New Left Review.* New Left Books.

—— (1981) *Culture.* Fontana.

Winnicott, Donald W. (1947) 'Hate in the Countertransference', in Winnicott (1975), pp. 194–203.

—— (1951) 'Transitional Objects and Transitional Phenomena', in Winnicott (1975), pp. 229–242.

—— (1952) 'Psychoses and Child Care', in Winnicott (1975), pp. 219–28.

—— (1965) *The Maturational Processes and the Facilitating Environment: Studies in the Theory of Emotional Development.* Hogarth.

—— (1971) *Playing and Reality.* Tavistock Publications; reprinted Penguin, 1971.

—— (1975) *Through Paediatrics to Psycho-Analysis.* Hogarth.

—— (1989) 'The Fate of the Transitional Object', in *Psycho-Analytic Explorations.* Karnac, pp. 53–8.

Wolfe, Tom (1988) *The Bonfire of the Vanities.* Cape.

Wolfenstein, Eugene V. (1977) 'Race, Racism and Racial Liberation', *Western Pol. Quart.* 30: 163–82.

—— (1981) *The Victims of Democracy: Malcolm X and the Black Revolution.* University of California Press; reprinted Free Association Books, 1989.

—— (1991) 'On the Uses and Abuses of Psychoanalysis in Cultural Research', *Free Assns.* (no. 24) 2: 515–47.

—— (1993) *Psychoanalytic Marxism (Groundwork)* . Free Association Books.

Wolstein, Benjamin, ed. (1988) *Essential Papers on Countertransference.*. New York University Press.

Worledge, Nicola (1993) 'Psychoanalytic Aesthetics: The Contribution of the British School', doctoral research, University of Kent.

Wright, Peter (1987) *Spy Catcher: The Candid Autobiography of a Senior Intelligence Officer.* N. Y.: Viking.

Young, David M. (1990) 'Ratlines'. Exposed Film to Channel Four.

Young, Robert. M. (1960) 'Freud and Psychoanalysis in Physiological Perspective: A Study of Some of the Historical and Philosophical Aspects of the Mind-Body Problem from the Viewpoint of Psychoanalytic Metapsychology', term paper submitted for Second Year Psychiatry, University of Rochester School of Medicine and Dentistry.

—— (1966) 'Scholarship and the History of the Behavioural Sciences', *Hist. of Sci.* 2: 1–51.

—— (1966a) 'The Divided Science', *Delta* 38: 13–18.

—— (1967) 'Animal Soul', in P. Edwards, ed., *Encyclopedia of Philosophy.* N. Y.: Macmillan, vol. 1, pp. 122–27.

—— (1967a) 'Philosophy of Mind and Related Issues', *Brit. J. Philos. Sci.* 18: 325–330.

—— (1968) 'Association of Ideas', in P. P. Wiener, ed. (1968–74), vol. 1, pp. 111–18.

—— (1968a) 'The Functions of the Brain: Gall to Ferrier' (1808–1886)', *Isis.* 59: 251–68.

—— (1970) *Mind, Brain and Adaptation in the Nineteenth Century : Cerebral Localization and Its Biological Context from Gall to Ferrier.* Clarendon Press; reprinted Oxford University Press, 1990.

—— (1972) 'Franz Joseph Gall', in C. C. Gillispie, ed., *Dictionary of Scientific Biography.* N. Y.: Scribner's, vol. 5, pp. 250–56.

—— (1972a) 'David Hartley', in *Ibid.*, vol. 6, pp. 138–40.

—— (1973) 'The Human Limits of Nature', in J. Benthall, ed., *The Limits of Human Nature.* Allen Lane, pp. 235–74.

—— (1977) 'Science *is* Social Relations', *Radical Sci. J.* 5: 65–131.

—— (1979) 'Science is a Labour Process', *Sci. for the People* 43/44: 31–6.

—— (1979a) 'Why Are Figures so Significant? The Role and the Critique of Quantification', in J. Irvine *et al.* , eds., *Demystifying Social Statistics.* Pluto, pp. 63–75.

—— (1981) 'Science, Technology, Medicine and the Socialist Movement', *Radical Sci. J.* 11: 3–70 (written collectively).

—— (1981a) 'The Naturalization of Value Systems in the Human Sciences', in *Problems in the Biological and Human Sciences.* Milton Keynes: Open University Press, pp. 63–110.

—— (1985) 'Darwinism *is* Social', in David Kohn, ed., *The Darwinian Heritage.* Princeton University Press, pp. 609–38.

—— (1985a) *Darwin's Metaphor: Nature's Place in Victorian Culture*. Cambridge University Press.

—— (1985b) 'Is Nature a Labour Process?', in L. Levidow and R. M. Young, eds., *Science, Technology and the Labour Process: Marxist Studies*. Free Association Books, vol. 2, pp. 206–32.

—— (1986) 'The Dense Medium: Television as Technology', *Political Papers* 13: 3–5.

—— (1986a) 'Life among the Mediations: Labour, Groups, Breasts', talk delivered to Department of History and Philosophy of Science, University of Cambridge.

—— (1986b) 'Sigmund Freud: Scientist and/or Humanist', *Free Assns*. 6: 7–35.

—— (1987) 'Darwin and the Genre of Biography', in George Levine, ed., *One Culture: Essays in Science and Literature*. Madison: University of Wisconsin Press, pp. 203–24.

—— (1987a) 'Racist Society, Racist Science', in D. Gill and L. Levidow, eds., *Anti-Racist Science Teaching*. Free Association Books, pp. 16–42; reprinted in D. Gill *et al.*, eds., *Racism and Education: Structures and Strategies* . Sage, 1992, pp. 303–19.

—— (1988) 'Darwin, Marx, Freud and the Foundations of the Human Sciences', *Cheiron Newsletter*. Spring, pp. 7–12.

—— (1988a) 'Second Nature: The Historicity of the Unconscious', talk delivered to the Centre for Psychoanalytic Studies, University of Kent.

—— (1989) 'Persons, Organisms . . . and Primary Qualities', in J. Moore, ed., *History, Humanity and Evolution: Essays for John C. Greene*. Cambridge University Press, pp. 375–401.

—— (1989a) 'Postmodernism and the Subject: Pessimism of the Will', *Discours Social/Social Discourse* 2: 69–81; also in *Free Assns*. 16: 81–96.

—— (1989b) 'The Role of Psychoanalysis and Psychotherapy in the Human Sciences', paper presented to Zangwill Club, Department of Experimental Psychology, University of Cambridge.

—— (1989c) 'Transitional Phenomena: Production and Consumption', in B. Richards, ed., *Crises of the Self: Further Essays on Psychoanalysis and Politics*. Free Association Books, pp. 57–74.

—— (1990) 'The Mind-Body Problem', in Robert C. Olby *et al.*, eds. *Companion to the History of Modern Science*. Routledge, pp. 702–11.

—— (1990a) 'The Culture of British Psychoanalysis', paper presented to the Philadelphia Association, London.

—— (1990b) 'Scientism in the History of Management Theory', *Sci. as Culture* 8: 118–43.

—— (1991) 'Psychoanalytic Critique of Productivism' *Free Assns*. (no. 24) 2: 507–14.

—— (1992) 'The Vicissitudes of Transference and Countertransference: The Work of Harold Searles', *J. Arbours Association,* 9: 24–58.

—— (1992a) 'Science, Ideology and Donna Haraway', *Sci. as Culture* (no. 15) 3: 7–46.

—— (1993) 'Darwin's Metaphor and the Philosophy of Science', *Sci. as Culture* (no. 16) 3: 375–403.

—— (1993a) 'The Profession of Psychotherapy in Britain', *Free Assns.* (no. 29) 4: 81–86.

—— (1993b) 'Psychoanalytic Teaching and Research: Knowing and Knowing About', *Free Assns.* (no. 29) 4: 129–37.

—— (1993c) 'Racism: Projective Identification and Cultural Processes', paper presented to Sixth Annual Conference on Psychoanalysis and the Public Sphere, University of East London and to course on racism, Birkbeck College, London,

—— (1993–94) 'When Did Oedipus Do It? Kleinian Ideas about the Oedipus Complex', *Viewpoint* Autumn/Winter.

—— (1994) "What Psychoanalysis Has to Say to Philosophy', paper presented to Philosophy Society, University of Kent.

—— (1994a) 'The Cussedness of Psychoanalysis', paper presented to Psychology Seminar, University of Manitoba.

—— (1994b) 'Whatever Happened to Human Nature?', Distinguished Visitor Lecture, University of Manitoba.

—— (1994c) 'Is "Perversion" Obsolete?', paper presented to Psychiatry Grand Rounds, University of Manitoba School of Medicine.

—— (1994d) 'We Are All Inescapably Social Darwinists', paper presented to Darwin Interdisciplinary Seminar, University of Manitoba.

INDEX